the Traitor

BY ANDRÉ GORZ

FOREWORD BY JEAN-PAUL SARTRE

TRANSLATED FROM THE FRENCH BY RICHARD HOWARD

1959

SIMON AND SCHUSTER · NEW YORK

Here the Traitor reveals his
original situation, which is
(virtual) treachery. In so
doing, he "betrays" us, since
this situation is our own as
well. But it is by announcing
our position that we betray,
to the degree that we claim
to be altogether on one side
or the other. As for him, he
does not betray, since he
unremittingly makes explicit,
represents his ambiguity: his
double relation and his double
exclusion.

—FRANÇOIS JEANSON,
Sartre par lui-même

Contents

the Traitor

Foreword: Rats and Men

"They corrected his strabismus with glasses, his lisp with a metal loop, his stammer by mechanical exercises, and he spoke perfectly, but with a voice so low and so fast that his mother was forever complaining, 'What are you saying? Talk louder! What are you mumbling about now?' and they nicknamed him Mumbler . . ."

This muffled, monotonous, courteous voice is the one you are about to hear, and you will recognize it among all others from now on. To whom does it belong? To no one. As if language had begun speaking all by itself. Occasionally the word "I" is mentioned and we expect to catch a glimpse of the speaker of this speech, the subject who selects the terms. Pure illusion; the subject of the verb is merely an abstract word, the sentence has followed its familiar course, has taken a personal inflection for the sake of convenience. As a matter of fact, someone *is* here—"a thin fellow with hollow cheeks and eyes, receding forehead and chin, a long neck poking forward above a slightly hunched back, with the gait of a heron and parsimonious gestures, as if he were trying to contain his being within himself." But he has nothing to say. He is an "object," every proposition reorganizes him, designates him. If it weren't for this mute creature, the voice would be quite uninhabited; he lives in it, extends his verbal body through the words; the voice tells us that "he" is apprehensive, that "he" has finished a philosophical work, that "he" is preparing to show it to someone named Morel.

"What do we care about this anonymous whispering?" you will ask. "What we want is books constructed by real authors. Literature is like a high-wire act—our only pleasure is being able to appreciate the artist's work; we attach no more importance to the shudders that run through an abandoned language than to the wind in the reeds." Then put down this book. In its last pages, as a matter of fact, a certain Gorz, emerging from the slime, affirms his retrospective rights over the language that has engendered him. He has not wanted to create a work of art, he says. You will readily believe him. From the first moment you hear this forsaken voice, you will notice its continual uncertainty, the flaccidity of all natural things; it is a kind of arid guest, unconscious of itself and always on the verge of being choked by its own words. Yet art is a motionless image of movement; when you begin reading a novel, even confessions, everything has long since been consummated, "before" and "after" are nothing but operative signs, the dawn of love and its death agony exist simultaneously, each spread out upon the other, in the eternal indistinction of the moment; to read is to make a time transfusion; the hero lives on our life, his ignorance of the future and the dangers that surround him are our own; it is with our patience as readers that he creates for himself a parasitic duration whose course we break off and resume as we please. As for style, that great, vainglorious flourish—style is death. Its illusory speed sweeps us back into the author's past. The latter may groan all he likes, may torture himself under our very eyes; he feels nothing, he is telling himself. By the time he picks up his pen the die has long since been cast, his friend has betrayed him, his mistress has left him, and he is determined to hate them or to hate the human race. He writes to communicate his hatred, and style is a hammer to crush our resistance, a sword to slice our rationalizations to ribbons. Everything is ellipsis, syncope, flea-jumps and false collusion; rhetoric becomes terror; rage and insolence, humiliation and pride control the attack and the turn of a phrase. The great writer—this madman, this maenad—hurls himself upon language, conquers it, enslaves it, mistreats it, *faute de mieux;* alone at his desk, he is an autocrat. If he slashes his paper with a streak of lightning that will dazzle twenty generations, it is because he looks to this verbal ukase for the symbol of respectability, of the humble powers his contemporaries persist in refusing him. A dead man's vengeance, for scorn has long since killed him; these thunderclaps conceal a defunct child who puts himself ahead of everything else; the child Racine, the child Pascal, the child Saint-Simon—these are our classics. We enjoy strolling among the tombs of literature, that calm cemetery, spelling out the epitaphs and momentarily resuscitating eternal words. It is reassuring that such phrases *have lived;* their meaning is fixed forever, they will not take advantage of the brief survival we deign to accord them and start up inopportunely, sweeping us on toward some unknown future. As for the novelists who are not yet so fortunate as to be in their coffins, they play dead. They will fish words out of their stock ponds, kill them, gut them, season, cook and serve them up—*au bleu, meunière,* or *grillés.*

The Traitor will be set both within and beyond the scope of a literary enterprise. This Gorz is not dead; he is even impertinent enough, at the beginning, not to be born yet. Therefore, no rhetoric. Who would there be to persuade us? And of what? Nor is there any question of tapping our duration to feed a fictional hero or direct our dreams by words. There is only this voice—this voice searching and ignorant of what it is searching for, desiring and ignorant of what it desires, this voice speaking in the void, in the darkness, perhaps to give a meaning by words to the words which have just escaped it, or perhaps to disguise its fear.

For it is afraid; we can no longer doubt the fact. It said, "*He* is afraid, *he* is apprehensive because he has finished his book." But the voice claimed impassivity; it was merely a sonorous medium where various objective meanings collected, it discussed the passions of the thin chap with hollow eyes without suffering them. But we are not fooled. At first imprisoned in this alien body, in the individual referred to, the passions have spread outside their envelope, can no longer be localized; suffering colors the voice in every register, creates the inert urgency of this mumble; these groping, scrupulous, modest words have caught the fever. This is the voice of anxiety speaking. This time we have understood, the individual referred to is the individual speaking; but the two do not manage to create a single person. There exists at least one man on earth who eats, drinks, works, sleeps, who looks just like us, in short, and yet is condemned by some obscure spell to remain Someone Else in his own eyes.

Has his inner life been kneaded and pulverized to the point of leaving only a swarm of words in a decomposed body? Or is his consciousness still intact, so deeply buried that it no longer recognizes him at such a distance? No one knows yet, for this divided creature is no one. There is the dummy with hollow eyes, this pure object which has no control over itself, and there is this tiny tumult of words that dies away in the empty darkness and does not hear itself. As a matter of fact, to whom is this voice speaking? To us? Certainly not. To talk to men, you must already be a man. This voice does not care about being listened to; it is the division that deepens itself by trying to fill the gap; it is the stitches of language that have begun to unravel. Without references, roused by a nameless anxiety, the words work on. If they are determined to designate this human carcass, it is because they are obscurely trying to assimilate it, to dissolve it into themselves. The voice is born of a danger. It must destroy itself or gain the right to speak in the first person.

That is why this soliloquy is so disconcerting—we overhear it. You will smile at my naïveté, you will say, "After all, Gorz *published* his book." Yes, when there was a Gorz to make the decision; but he has added nothing, altered nothing of this beginning that seemed to be going nowhere and was intended for no one. I remember being told, whenever I chattered too much as a child, "Keep still, you sound like a trickle of warm water." A trickle of warm water is about to be turned on inside you now. It will consist of these long inchworm sentences interrupted by parentheses, swollen with the retrospective particulars they have engendered, expunged by scruples and regrets, suddenly inverted by backward glances. Where is order? Where is ceremony? Where is mere politeness? In vain you will try to cling to these first declarations; they are constantly being transformed by the action of those that follow. What you read on page 30 you learn, on page 80, *he* did not really believe—*he* merely supposed he believed it: on page 150 you learn *he* did *not* suppose he believed it, and on page 170 you find out *he* had not even written it—*he* had written a certain sentence imagining he was writing another one; and on page 200 you discover that imagined and written significations are strictly interchangeable and are both false besides. But you must not assume you are witness to a confession deceptive at the start and gradually inventing its own sincerity. Here there is no confessor in either sense, no confessional, and nothing to confess; when the voice began—I know, I can bear witness—it had nothing to say, its truth did not exist. It spoke words by chance because it had to begin somewhere; such words are transparent, they refer only to themselves and conceal no strategy of exposition in the defenseless stammer. Nothing is more sincere, nothing less artificial than this enterprise. It begins in anguish, in penury, here, under your eyes, by these very words; it loses its way and we miscarry with it. *It is true* that it loses itself and will find itself. *It is true* that it breaks free and grows rich.

Accustomed to the mind's calisthenics, we imagine, from the first words, that we have grasped the movement of this thought, the intention that presides over the construction of a paragraph; these sudden anticipations, these implied conjectures, these guesses and forebodings ordinarily permit us to understand the way of the world and the actions of men. We easily outstrip the developments still to come and wait for this language-in-action, comfortably installed at the finish line. But in the present instance such a procedure is of no use. We discover an intention, and in so doing were not mistaken, only the intention changes in its course. No one is there to maintain it; "the master is in the Styx," or, rather, "in Limbo," and there are only these trinkets of sonorous inanity which change as they incarnate themselves and each of which, by its mere presence, modifies all the rest. Leaning against the goalpost, we see the verbal stream flowing toward us, and then, suddenly, it contracts, wavers, slips down another slope and leaves us in the lurch. The indefinite recurrence of our disappointments makes a prattling disorder out of what will later seem an order-in-the-making.

For this slow, unpredictable progress *is* an order, a truth in the process of becoming; this is a whole human life shifting from the abstract to the concrete, from poverty to plenitude, from the universal to the individual, from anonymous objectivity to subjectivity. There are reasons for our surprise. Books are corpses, yet here is one which, scarcely in our hands, becomes a living creature. We must open it, of course, turn the pages and awaken the signs, but the mere movement of reading will provoke an unforeseeable occurrence of which neither the moments nor the end are given in advance; you imagine you are lending it your own duration, and it is the book that imposes its duration upon *you;* you will discover the laws of this dangerous language at the very moment it is engendering them, but you will know at the same time that they will be unceasingly changing and that the whole system transforms them to the very degree it is based upon them.

This hoarse, muffled voice, this breaking voice will live in your ears. Its slowness is a kind of speed, for it guides us toward a real future, the only future that is not a masquerade of memories, toward a place no one knows, which does not exist, and which, nevertheless, will be. It strips away its appearances; neither warm nor soft nor fluid, it reveals the inflexible order of enrichment; each sentence gathers within itself all that have preceded it, each is the living medium in which all the rest breathe, endure and transform themselves; in fact, there is only one sentence, rolling over all kinds of terrain, sustained by all kinds of soil, always heavier, fuller, denser, swelling to the bursting point, to the point of becoming a man. From moment to moment the sentence runs a real risk: it might explode, might come to a pitiful halt and fall back on itself, a great, inert mass clotted in the desert of the present; we sense this risk inside ourselves as we read on, anxiously. Of course, the book seems to be finished; after this page come others, but what does that prove? Everything can end up in nothingness or, worse still, in quicksand. What reassures us, however, is that behind the hesitations of life and language we glimpse a kind of arid passion, cold and sharp, a steel wire stretched between the lacerations of the past and the uncertainty of the future—an inhuman passion, unconscious of itself, an anxiety casting about for its cause, the maniac silence at the heart of language. It drills through the readers' time and draws after it this whole cavalcade of words; we will trust it.

If the work of art cries to all comers the name of its artist, the Late Great who has settled everything, then *The Traitor* is not a work of art; it is an event, a sudden precipitation, a disorder of words assuming an order. You hold in your hands this surprising object—at work in the process of creating its author. Of the latter we know nothing save this one negative characteristic: he will not be, he cannot be that sacred monster known as the Writer; if, at the end of his struggle, he finds himself, it will be as Anyman, a man like the rest, for the voice is in search of a man, not a monster. Therefore do not expect the gesture which is style; here everything is action. But if you prize a certain flavor in our great authors' words, a particular harmony in their sentences, a physiognomy of the feelings and of thought, then read *The Traitor*. At first you will lose everything, but everything will be restored to you; it is its renunciation, its passionate search, the break in its tone that make this voice inimitable; in this writing without subject, the radical impossibilty of style ultimately becomes a transcendence of all known styles, or, if you prefer, the style of death gives way to a style of life.*

The undertaking is scarcely one that will please. We like whoever likes us; if you want to be read, you have to know how to give yourself, how to pluck your words cunningly to make them resound, how to let your voice grow husky with feeling. But *he,* the object, the "third person," how could he like us? How could this voice like us? We are confronting a man cut in two, trying to join his stumps together. This occupation leaves him no leisure; perhaps tomorrow there will be time for such trifling. To which you will doubtless reply that your time is short too, and that the problems of joint surgery do not interest you. But how do you know? I happen to read science fiction, invariably with pleasure, for this genre offers an exact measure of our fear of ourselves. One piece particularly delights me: Men from Earth land on Venus; no sooner have they stepped out of their rocket than these future colonists happily start hunting for the natives of this planet, their future subjects, who do not show themselves at first. You can imagine the arrogance of the king of nature, the intoxication of his victory, his new freedom. Everything soon collapses before the intolerable evi-

---

* I do not claim to establish Gorz's superiority, but his originality. Like everyone else, I love death as much as life, for both comprise our fate.

dence: the conquerors are in a cage, their every movement foreseen;
every path they decide to take has already been determined for them
—by someone. Invisible as they lean over the glass cage, the Venusians submit these captive higher mammals to various intelligence
tests. Such, it seems to me, is our common condition. With this difference: that we are our own Venusians and our own guinea pigs.
Open *The Traitor* and you are a colonist, you observe with a shrug
of the shoulders a curious creature, perhaps a native running terrified across the soil of Venus, but it will not take you two minutes
to realize that the native is a rat and that this rat is none other than
yourself. The book was a trap, and we have fallen into it; now we
are scampering down the corridors of this oversized labyrinth under
the experimenter's eyes—that is, under our own. The experiment is
taking place; we are trying to find out if there is a single action in
this rigged world of which we can say, *I* have done it. Do we recognize our undertakings? Do they not become "Other" in becoming real? And do not "Other People" pursue them in our place,
Other People who are dearer to us than ourselves and who feed
upon our blood? Scarcely has this stranger in my heart of hearts
determined my behavior for me than I hear the uproar of the crowd
that inhabits me; a sudden agitation seizes all these people I do not
know, they condemn my initiative and protest that it concerns only
me, ignores them! *Je suis un autre,* says the Traitor, after Rimbaud.
I consider this to be quite modest. In his place, instead of saying,
"I am Someone Else," I would say, "I am Other People," and I
would refer to myself in the third person plural. Each of my acts,
registered upon the passivity of being, becomes a turnstile whose
imperious inertia defines me as its man, in other words, its slave,
the Other Person I must be in order to provide the first impulsion
and incessantly renew it. My slightest action, my sincerest commitment suggest inanimate faces; I must slip into this merry-go-round
and revolve like a circus horse in order to make it turn with me.
He, the author writing this Preface, is Someone Else, at this very

moment someone I don't like. I like the book and I said I would
write a preface for it because you always have to pay for the right
to like what you like; but once I picked up my pen a tiny invisible
carrousel started up just above the paper. This was the foreword-
as-a-literary-genre, which requires its specialist—an Olympian old
man, a silver-haired Academician. I wasn't an Academician? It
didn't matter; *he* would become one for the occasion. How dared
I present someone else's book if I wasn't on my own deathbed?
He would get inside the character's skin, make himself great-
elderly-diaphanous-and-astounded; *he* has written the foregoing
with a long pale hand which my own stubby fingers were manipu-
lating, *he* thrusts his tentacles into me, sucks up my words and my
ideas to produce his slightly superannuated graces. If I try to
wrench myself from his grasp, to write naturally, it is worse still;
I no longer know what is natural, *he* filters it out and transforms it
into *bonhomie*. He will hold onto the pen until the end of this exercise and then he will disappear. But whatever I start on next—pam-
phlet, lampoon, autobiography—other vampires lie in wait for me,
future intermediaries between my consciousness and my written
page.

At least I can hope that the intruder will go away, but it is just
as likely he will stay on, that I am the victim and the accomplice
of his permanent installation. One day Mirandola felt called upon
to bring out under the pseudonym Jouvence one of those vehement,
vital books which exhort the reader to courage and which for this
reason are considered courageous. The work was successful; men
who had been down and out glimpsed between the lines an austere
and sacred countenance which restored their hopes. In short,
Mirandola's book, once it cooled off, created Jouvence, its true
author. Today, Jouvence is recognized for his public utility, his
virtues are taught in our primary schools, he constitutes a part of
our national patrimony and often represents France abroad; he
lives on Mirandola, and Mirandola dies of him. The other day at

some opening night or other, Mirandola and Jouvence were given only a side seat in the balcony; Mirandola is modest, almost timid, yet he took it upon himself to protest loudly, trembling with rage. "I wouldn't have said anything if it had been just I," he exclaimed as he stalked out, "but I couldn't let them do it to Jouvence!"

Is it his fault? Is it yours? After all, we don't ask for these undesirable guests; it is other people who impose them upon us. Other people or their instruments, those petrified fingers continually pointing at us—the little black bag and the patient making the doctor out of a fat scatterbrained man, creating an angelic dictator, an enlightened despot who pursues our welfare against ourselves while we look forward to his orders, his remonstrances, his adorable severity. Sometimes we would like to muzzle the vampires and to show ourselves as we are; no one is listening, it is They who are expected. Faced with disappointment or general indifference, we ruefully decide, "If that's the way everyone wants it . . ." and then we unleash the monsters; it always turns out badly. Soon after the war I made the acquaintance of a foreign painter who came over from London; we used to chat in a café. He was a Traitor too, or thought he was. He liked himself so little that other people detested him; it was his name that they liked. I thought he was quite charming. Authoritarian and weak, mistrustful and naïve, drunk with pride and shame, mischievous and kindhearted, fascinated and inconvenienced by his celebrity, he was still quite stupefied at having behind him a considerable body of work which he nevertheless despised. This Don Quixote could respect himself only by winning on another battlefield the war he knew in advance he would never even manage to declare. It all came to an end, in fact, two years later in a burst of laughter. Unstable, unhappy, romantic, he depended on the time of day, on the light in the sky, on a note of music, on women, and especially on men, on all men. All together we might have saved him; lacking this unanimity he vacillated between arrogance and a defenseless kindness. Sometimes, to forget his Treason, that old, badly cared-for blennorrhagia, he let himself be entirely devoured by the celebrated creature he represented for others, and then there remained of him nothing more than a shiny bug; and sometimes fear, warmheartedness and good faith changed him into himself, an ordinary man who painted pictures. On this particular day, a little old man at another table was staring at us. I knew this little old man too; it was one of his compatriots, an *émigré* like himself, but one who had had no luck. Finally, unable to resist any longer, the little old man came over to introduce himself to my friend, who, off his guard, naïvely returned his smile. Glory and genius vanished together; there remained only two exiles who recognized each other without knowing each other, neither of whom was happy, and who talked together like friends.

It was the unluckier of the two who reignited the halo around his interlocutor's head; there had been a misunderstanding, he had not been speaking to the man but to the Painter. You mustn't ask too much of artists; provoked by a respect that was all too manifest, by a few servile inflections, the Great Man appeared; he was perfect—understanding, modest, so inspiredly simple that he drove his compatriot away. The latter hastily gathered up the papers that littered his table and left the café with a bitter, disappointed look, unaware that he had been the artisan of his own misfortune. The painter and I sat there together, and after an uneasy silence the great man murmured something I shall not forget: "Another failure!" And that meant: *He* had decided he would forget his name, his fame, his voluminous presence; *he* would be merely an exile sitting across the table from a companion in exile. But since it was the Incomparable Artist that was expected of him, *he* resigned himself to it, *he* lent his body and his voice to this Other Person who was not even his private parasite, who at that very moment was infecting over a thousand people from Peking to Valparaiso by way of Moscow and Paris, and he heard it speak out of his own mouth, with that dreadful sweetness meaning "Oh, no, it's nothing, *I'm* nothing, I've done nothing more than you, I've been lucky, that's all." And he realized that he had once again missed his chance, and that his chance would turn up again every day, every moment, and that every day, every moment, he would miss it.

The test is not over; we are still scampering through the labyrinth. The voice is still speaking. These tourists, these hitchhikers who inhabit us by the month or the day are not concerned by this investigation. We will not be asked to account for the furnished rooms, the halls of mirrors we rent out to our transient guests; everyone will be released after identifications have been checked, save for one mysterious and seldom seen visitor, a usurper who claims to be a prisoner and who is actually nothing more than our oldest lodger. This individual is precisely the person whom the voice persists in calling "he." Besides, listen to the voice now, it's not quite the same any more. At the start, it confined itself to a commentary on our occupant's actions; later, it revealed that this person was under observation, it described the tests he was made to undergo, and it gave the results. Now, louder, more insistent, sometimes brutal, it interrogates; the Venusians have turned into secret police and the rats into suspects. Of course, at first we are led to believe we are merely witnesses of a preliminary investigation. No one seems to bother about us. It is someone named Gorz who is on the stand; his name has just been pronounced, he is unremittingly questioned, his alibis are exploded, they are trying to force him to contradict himself. What was he doing in Vienna on a certain winter day in 1936? And before that, in his earliest childhood? And later on, during the Anschluss, he admits he frequented young Nazis, admired them. Why? Then he claims to have broken off with them. Did he really? Of his own free will? Can he honestly say, "*I* broke off?" Wasn't he forced by circumstances? By his "objective nature"? And where did he get this objective nature from? From whom? From what? Silent, embarrassed, we attend this interrogation and do our best to feel indiscreet. What luck if we could remind ourselves, I was not in Vienna under Chancellor Dollfuss; this business has nothing to do with me. But no, we are stuck, and we know it. At the very moment we explain to the guards that our presence in the torture chamber is due to a misunderstanding, we have already long since started on our own confessions. Executioners and victims, as always, it is we, the police, who begin questioning the Traitor. But as soon as he denounces his first inhabitant, that misshapen dwarf who might be dead or in hiding or whose sly face has just now pressed against the window to mock us, we remember suddenly the little weakling that inhabited us so long, and we try to reconstitute the suspect circumstances of his disappearance: In 1920 I existed, and *he* still existed, so who had so cruelly mutilated him? I remember I didn't like him much, and then I didn't see him any more; there was a murder, I think. But which of us killed the other? The voice is still talking; it has found words for the seam, the scar, the chasm that separates us; the first guilty parties have left their fingerprints on a knife; it won't take us long to identify them.

In fact, the world still seems to be inhabited by savages stupid enough to see reincarnated ancestors in their newborn children. Weapons and jewelry belonging to the dead man are waved under the infant's nose; if he makes a movement, there is a great shout— Grandfather has come back to life. This "old man" will suckle, dirty his straw and bear the ancestral name; survivors of his ancient generation will enjoy seeing their comrade of hunts and battles wave his tiny limbs and bawl; as soon as he can speak they will inculcate recollections of the deceased. A severe training will "restore" his former character, they will remind him that "he" was wrathful, cruel or magnanimous, and he will be convinced of it despite all experience to the contrary. What barbarism! Take a living child, sew him up in a dead man's skin, and he will stifle in such senile childhood with no occupation save to reproduce the avuncular gestures, with no hope save to poison future childhoods after his own death. No wonder, after that, if he speaks of himself with the greatest precautions, half under his breath, often in the third person; this miserable creature is well aware that he is his own grandfather.

These backward aborigines can be found in the Fiji Islands, in Tahiti, in New Guinea, in Vienna, in Paris, in Rome—wherever there are men. They are called parents. Long before our birth, even before we are conceived, our parents have decided who we will be. They have called us "he" years before we could say "I." We existed at first as absolute objects. By means of our family, society assigns us a situation, a being, a set of roles; the contradictions of history and class struggle determine in advance the character and the destiny of generations to come.

Algeria 1935: The parents are exploited, oppressed, reduced to poverty in the name of a racism which refuses them their status as men, Arabic is taught as a dead language, there are so few French schools that the great majority of Algerians are illiterate; rejected by France, without rights, without culture, without a past, they find relief and assistance only in religion or the negative pride of a dawning nationalism. Are not their sons, the fellahin of 1957, predetermined? And who has predetermined them thus, if not the French *colons*? Who has forced upon them, since Bugeaud, this destiny of wrath, despair and blood? Who has built these infernal machines which must one day explode and destroy the colonial system? Everywhere, the role is there, waiting for its man. For this one it is the role of a Jew; for that one, the role of a property owner. But these occupations are still too abstract. They are made specific *en famille;* we have all been forced to reincarnate at least one deceased person, generally a child who is the victim of his next of kin, killed at an early age, and whose wretched ghost survives in the form of an adult—our own father or mother. Zombies. Scarcely out of the womb, each child of man is taken for another; he is pushed and pulled to make him play his part like children the

comprachicos stuffed into porcelain jars to keep them from growing. At least the latter were not the sons of their executioners;
sometimes they were bought, often kidnaped. But who is not a
kidnaped child, more or less—stolen from the world, stolen from
his neighbor, stolen from himself? The custom has been perpetuated; it is from kidnaped children that kidnapers are made. We
knew all this, we have always known it. A solitary voice constantly
told us so, but we preferred to pass it over in silence, it was speaking in the desert, in our desert. *He* was doing this or that in our
place, and we were *his* straw man; out of cowardice, out of complacency, we declared, "I did it," and everyone pretended to believe
us on condition that we did the same for them. Thus for thousands
of years humanity, ashamed of yielding to fear, to blackmail, covers
up for the profitable racket that has been feeding on it. Fortunately,
someone has just given away the show, a "traitor," someone like
the American dockworkers who, disgusted by their own cowardice,
inform against the gangsters exploiting them and are later found in
the Hudson. A traitor, a man with as many cracks and crevices as
ourselves, but a man who could no longer stand the double-dealing.
He has broken the silence, refused to cover up for the intruder who
was impersonating him, refused to say, "I did it." Suddenly the
Others—the Zaras, the loas, the dark angels, the sons of Cain, all
our parasites—are shown naked. Naked but not dead. We are torn
between scandal and terror; from one minute to the next we expect
the mobsters' reprisal, an informer's execution. In fact, we have
gained nothing; we find our own cracks, we discover our occupants,
that is all. But we are undeceived. We thought that this little gnaw-
ing noise came into us through our ears, but no—it is in our hearts
that it was born; this time we have recognized the universal mumble of enslaved consciousness, the human voice—and we are not
likely to forget it.

Which, of course, does not keep the Traitor from belonging to a very particular species; he has his own way of being anyone at all. Neither the Extravagant Doctors nor the Braggart Heroes have chosen him as their domicile. If he refers to himself in the third person, it is not out of excess but by default. The temperate actions committed in his name he regards as *his* only if he manages to find motives for them; he has conducted hundreds of investigations, always in vain; from which one might conclude that he cares about nothing. *He* travels without wanting to travel; *he* meets people, makes visits, invites guests without enjoying company; on other occasions, *he* goes to earth, shuts himself up without any desire to be alone. Is he blasé? Not at all. To rid yourself of this world's goods, you have to have cared for them once. And we certainly cannot reproach him for "having come back from somewhere, anywhere, without ever having been there." For there is nothing of the *revenant* about him; he has never left, this is his real misfortune. Why? Because he didn't want to enough. His heart, moreover, shows no trace of that arrogant insatiability which has served as our alibi for three literary generations. The infinite, the eternal Elsewhere, the Dream—he couldn't care less, thank God. Some men I know feel justified in despising the world by comparing it with some perfect prototype. But the Traitor despises no one, nothing. Then is it Drieu La Rochelle's famous "empty suitcase"? No. The valise trick was good for the years between the wars—you opened it, you asked the spectator to see for himself that there was nothing in it besides a pair of pajamas and a toothbrush. Today we know that the valise had a false bottom, that it was used to carry arms and drugs; the *jeunesse dorée* skillfully concealed in it anything that could be used to destroy the race and precipitate the succession of the Inhuman. But the Traitor has no interest in blowing up the world; the Inhuman is already his fate, since he does not share the objectives of men. In a word, I classify him with the Indifferents. This subgroup is of recent origin, its representative

members are no more than thirty; no one knows yet what they will
become. All we know now is that we lose all means of understanding them if we insist on saddling them with an aristocratic non-
chalance. What distinguishes them, in fact, is their eagerness. Gorz
has a job, cultivates his body and his mind, lives with a woman.
If you met him carrying his elegant leather briefcase at the Palais de
Justice or the Bourse, you would take him for someone like yourself. He is punctual at his office, scrupulous to the point of being
niggling; no one is more affable; in his daily relationships he betrays only a faint shadow of reserve which his colleagues smilingly
explain as timidity; but ask him to do you a favor and he drops
everything to execute it as fast as he can. Superficial observers will
judge him to be insignificant. As a matter of fact, he speaks infre-
quently, he looks like everyone else; this effacement and this skill-
ful mimicry will assure his popularity. But when you look at him
more closely, this impostor is exposed by his very zealousness.
Most people, convinced of their status as men from father to son,
and since Adam, treat their human nature with some negligence;
they have rights to it so ancient and so little contested that they
calmly follow their personal inclinations, certain that they can take
a piss, if they want to, or kill a man, quite humanly. But the Indifferent does not recognize his own right to his inclinations; he has
to force himself to take a drink or get into a fight, drink without
thirst, take revenge without anger for an affront he has not suffered,
all in order to do as the rest do. His first impulse is not to have
one—that is what he must conceal, constantly deny; this curious
product of our societies, terrified of falling to the level of the angels
or that of conditioned rats, forces himself to imitate the Adamites
in every detail; he disappears. In the excellent little book in which
he describes his war experiences, Paulham calls himself "the diligent soldier." The Indifferent, on the other hand, rouses suspicion
for the simple reason that he is a diligent *man*.

Too diligent to be honest. If he is so anxious to pass for a man like myself, it must mean that he isn't one. Could the human community contain *false* men? Men who cannot be distinguished from the real ones? Then how could you know if the real ones exist at all? Who is to check their qualifications? I have occasionally heard that man was his own future, on other occasions that he was his past—never his present. We are all false men; the Traitor has given away the game again; by his passion to make himself human, he reminds us that our race does not exist. The author of this book is a rat, as we might have suspected. And what is more, a rat possessed. By another rat? By the rat-in-itself? Certainly not. This Other Person a lonely voice continually refers to, this pure object, this receding perspective, this absence—is man, our tyrant. We are all exposed, rats a prey to man. Now the Indifferent's folly is immediately recognizable, it is our own. We all pursue a ghost down the corridors of an experimental labyrinth; Gorz is at the head of the line. If he catches that ghost and eats him, if he assimilates into his own substance that parasite he has fed so long on his anxieties and exhaustions, then our race is possible; somewhere, between the rats and the angels, it is in the process of being born; we will get out of the labyrinth.

Once again, the sense of this book has been transformed. It is not a question of knowing oneself but of changing life; we are not being spoken to, but whether we like it or not it is of us that the fundamental question is asked, By what activity can an "accidental individual," as Marx calls him, realize the human person in himself and for everyone else?

This book is organized like a feed-back machine: the present ceaselessly metamorphosizes the past from which it issues. In the early pages, the voice seemed to gather up words accidentally, no matter where, to escape its anxiety and to have something behind it, no matter what—anything but silence. And that was true; at that moment, that was true. But the question of man has been asked. A new light is now shed on the beginning of the enterprise, a metamorphosis: Before the voice, Gorz already existed, was already suffering from his indifference, was protecting himself against it with the means at hand. Suddenly he changes his tactics and reverses his relation to himself. This rupture constitutes in itself an absolute event, but it would be wrong to construe it as an interior adventure whose chief merit would be to have produced a book; in fact, it is in the book that the event occurs, it is through the book and by the book that this rupture develops and becomes conscious of itself. *The Traitor* does not claim to *tell us* a convert's story; it *is* the conversion itself.

Gorz is thirty-two; for thirty-two years, whatever he does, it invariably seems to him that he might have done the opposite and that the result would have been the same; that is, null—or, worse still, insignificant. For thirty-two years, his existence has escaped him, he has no proof of it beyond an insurmountable boredom: *I'm bored, therefore I am*. But he has struggled, has searched, has thought he found the way to carry it off, deciding, "Because I belong nowhere, to no group, to no enterprise, because I am exiled from all such groups and enterprises, there is only one alternative: either to be a marginal note of society and history, the supernumerary of the human race . . . , reduced to the boredom of living, to the acute awareness of the contingency of everything around me, or to raise myself conscientiously to the absolute—that is, to regard everything, philosophically, as a moment of the spiritual adventure and then . . . to recover, starting from such speculative interests, a taste for the concrete. . . . I can achieve . . . the real only by starting with the Idea." In other words, since he is so constituted as to be unaware of possessing any particular desire, he will put his indifference to good use. Because he cannot —or will not, nothing is certain yet—be a certain Gorz, he will make himself into the Universal Man; he will determine his behavior by concepts and give himself this rule: Always act so that the circumstances and the moment serve as a pretext for your actions in order to realize in and beyond yourself the generality of the human race. This is why he undertook, at twenty, to write a philosophical work; when you are immunized from birth against the violences of fear, concupiscence or anger, you must either do nothing at all or base everything on reason, even the act of opening an umbrella if it is raining.

Everything is clear now. We are no longer surprised that he has "betrayed"; he is one of those people who have their heads full of words, who analyze everything, who always want to know the why and the how; a critical and destructive spirit—in short, a damn intellectual. I wouldn't dream of denying it—that's even why I like him; I'm one myself. Not long ago a literary paper asked the prince of counterfeit what he hated most of all; he didn't hesitate a moment: "Intellectuals." I happen to be the friend of this forger. He is a true poet and a good man; but I wonder what was the matter with him that day. Everyone knows his hunted looks, his arias about time, death and destiny, anthology pieces from a perpetual and suppliant vindication, these congestions of words in his throat, his charming hands that are words too, turning palms outward to implore pardon, this harassed, exhausted intellect, but still running, leaping nimbly from one idea to the next without realizing that it is merely turning the treadmill in its cage, these skyrocket improvisations whose scaffolding can be found in the texts of the day before and which, as they fade and go out, offer glimpses of the incurable sadness of that frozen stare. This man seeks a tribunal for himself only in order to corrupt it; if he meets you, you will be judge and jury, he will not let you off from a single detail of his behavior and will let you go only if you have acquitted him. But don't fool yourself, he knows it all, he knows he was condemned at the century's start to the sentence he wants to head off, he knows he is a convict and has been working out that sentence for over fifty years; for he is condemned to plead even in old age the cause which his adolescence has judged without appeal. What would you call this Devil's Advocate if not an intellectual? I know others, of course, who would oppose such chatter with the great silences of the earth or of the peasants. But if you open them up, what a hub-bub! Their heads are humming with words that describe other people's silence. Gorz is the first, I think, to have formulated the problem concretely; and I am grateful to him for that. It matters little whether you speak about language or about silence, about the poet's confused intentions or about reason's clear and distinct ideas; what matters is that these speakers must speak, are compelled to speak. In the cause of the heart's shadows, our forger has offered more reasoning than Kant to establish the rights of Reason. He was compelled to; discourse, concepts, argumentation—this is our fate. Why? Because the intelligence is neither a gift nor a fault, it is a drama—or, if you prefer, a temporary solution which generally becomes a life sentence. Someone once told our Traitor, "You stink intelligence the way some people stink under their arms." And it's true; intelligence stinks. But not more than stupidity; there are odors for every taste. Stupidity smells of animals; intelligence, of men. To begin with, this is because there are certain lacerated, condemned, exiled individuals who try to surmount their conflicts and their solitude by pursuing the fleeting image of unanimity; it is that image we see reflected in their eyes, that image their timid smiles offer us. Apropos of anything and everything, the appeal is there, permanently etched on their faces; the voice insists, what-ever it says, on universal agreement; but humanity, weighed down by its particularities, by its close-packed interests, by its passions, detests anyone who would dissolve its differences and its hates in the formal harmony of assent.

And then, intelligence is scrupulous: It wants to start every-thing over at the beginning, even what everyone thinks he already knows how to do. It takes apart walking or breathing and puts them back together again, it learns how to wash an ear, how to blow a nose, according to principles. That is what makes intellectuals walk like wounded men learning how to use their artificial limbs. But you must understand them—they are reinventing everything to compensate for the great rummage sale that has liquidated their every impulse, every obstinacy; they need it to replace the signals that have not been inscribed on their flesh, the habits they have not been given, the paths they have not been shown—in short, to live. I remember seeing a puppy after the partial ablation of its cerebellum. It moved across the room and only rarely bumped into furniture, but it had become thoughtful; the animal carefully established its itinerary, deliberated before avoiding an obstacle and took a long time to accomplish the movements previously made without paying any attention at all. In the language of the period, the animal's cortex had assumed the functions of the lower centers; what we had was an intellectual dog. I don't know if the creature was very useful or very harmful to his fellows, but we can suppose it had lost what another exile, Genêt, has so aptly called "the sweet natal confusion"; ultimately, the creature must either crack up or reinvent the dog. And the rest of us, rats without half our brains, are so constituted that we have to crack up or invent man. Moreover, we are well aware that he will be invented without us, by work and by conflict, that our models grow obsolete from one day to the next, that not even a knucklebone will figure in the finished product; but the creation would be performed in the dark, blindly, by tinkering, by puttering and patching, if we, the lobotomized, were not here constantly repeating that you must work according to principles, that it is not a matter of darning but of cutting, that our race, finally, will be the concrete universal or not be at all.

Gorz's intelligence is immediately and strikingly apparent. It is one of the sharpest, the most agile that I know; he must have great need of this tool to have sharpened it so well. But when he undertakes his philosophical treatise, he still does not escape the contradiction proper to intellectuals. He wants to act only in terms of the human condition; yet, once performed, the action buries itself in the particular; what remains is the fortuitous realization of one possibility out of a thousand. Why particularly that one? The worst is that it compromises him; he cannot even breathe without adding a new brushstroke to a portrait-without-a-model which is none other than his own. He would have to become every possible Gorz at once for these futile equivalents to cancel each other out, in order to be, finally, *only* man by becoming *all* man. But no—"We are born several and we die alone," says Valéry's Socrates. Gorz cannot keep from living or from shrinking with use. His universal intelligence exceeds his personal adventure and is disgusted at the appearance of the physiognomy of the Gorz who will die alone; his intelligence refuses this solitary, does not even want to recognize him. It would accept him gladly as anyone at all; now he is not even that; a series of accidents has given him a definite individuality that distinguishes itself from the rest by a number of inanities.

We all know this listless, sugary anguish—we, that is, we intellectuals. We think we are universal because we play with concepts, and then, suddenly, we see our shadow at our feet; we are *here,* we are doing *this* and nothing else. Once, in Brooklyn, I thought I was going crazy. It was my own fault—I was strolling, and you don't stroll in the United States. Therefore I was crossing sidewalks, passing apartment buildings, staring at people on the street. And from one street to the next, apartment buildings, people and sidewalks were all the same or, at least, seemed all the same to me. I turned right, left, turned back, continued straight ahead, always to find the same brick buildings, the same white steps in front of the same doors, the same children playing the same games. At first I liked this—I had discovered the city of absolute equivalents; universal and anonymous, I had no more reason to walk on *this* sidewalk than on the same one ten blocks ahead; recommenced a thousand times, the wave of stone carried me on, made me share in its inert renewal. What gradually exhausted me was to be advancing constantly *to get nowhere;* I walked faster, I was almost running, and I was still in the same place. Suddenly I was conscious of an infinite refusal; all these standardized products, all these stubs of streets running side by side, resembled each other further in that they were equally empty of me—except for one, in fact, which was in no way different from the rest, in which I had no more reason to be than in the neighboring blocks and which, for an unknown reason, or even with no reason at all, tolerated my presence. Suddenly my movements, my life, my own weight seemed illegitimate to me. My person was not real, since I had no particular reason to be at this point on the forty-second parallel rather than at any other; still, I was an individual being, irreducible since my position by latitude and longitude rigorously defined me. Neither everyone nor someone, nor quite something—a determination of space, a guilty and contagious dream that haunted, in spots, the overheated asphalt, a fault in being, a defect. An obstinately moving body, my presence in the mechanical universe of repetition became a crude accident as stupid as my birth. Ubiquity would have saved me; one must be legion, prowl a hundred thousand sidewalks at once—that alone would have allowed me to be any stroller in any Brooklyn street. Since I could not abandon myself, or multiply myself, I dashed into the subway, returned to Manhattan and, back in my hotel, recovered my usual, ordinary *raisons d'être,* scarcely convincing, but human.

There is no subway for young Gorz, no hotel and no *raison d'être.* He is outside even in his room, hence illegitimate everywhere; and hoaxed into the bargain: he thinks he can escape his insignificant person by parading the disgust it inspires in him; now, it is first of all this disgust that singles him out; the peculiarity of intellectuals is precisely their vain desire for universality.

But he has just finished his treatise, he steps back to get a better look at it, and the entire hoax vanishes; the notion of the universal contracts, condenses, assumes a contour, a physiognomy—it resembles him; he is at the origin of a supernumerary object—this bundle of typed pages—and at the same time he is imprisoned within it. For a long time now other people have claimed to recognize him by his most ordinary gesture, his way of eating, sitting down, opening a telegram— "Oh yes, that's you all right, that's just like you, I'd know you anywhere by that, what you just did is pure Gorz, the spit and image." God knows it made him angry enough, but has he not just performed a voluminous gesture that has closed over him? The others will be all too pleased, they will lean over the transparent walls of his prison and they will recognize him. "That way of writing, *mon vieux,* that way of correcting yourself, of entering into your subject little by little, of testing the water with your toe before jumping in—why, that's you, that's you all right, and those ideas, they're pure Gorz, only Gorz could have such ideas!" Like a devil in a bottle, whether he opens cans, other people's concepts or his own umbrella, he has only one and the same gesture, only one way to enter the views of a seventeenth-century philosopher and a girl friend's apartment. One by one he takes up the sentences of his book. Gestures! Gestures! Gestures! Gorz is here, under his eyes, stretching out his long neck, pinching his thin lips. *"Tel qu'en lui-même enfin . . ."* * In short, he has tried to live, and he has failed. Now he knows he was condemned to fail and that he was secretly determined to besides.

It is at this very moment that we first hear the voice—a tiny, almost unintelligible mumble born of anxiety and recrimination, ruminating this surprising and foreseen defeat. The voice merely establishes a fact: That's him, that's him all right, the spitting image. Which is enough for everything to collapse. It was other people who claimed to know this parasite that fattened on his acts, while the Indifferent's universal gaze passed through him like light through a windowpane. Suddenly he is there, opaque, encumber-

* "As into himself at last [eternity transforms him]," from the first line of Mallarmé's sonnet on Poe.—TR.

ing. "Confess—you saw him, you spoke to him, we know you did; your alibi is totally unconvincing, we know the time and place of your meetings. You're finished!" The voice changes to a confession: "All right, yes, I know him better than anyone else, I've always known him, I'll tell you everything I know about him!"

Was I not right just now when I said we should always speak of ourselves in the plural? There are two people living on this unfortunate creature: there is the Universal Man, an elusive, well-armed tyrant, and then there is the other one, the failure. One becomes a certain Gorz by trying to be merely man; and, to tell the truth, one wants to become man because one refuses to be a certain Gorz. But then, who refuses to be Gorz if not Gorz himself? This refusal explains and defines him. If one accepted being—in other words, accepted having been the greedy boy with the long neck who wants to preserve his futile universality—if one unremittingly spoke of him, if one detailed all his private obsessions, if, instead of passing through him, the intellectual gaze brought him to light, would not this "original" disappear with the stubborn negation that comprised his originality? Of course, it is not Millennial Man who would come to take his place, but another private individual whose fundamental obsessions would merely risk being more positive. What is there to be gained? Is the game worth the candle? As a matter of fact, it is too late to reckon profit and loss; the voice is speaking, the enterprise has begun. The Traitor has chosen as his goal his own particularity.

It is not a question of knowing that particular nature, not even of changing it, but first of all of changing *oneself* by wanting to know it. The Indifferent has no such foolish project as to describe himself; he wants to modify the fundamental relation that unites him to Gorz. When he turns back toward the child and the adolescent he has been, when he questions his witness, his investigation is already an action. He calls a halt to his headlong flight, forces himself to look at himself without disgust, transfers to himself his taste for generalities and, lacking All Man, he claims first to become for himself All Gorz.

This is not easy; having neglected himself so long, he is lost inside himself, like Crusoe on his desert island. How rediscover the lost paths? Creepers and briars cover everything. He can still glimpse certain memories, but what is a memory? What is the truth of this inert miniature? And its importance—what is its importance? Is it the part that explodes in the present like a bomb? Is it the present making itself up to look like the past? Or both together? To answer these questions we must know: Who is this Gorz I am? Who made me so that I am Gorz, so that I refuse so fiercely to be Gorz? But how decide? Where are the tools? Of course, there is no lack of offers; there are well-tried methods which hurriedly propose themselves and even make little test demonstrations to prove their effectiveness. "Your class," says one, "is decaying. Without principles and without hope, it expends all its strength maintaining itself and has not enough heart, or, if you prefer, enough naïveté, to undertake anything new. Your indifference betrays the anxious uncertainty of your class; existence seems without a purpose to you because bourgeois life no longer has a meaning. As for your philosophical malaise, how else account for its origin? The bourgeoisie no longer has any confidence in its old idealism and tries to conceal it with new tinsel; you have taken these bright rags into your hands, you have seen the threadbare warp, and you have been disgusted, unable to satisfy yourself with these outworn notions, unable to find a new rationale." He listens, he approves, he is not altogether convinced; he has no difficulty admitting he is a young bourgeois. Without needs, quite abstract, a "pure consumer of water, air, bread and other people's work, reduced to . . . the acute awareness of the contingency of everything around me." But he knows many other bourgeois his age who do not in the least resemble him. Of course, he could, without abandoning the method, recover the historical and social circum-

stances which might explain his peculiarities. He tells us himself
that he is Austrian, half Jewish, that he had to leave Austria during the Anschluss and that he lived in Switzerland for several years.
He is convinced that these factors are not without an influence on
his present attitude. But just what influence is here at work? And
how is it wielded? And in a more general manner, is there anything more surprising, more obscure than the action of people,
of events or of objects on a man's development? Around him everyone is in agreement: we are conditioned; he finds no one to doubt
the existence of this conditioning and to question its nature; these
are things handed down from father to son; their quarrels begin
when they try to classify the conditions and to determine their
importance. But all these people are inheritors; these presuppositions, these supposed evidences comprise an ancient legacy which
each generation palms off on the one following, and of which no
one has ever made an inventory. The Indifferent, on the other
hand, has inherited none of their convictions; the Exile from all
groups must also be exiled from all ideologies. When he comes
to consider that he is "the son of a Jew" and at the same time that
he has an "acute awareness of the contingency of everything," he
admires the isolation, the opacity, the lofty irreducibility of these
two facts at such variance with each other. Considering them quite
naïvely, it is as if they were two miniatures of medieval cities
girdled with ramparts and moats; each was painted long ago and
framed, and they were hung at the same level on the wall; between them there is no visible connection for they do not exist in
the same world. Yet he is not unaware that people come and go
in this private museum of theirs, that they pass from a Circumci-
sion to a Flagellation without even looking for the painters' names,
saying: "*That* is because of *this;* I am the unfortunate product of
my race, of my father's Jewishness, of my friends' anti-Semitism,"
as if the real link between these mysterious images of himself were
quite simply the wall on which the pictures had been hung; but

when he thinks of the peaceful assurance of these heirs, he falls into a trance of wondering.

This is when the other method seems more likely, this strange dogma based on absolute skepticism. Does he remember his early years, the aversion that his mother felt, that she was able to inspire in him, for the Jew she had married, the intolerable tension of the family group, the severe training he was made to undergo as soon as he could speak? Then let him ask whether he was not the victim of a tyrannical, castrational mother, and if it is not from this obscure period, from this oppression submitted to in bewilderment, that he must date the appearance of the "complexes" that today divide him from the world. *"He,"* finally—would *he* not be the Honorary Aryan, a character an outraged wife wants to impose upon her son because she ceaselessly reproaches a certain Jew for being the only husband she could find? The docility of a molded child survives in the adult as apathy.

To which he replies that his education has in fact given him certain complexes. His mother wanted to make him this Other Person whom he has in part become; during his first years, he suffered, as now, from an anxious and overzealous indifference. But he cannot understand how these famous complexes perpetuate themselves. He was apathetic at eight, he is apathetic today. Is it the same apathy? Has it been preserved by an inert perseverance of being? But he will not believe so easily in human passivity; all his experience rejects this notion, despite its convenience, and the metaphysic that supports it as well. Will he admit, on the other hand, that he has coddled his complexes, that he feeds and fattens them now, that the adolescent and the adult have developed, emphasized, enriched the child's first characteristics by a kind of continuous creation? Then he would be responsible for everything, it is he, from day to day, who makes himself indifferent.

He cannot reach a conclusion so quickly. None of these interpretations is completely satisfactory, none is altogether clear in his eyes; a traitor once again, like the child in the fairy tale who sees the emperor naked, he takes inventory of our philosophical heritage, finds the coffers empty, and says so ingenuously enough. Why, moreover, should he be interrogated by the other people's methods, why should he hand himself over to the psychoanalytic or Marxist third degree? It depends on him, in fact, to put these investigation procedures to the test in the questions he asks himself about himself. This Oedipus interrogates his own past, the validity of his memory, the rights of experience and the limits of reason, and the legitimacy, finally, of the prophetic gifts claimed by our Tiresiases. But he turns his back on the universal. He invents the method by reflecting on his own case, it will substantiate itself by his success; in order to bring himself to light as an individual totality, he must confine himself in the experience of his individuality, which he will invent for himself by inventing his own interrogation and the means of answering it. The Traitor erases everything and begins himself all over again. That is what gives us, today, the opportunity to read a *radical* book.

For a long time we have been listening to "his master's voice." Now it is Gorz speaking. The monologue's end catches up with its beginning, envelops it, absorbs it; the meaning of the work appears in broad daylight. First of all there was a question, asked in the darkness by no one: Under what conditions could the man named Gorz say "I"? But, immediately afterward, a creature still indistinct emerged from the shadows. It is not merely a question of determining these conditions, the book becomes Gorz's living effort to satisfy them. *He* knows, now, that *he* will have done nothing if he does not wring the necks of the vampires that dress, wash and feed him in order to feed upon him. The first action of my hands, depending only on itself and the obstacles to be overcome, turning back on itself to develop and check itself—that is the action which will say my first "I"; this imperceptible pressure of an action upon itself, that will be I. And who keeps him from acting? He knows that too: it is the too prompt desire to be too quickly universal. He reminds himself now that his future action will necessarily borrow *his* eyes, *his* mouth, *his* arms, that it will have *his* expression; and, above all, that it will be more rigorously defined every day by the ephemeral agitation it will communicate to the objects around him. Taken outwardly, that's all a man is—an anxiety working over matter in the limits of a rigorously defined area. Singular old enterprises impose their singularity on a new enterprise which refers to all the rest in order to singularize them still more: "I" is this perpetual coming and going. Whatever it does, it will be itself; but one must accept oneself in order to act. Who keeps him from doing that? What is the reason for his futile desire for universality? He discovers an accumulation of failures piled up in his heart: his childhood; he attempts to sweep it away, but that is not enough. He can no longer conceal from himself the fact that he is constantly reinventing his bastardy, the weight of his old miseries, his old weaknesses; because he is not everything, it is he, today, who flings himself into a proud passivity so that everyone will know he receives his determinations from the exterior and without consenting to them; it is he who annihilates himself of his own free will or, at least, who absents himself, letting the habits other people have made him acquire assure his place in the world, assume the natural and social functions of his body; it is he who has voluntarily decided, like Saint John of the Cross but without mysticism, to do nothing at all in order to be free to "be nothing at all." Then is he free? Of course; he never doubted it. They have made him, marked him, poured him into the mold—and he is free? Yes; predestination and free will create in him one and the same thing. How can this be? He will try to say, to tell himself; but his purpose remains practical: It is, for him, a question of inventing the dialectical movement that can sum up the changing relations of past, present and future, of objective and subjective, of being and existence, of mechanism and freedom, in order to be able to affirm himself and at the same time perpetually dissolve himself until at last he can generate in his heart the authentic impulse that ravages him as it leaves his hands and reaches external completion in that holocaust of objects called an "action."

Such is his task. He has just understood it, he puts what he has understood on paper; and, at that moment, he realizes that his most intimate desire leaves his heart through his hands; that he is already launched on an enterprise; that yesterday's words and today's and those of the month past gather together, organize to show him his new face; that he is dissecting himself by words so that he can someday create himself by actions; that this destruction creates him, that it determines him irreversibly, that it transforms him little by little into that incomparable and ordinary creature each of us is for himself while our vampires are asleep; that he has, finally, "jumped in," condemned, whatever he does, to have no other springboard ever again but himself. This is the moment. *Hic Rhodus, hic salta;* the enterprise turns back on itself, provides a thousand fluctuations of consciousness, the thousand rings of reflection, brushes against itself, smells itself, sees itself. The enterprise is the voice. The voice recognizes itself. In it, action discovers itself and says "I." I am making this book, I seek myself, I write. Somewhere a hollow-eyed chap sighs, intimidated, "How pompous to use the first person!" and then dissolves. Gorz appears. I am Gorz, it was my voice that was speaking, I am writing, I exist, I have submitted to myself and I create myself, I have won the first round.

Is it worth crying victory? Who is Gorz, after all? Someone "of no social importance," a failure of the universal who has flung out these abstract speculations to fascinate himself with his own insignificant person. Where is the gain? Where is the progress? This is a question Gorz will not answer, I imagine; but we can answer for him. For we have followed step by step this fantastic Cuvier who

finds a bone, reconstructs the whole animal from the meager remains, and realizes, at the end, that the creature he has put together is none other than himself. The method was valid only for
him, he has said so a hundred times; he can experience it only in
his own case. But we have followed him, we have understood the
meaning of his actions along with him, we have watched his experi-
ments, seen the muscles reborn around the knucklebone, the organ-
ism reconstitute itself step by step, author and book create each
other by means of each other. Since what we understand belongs to
us, Gorz's method is ours; when he tries to interpret his life by
Marxist dialectic or by psychoanalysis without ever quite succeed-
ing, his failure involves us, we will be able to make the test, and we
know the result in advance. And when he asks his own object, that
is, himself, to create his method for him, we grasp at once the significance of this singular attempt. For we are like him in this, that
each of us, too, is a unique someone. Then what is this object that
makes itself into a subject by invoking a method? Gorz, or you
and I? You are not indifferent, you will have other questions to
ask about yourself; by inventing himself, Gorz has not relieved you
of your duty, the duty of inventing yourself. But he has proved that
the generalizing invention is possible and necessary. Closing this
book, each reader confronts his own underbrush, the poisonous
trees of his private jungle; it is up to him to hack out his own paths,
to clear his own ground, to drive off the vampires, to burst the old
iron corsets, the exhausted actions into which resignation, fear and
self-distrust have laced him. Will we recover the universal by putting
our chips on the individual? No, that would be too easy. We are no
longer altogether animals, without quite being men; we have not yet
taken advantage of that dreadful catastrophe which has fallen on
some representatives of the animal kingdom—thought. In short, we
shall be victimized mammals for a long time still; this is an age of
fury, fetish and sudden terrors, universality is only a dream of
death at the heart of separation and fear. But for several decades

now our world has been changing. At the very depths of its hatred, reciprocity reveals itself; even those who enjoy emphasizing their differences must be willing to ignore a fundamental identity. This new disturbance, this modest but stubborn attempt to communicate across the incommunicable, is not the stale and always somewhat stupid desire for an inert and already realized universal; this is what I should prefer to call "the movement of universalization." Nothing is possible yet; no agreement is foreseen among the experimental creatures; our universals separate us; they provide the permanent occasion of private massacres. But if one of us, stirred by anxiety, turns back on his singularity to go beyond it; if he tries to recognize his solitude in order to escape it, to launch the first bridges, whatever the cost—in a strange, empirical language like the speech invented by the aphasiac—between the islands of our archipelagos; if he replaces our intransigent loves—which are disguised hatreds—by applied preferences; if he tries, in circumstances that are always individual and out of date, to ally himself with others whom he scarcely approves of and who do not approve of him, to make the reign of injustice a little less unjust, then he will force those others to reinvent this same stubborn effort, to ally themselves by the recognition of their diversities. This is what Gorz has attempted; this Traitor has broken the tables of the universal, but in order to find the movement of life, that slow universalization which realizes itself by the affirmation and the transcendence of the particular. The immediate consequence: At the very moment when at last he can say, *I* am doing this, *I* am responsible for it, he realizes that he is speaking to *us*. For today there are only two ways of speaking about the self: the third person singular and the first person plural. We must know how to say "we" in order to say "I"—that is beyond question. But the opposite is also true. If some tyranny, in order to establish the "we" first, deprives individuals of the subjective image, all "interiority" disappears and all reciprocal relations with it. "They" will have won forever, and "we" never stop running through their experimental labyrinths, crazed rodents at the mercy of vampires.

Gorz's book concerns us all. If he stammers at first, if he doesn't know where he's going, if he transforms himself incessantly and if we feel his fever and his chills in our own hands, if he contaminates us without seeing us and if, finally, he speaks directly, intimately, to each reader, it is because he is altogether alive with the movement that animates us, the movement of our times. Radical and modest, vague and rigorous, banal and inimitable, this is the first book after the defeat; the vampires have made a memorable carnage, they have extinguished hope; we must catch our breath, play dead a while, and then get up, leave the charnel house, begin everything all over again, invent a new hope, try to live. The centuries' great slaughters have made Gorz into a corpse; he revives by writing an Invitation to Life.

—JEAN-PAUL SARTRE

We

Hic Rhodus, hic salta.

He stared at the silhouettes appearing behind the window curtains across the Place de Rennes. The die was cast; he had to make a move. For ten years he had clung to this manuscript. He had set out to solve the world's problems. With no certainty save that certainties can be acquired and remain subject to dismissal, he had thought he could begin living the day he answered this question: When, how, for whom can life have a meaning?

The silhouettes wavered behind the curtain. The light went out. He glanced at the shadows of the doorway. That was where they would come out, and the manuscript would stay on the shelf, a corpse. Would they even read it? Not tonight. Tomorrow maybe. He wanted to be angry with them, but could not.

Hic Rhodus, hic salta. He had promised himself to write these words in his journal the day he finished writing this book. He had clung to it for ten years; it had become his justification. He had discovered that when a man is incapable of living, or when life has no meaning for him, he always invents this way out for himself: to write about the nonmeaning of life, to look for an explanation, an escape, to demonstrate that all roads are blocked save one—this demonstration itself, and the remedy it provides against the experience it contradicts. Writing had become a passion; he had purged himself of all problems; he had resolved them in the abstract. And when, after nine years, he had felt he was near the end, the beginning of the end, he had realized that the essential thing was eluding him. The essential thing: himself. He felt empty and bone-dry. He wondered if he would even suffer if his book (ten years!) were refused. "The Essay" had slowly died as he drew near the end, had fallen outside himself; it had given him something to think about for ten years, but these ruminations had not reached him. He was the same as he had been before, with this exception: he had learned to think about life. He had not learned to endure himself. He had escaped himself by posing his problems in the abstract, and he found himself intact. Now everything had to be begun all over again; he must take a look at himself rather than at "man in general." He must stop believing a problem can ever be "solved." He must reach this certainty: A philosophy cannot dispense with life— the question persists and you have to put up with yourself indefinitely.

Then it had begun to seem laughable. This book had not come from *him*. It was a lie. It was not looking for his way, it was looking for The Way. And all it had given him was his feeling, today, of mounting anxiety: I have not tried to resolve problems, but to get rid of them. Using a technique not my own, I have tried to make everything abide by the laws of this technique. I have wadded reality together and tied it up with Morel's string. I have asked myself the questions he left open (What is pure thought? Morality? Authenticity? Value?), but I have refused to live them. I have lined up various cogitations, supposing that by repeating what he had shown I would discover the Truth. I have done nothing except imitate without understanding.

That is why he finds himself empty today, the earth giving way under his feet. No need to wait for Morel's verdict. He knows it will be negative. Ten minutes' conversation with Morel and he came back to all the questions of ten years before, questions he hadn't known how to ask, with this one into the bargain: What made me think I was competent to begin this anyway?

Betrayed. The question shimmers before him like a trap. Atheist he might be, but the question betrayed his profound religiosity. He had a God. God, for him, was called Morel, and all he had done for ten years was to pray to Morel as you pray to God: spiritual exercises in order to enter into communion with Morel; exegeses of texts in order to receive the absolute Truth from Morel's mouth (Morel's pen). Competent to begin! To begin what? As for my questions, who else would be competent to begin? But that was just it, they were Morel's questions, not mine; his. I didn't care about "me"—I didn't like "me." I liked Morel, because it was easier; you got rid of yourself to become—by immolating yourself on the altar of—Morel. Like Kay. Kay doesn't love herself, so she loves me; I am the anti-Kay in whom Kay lovingly abolishes herself. And I, I'm nothing unless I abolish myself worshiping Morel. I'm a fake. I've often wanted to scream at Kay, "You're in love with a fake," to tell her I don't exist, that I'm the empty vessel waiting for the Lord's wine. I loaded her up with all of Morel's books, and if she hadn't said she liked them, I think I would have dropped her. (And when she happens to disagree with Morel, he becomes exasperated and refuses to argue; he explains why Morel thinks as he does and is furious that this explanation is not enough.) She expects a personal contribution from me, but I have nothing to give her.

I want to see Morel and tell him, "Don't waste your time, I'm worthless; it's all a cheat; just intellectual games, words." And

then he'd send me away. "Unworthy son," he would say, "I condemn you to eat dry sand forever." I'll say, "Yes, yes," sobbing,
and I'll feel the floor swaying, as it did when the school principal
told me, "Dirty Jew, we're doing you a favor keeping you on," and
when the priest said, "Can't your father go to mass?"

Let them condemn me. He had been asking for it a long time
now. He who is damned is saved, for the damned are never alone.
There is always a God pointing his finger at them, they are saved
in and of themselves. Respectful, obedient, impotent, their entire
infernal existence is a submission: there is God and the Law above
them; they are relieved of themselves, in security.

The worst, and the best too, that could happen to him is that he
might lose his respect for Morel; then there would be nothing
left. If Morel could make a fool of himself, then he would have to
find his own truth by himself. But Morel will pump me. He won't
say: "This is good and that's bad." He'll want to know how I got
there, and then I'll show him my nothingness: intellectual speculation, logical delirium, eclecticism; as he said of X, "He takes a little
here and a little there, but he lacks unity, a sense of synthesis." I'm
going to disappoint Morel terribly; he liked me because he thought
I was trying to find . . . But I haven't tried; this interminable
labor was nothing but a sterile evasion.

He turns back, he rereads his words, he recognizes himself. Take
any event, pursue your sense of it as far as you can go, and it will
be like pulling one thread in a tangled skein—the entire skein
comes with it. He was all there: his arrogant humility, his weakness for "lucidity," his taste for self-destruction. And, as always,
everything he said had a ring of truth in it: he was objectively right,
his philosophical intentions *were* an escape; but the discovery of
this truth manifests a still deeper truth: the taste for self-destruction. So he can ask himself, "Is it this depraved taste that allows
me to see clearly, or does it falsify my sense of the event, or does

the event, by a quasi-miraculous coincidence, justify this depraved taste?"

He is dealing with philosophy's most disturbing question; it will take him hundreds of pages to elucidate it, and this is now his aim, an aim he still doesn't dare claim as his present task, for he doesn't know how or even if he'll achieve it. All he knows is that the event seems to justify his taste, his profound choice, to such a degree that there is always reason to wonder, Is it the event which has provoked the choice, or the choice that has provoked the event? Given his condition, was another choice possible? And given his choice, another condition? What is the proportion of (historical, social, individual) fatality, and what is the proportion of freedom? An impossible question; neither can be fixed. They must be taken together, in their experienced unity. But where begin?

Not by trying to explain the event by psychoanalysis; not by trying to explain the person by the event. Fatal as it may be objectively, the event is always the image of the person to whom it happens as well; whatever happens to me, it is I who happen to myself. The proof: He always recognizes himself in what happens to him—not, of course, in the raw event, inconceivable in itself, but in the meaning which this event, immediately integrated into his situation, assumes for him, in the familiar, anticipated countenance it turns toward him, though in reality it has not been anticipated. This is the "mystery of life." It's not so mysterious after all; in every event he recognizes himself, recognizes his destiny (tells himself, "I could have guessed that, it's no surprise, you've got what you deserve"), recognizes a will he has actually never produced, because, from the fact that this event happens to me, it becomes me, an occasion for me to perpetuate my being, to recover myself as I am, with a "miraculous" air of the *déjà vu* about it, although it may be altogether unique. So with this business of Morel: Morel has still not said anything to me; I'm doing the talking. I'm the one who heaps abuse upon myself in advance (a deterrent accusation—he anticipates abuse in order not to be crushed when and if Morel heaps abuse upon him; pride), because I cannot believe in what I have done; because he has always doubted his success, because it seemed impossible he should succeed in such an undertaking, because he has begun it with every expectation of failure—the big one, the final catastrophe, as when you work ten years on something, stake your life on it, aim at the highest, so when the failure does occur, everything will collapse, nothing will remain. Nothing save the impossibility, now complete, of being anything at all. That is what I call "a successful failure": one that cures you of the little fiascos you incur all your life without wanting them, one that will at least be entirely attributable to me and will raise me above everything; it is the annulment of my life, my nonwork. My hell. It will cast him back into that nullity which is his condition in fact and which can only be transcended philosophically. Because I belong nowhere, to no group, no enterprise, because I am exiled from groups and enterprises, there is only one alternative: either to be marginal in regard to society and history, the supernumerary of the human race, the pure consumer of air, water, bread and other people's work, reduced to the boredom of living, to the acute awareness of the contingency of everything around me, or to raise myself conscientiously to the absolute—that is, to establish everything philosophically as a moment of the spiritual adventure and then, having gone so far, to recover, starting from this speculative interest, the taste for the concrete.

This is the first rational thing he has said in six pages; the rest is sterile lucidity. Which leads to another question. What he has called his desire for failure, his evasion, his logical delirium, boils down to this: Given my condition, I can achieve the concrete only by starting from the abstract, the real by starting from the Idea; given my condition, it is impossible for me to believe in anything I do, to believe in my own reality, in any form of success. Living in this condition of nullity, I cannot imagine emerging from it. And I shall not start emerging from it until I learn from other people— and for me "other people" means Morel first of all—that I really have done something, that I'm not a blank in being, but an existing man. If I achieve this recognition of my reality, my history will begin; but I can no more imagine this history than the Chinese can imagine the accomplishment of their tenth five-year plan. I have not worked in order to fail; I have worked in order to emerge from failure without knowing how I would manage afterward, and therefore quite ready, in case of a new failure, to fall back into my situation of nullity which I have not yet really transcended.

Here the ground is firm, at last he has the sense of having put things properly. But even to get this far, he had to start from the sentiment of nullity, doubt, impotence, failure, the taste for self-destruction—from the personal choice, from his complexes. If he does not start by acknowledging how he feels, he will not discover the condition motivating his way of being; if he does not start by an interest in the world's affective coloring, he will not discover the "destiny" he is living. The objective, materialist explanation cannot come first; how can he become conscious of his condition in fact, if not through the felt experience he necessarily has of it? How can he even conceive of changing his condition if he doesn't first disengage himself from it by reflection, doesn't first acknowledge the absolute subjective misery which this condition occasions?

No further. There is something ignobly satisfying in the explanation of himself by his condition (the vulgar Marxist explanation): Of course you're like that, because (because the world, society, your history are like that) you're a victim of circumstances. This is false and leads back to the same problem as before, the problem of the "miraculous coincidence": It is not my condition of objective nullity that has determined my desire for subjective nullity, it is the inverse. There was an encounter, an encounter between his immemorial taste for annihilation (. . . as a child of four or five, he still knew nothing of his "condition," he didn't know who his father was, that every group would reject him; at four or five he was already hiding under couches, tables, the piano, disappearing behind curtains or into closets; he would huddle into dark corners and make believe he was a tiny animal, a solitary captive fallen out of someone's hand or pocket, whom no one wanted, and then he would cry to himself quietly, comfortably, full of self-pity, and after he had mourned his exile he would harden himself by knocking his head against the wall until he saw stars, and then, to punish himself, to destroy himself further, he would do the things that were hardest of all: pull out his hair and eat it, lick the soles of his shoes after walking over dogs' refuse, or not drink water for three days . . .) and an objective condition of nullity, an encounter between infantile complexes and adolescent and adult problems which the child could in no way anticipate. Everything happened as if the spoiled, ascetic little boy had unconsciously prepared himself for a destiny which would justify him.

And this was the retrospective illusion, the hoax par excellence, the "miraculous coincidence"—miraculous, as a matter of fact, if he admits that his condition was imposed upon him ready-made, that he fell into it by accident as into a snare prepared only by God or by chance. But isn't it true that this condition is not attributable to him, that he fell into it? True, yes, that he one day discovered Father was a Jew. (One day—he was seven or eight—they were walking home from school past a fence where someone had pasted up a lot of butterflies with human heads, faces with big, fleshy, arched noses, drooling mouths, and *paiessl* curling down the cheeks, and Felix said, "That's your father." "My father doesn't look like that," he said. Felix laughed and said, "Oh yes he does, because he's a Jew!" And Borck burst out laughing and said that *his* father was a baron. Then he found out, and his mother told him that his grandfather on *her* side was a count and that a count was more than a baron because his crown had seven prongs and the baron had only five. But Borck said that didn't matter, it was your father who mattered, and a Jew couldn't be a noble. "My father was a captain during the war. What was yours? Jews are never officers. They don't know how to fight." And although his mother showed him a photograph of his father in uniform with a long saber, she had to admit his father hadn't been an officer and hadn't been in the fighting either. He had been a clerk and his saber was a general-staff clerk's saber.) True too that his mother took him to Switzerland on the eve of the war; true that, half-Jew in anti-Semitic Austria, then Austrian half-Jew in the Pan-German Reich, then Austrian half-Jew with a German passport in a Switzerland favoring the Reich, he was neither Jew nor Aryan, nor Austrian, nor German, nor Swiss—nothing, in short, except the nothing that he was. But true too that before knowing that he was this nothing, he already regarded himself as nothing, was nothing for himself. At five, his four-year-old schoolfellow gave him a smack and he ran home in a state of panic. "I won't play with him any more," he told his mother. "He hit me." "And you didn't hit back, silly?" his mother said. At six, Strauss, a Jewish boy, caught up with him on the way home from school and gave him a kick that stretched him in the dirty street, and he was afraid of Strauss, he did not fight back but kept out of his way for the next few days, but Strauss caught him again and rolled him in the mud. And his mother complained to the teacher and asked him to walk her son home. Protected by the teacher at the age of six, when he still didn't know anything.

His conclusion, then: He himself was responsible for the "miraculous coincidence" of his infantile complexes and his objective condition of nullity. This condition of nullity, although objective, was his own work. And because it was his own work it fit him like a glove. Not that he had invented this condition altogether, of course; but he recognized himself in it, established himself in it, subjectively an accomplice because subjectively prepared for it. Others, in his place, would have considered such a condition temporary, provisional. Not he; to him it seemed immutable, he abandoned the idea of being at home somewhere, disavowed his family, his Church, the Reich, Austria, the Jews, his mother tongue, everything, and decided that he would be the one thing which he was least of all—he would be French. To read, write, think in French (to think in French in a German school, in 1940, after the fall of France, was a splendid self-destructive *ascesis,* a transparent choice of nullity) and to despise everything around him that wasn't French. An objective condition of nullity, yes, but maintained, willed, rendered still more null by virtue of a choice anterior to it, a choice that had not been occasioned by that condition.

I said he must start with this choice! A Hegelian-Marxist notion that the human condition is man's own work; not because he has created it *ex nihilo,* but because it is his only insofar as he has already assumed it, chosen to live it, recognized himself in the meaning he gives it. For man adapts himself to his condition only insofar as the fact of living it has set up a choice which gives it value, a choice occasioned or awakened by "complexes" which cause him to feel comfortable in that condition, resigned to it, or proud of it. Had I not given a value to that condition, I would already be trying, here and now, to transform it, no longer its accomplice, no longer able to explain myself by it.

To start from the personal choice, what would be the use of wanting to change your condition if you didn't know what had made you choose it in the first place, establish yourself within it, if you didn't revoke this choice, a revocation which is your only reassurance that you're not going to reproduce the same condition all over again? To start from the personal choice—that is, to understand how you have arrived at your condition, how you have chosen yourself starting from there, how you have let yourself be infected by it, half victim, half accomplice, how it has been possible that you have agreed to live it.

His head has emptied itself out. He feels he is at the foot of a huge, slippery mountain. He has to climb it from all sides at once. He doesn't know where to begin. To understand yourself as the choice of your condition—of course, but since this choice itself is conditioned . . . He wants to know how it has been possible for him to adapt himself to his own condition. He says two apparently contradictory things (he adds "apparently" for caution's sake, hoping that the contradiction will prove to be dialectical, but actually he doesn't see how he will escape it). He has accepted or, better still, he has created his objective condition of nullity by virtue of a choice of nullity that reaches far back into his childhood; that is the subjective explanation. He juxtaposes to it an objective explanation: his infantile choice of nullity was encouraged to develop because he was placed in an objective condition in which he recognized himself, an accomplice. Very pretty; the difficulty has been forced to retreat, and the indigestible residue is the question, What has occasioned this infantile choice? Or, since it is this choice which explains his complacency toward his empirical condition, the way he has adapted himself to it, must he then yield himself up to a complete psychoanalysis, delving back into the infantile clamminess in order to revoke his original choice and therefore to transform his condition? Does not this priority he has accorded to the psychoanalytic viewpoint condemn him to perform first and foremost a subjective conversion, a katharsis? And how would he have the means to perform this conversion, since the condition he has made for himself, which is his choice sedimented in being, conditions him in return, consigns him to the nullity which he claims he wants to transcend?

He is not yet through with the theory; he must clarify matters. He sums up: (1) There is no concrete hope of transforming his condition if he does not at the same time revoke his choice of this condition. (2) His choice of this condition is conditioned by it, therefore there is no concrete hope of modifying it if he does not modify his condition at the same time. (3) His choice of this empirical condition is conditioned not only by the condition but by one anterior to it, the infantile condition. Three possible conclusions: (a) This is a vicious circle, since the subjective conversion supposes the transformation of the objective condition, and since inversely the transformation of the objective condition supposes the subjective conversion if it is to be effective. (b) The subjective conversion must (see 3) start with a psychoanalysis of the infantile choice, the infantile condition being the original basis of the total choice; but how can this psychoanalysis be effective, since there can be no question of transforming the infantile condition, moreover buried in oblivion? (c) (Here he has got hold of something, he begins to see a way, and it is only out of complacency that he continues accumulating difficulties.) The subjective conversion and the transformation of the objective condition must go hand in hand, react dialectically against each other, the former causing his condition of fact to appear in a new light, showing new ways out by an initial transforming action, consolidating the conversion and furnishing it, for at this point it is merely an abstract self-doubting, virtually disincarnated intention, with a content, a body it cannot derive from itself, the beginnings of a new condition, conditioning new possibilities.

A momentary temptation: to say that psychoanalysis of the infantile choice is therefore superfluous, that the way out (the way to salvation) is in action, that action, once initiated, will develop dialectically and, upon contact with concrete reality, will cause the unanticipated means of conversion, the new man, to appear. This is false. For how initiate the subjective conversion which will cause the objective condition to appear in a new light? By what means? How transform the instruments employed by the total choice to develop itself, on which it leans as on a total attitude, consolidated by habit, if you do not know them? And how know them if not by a scrupulous investigation of my history (and of history itself, from a Hegelian-Marxist viewpoint; for we cannot conceive our world, our condition, explicitly, since our concepts are a part of the world which we comprise and have no point of view as to the worldly and intellectual means of which they are the instrument; the only point of view they can acquire as to these means is historical—the study of their genesis, of their objective meaning, both imperceptible to the subject who "lives" the sociocultural heritage as closely as he lives his own body), which will reveal the themes, obsessions, dominant motifs of my life, the progressive elaboration, in contact with people and changing realities, of that arsenal of habits in which each being-for-itself is enclosed, just as a pudding conforms to a mold it has already left.

Again, he wonders if he has not produced contradictory declarations, and at the very moment he picks up his pen to write that he is wondering this (the first time he has permitted himself this luxury of writing down the questions, instead of writing only the result of his cogitations about them), he sees the issue appear again before him: the savory nebula in which thought dawns, fast taking form; this is a moment he likes to prolong, feeling, tonight, that his thoughts will be rare ones (not so much rare, perhaps, for a crowd of ill-assorted ideas rushes forward, but difficult to bring to birth). So on the one hand he declares he must start from the "personal choice," meaning by this the subjective—he must become aware of the original intention that goes hand in hand with the situation-in-fact it has elaborated, in order to modify it. On the other hand, he has just realized that this modification of the fundamental intention (the subjective conversion) has no means of functioning if it is not based on his becoming objectively aware of the instruments of which his original intention constitutes the existence, and with which it combines. Why not say right away that the subjective conversion must begin by an objective investigation? What does this mean?

It means so many things that he must be careful not to let the

idea vanish before he has managed to put it into words. First of all
it means that the first intention of subjective conversion is a formal
and empty intention (a pious hope, an abstract wish for "something to change," unaware of its content and its real possibilities),
for not only does this first intention not have the means to come
into being, it is even unaware what content it must apply its means
to once they are created. In other words, the subjective conversion
from which he says he must start is at first nothing but the abstract
intention of subjective conversion, a resolution to become aware of
his original choice through the instruments of revelation (skills, habits, obsessions, "natural" behavior) in which that choice is incarnated. And to become conscious of these instruments, he must be
able to stop using them, stop living them so closely that he has no
point of view about them. To know them instead of clinging to them,
of existing them, he must use different instruments of revelation: a
method affectively neutral, "scientific, objective," as Marx and
Freud both put it. A fruitful notion of the incarnation, which will
perhaps allow him to thread his way between Marxism and psychoanalysis. ("You cannot juxtapose these two techniques," Morel
said. "You must adopt a perspective which will create their unity."
And Morel said that such unity was "the person," was lived before
being thought. But how establish this unity in thought without
exploding?) The personal choice is not a "subjective" intention
deliberately creating the means of its own realization; it is an incarnated intention, enclosed within the mold of his body. In one
sense, the personal choice is "interiority" though it will not grasp
itself as such save by a turning back upon itself, when in hesitation
and anxiety it discovers its own nothingness; in another sense, it
is deployed altogether externally, existing in things as their signification for me, their quality, their potentialities. The personal
choice is inscribed in being like a certain face, a certain truth, a
version of the world indistinguishable from its reality. Forever developing yet endowed with the permanence of things, this world

tends to persist in his being, thereby lending a solid consistency, a quasi inertia to the choice sedimented within him.

His idea, then, is that there is an objective aspect to the personal choice; that the situation of being-for-itself and its choice are one and the same, for its situation is the incarnation of its choice, the sum of the instruments it is in order to produce and develop itself. The meaning of the choice is here, outside, existing in things (but also inside—in my body's qualities, my past, my being-for-others). His idea, now, is that all things (the world) are created, and that insofar as all things are the objective unity and dialectic of a creative choice, they are not only meaningful and human, but also the sedimentations of choices created by others, sedimentations which entreat our comprehension (and not our scientific knowledge) and therefore ask us to reproduce in ourselves the choices which have produced them.

He reminds himself that this is all somewhere between Hegel, Marx and Merleau-Ponty, and that he is still nowhere near out of it; he is afraid of once more losing himself in abstract speculations which, so far as he is concerned, lead to nothing, to everything save himself. But that remains to be seen. He is also astonished by that intellectual toy, Marx's concept of "work"—essence of the apparent world—though where Marx says "production" or creation, he would say "choice producing and incarnating itself." And he glimpses a vague possibility of making this concept into a bridge to phenomenology by arranging matters as follows: starting from the world as it presents itself to us and, by entirely re-creating it in the imagination, seeing how it has been possible—that is, what is its human signification, what is the project, the creative choice that has "created" and produced this world in being. And this is precisely Marx's procedure too: not relying on "appearances" but, starting from labor-as-value, finding the "essence" beneath appearances, that is, the project which has produced—and has alienated itself in—capital. The idea, then, that the world has a meaning, is a knot of tangled significations, that, upon appearing in this world, being-for-itself is at once enlisted in an anonymous project which is inherent in the facts and whose instruments are immediately furnished to it, to the exclusion of other immediate instruments. Enlisted: provoked to play a role, to choose between the roles the institutional world offers him at the start and on the basis of which —transcending or repeating them—he will make himself into a person.

Good; still to be discovered is the point of view from which he can interpret the anonymous project which a given interworld proposes to being-for-itself—a world which is an "order" already here and addressing itself to him, but which in truth is merely produced and reproduced over and over again by the creative choices which determine themselves for and start from him. Here the methods begin to diverge radically.

Then is the anonymous project (which every being-for-itself willy-nilly assumes by becoming its conscious defender, its involuntary accomplice, its victim or its critic) a project of this human order? Precisely not; that order is the alienation of the very work which produces it. No one recognizes himself in such an order. If we have produced it, we have not desired it but somehow produced it into the bargain, as the unforeseen result of an intention aiming at something else (much less than an order: a little comfort, security, pleasure, privacy). But from the fact that this order has been produced it has repercussions upon the anonymous social and cultural project of the group, making of this project—insofar as the group is not willing to surrender its purpose and its avowed ideology—"its solemn complement, its general rationale of consolation and justification, its idealist point of honor," and actually obliging that project to complicate itself, to produce the intentions of actions other than the actions initially intended. Actions not produced by express intention arouse intentions after the fact, the objective has repercussions upon the subjective, the men who have

produced an involuntary order are led to will that order. It is a
fruitful idea of Marx's, then, that the reality of this order is the
work which produces it despite itself and alienating itself in that
order; further, that this order is imputable to the dominant class,
that the latter therefore has to answer for it, but that this class itself
is transcended and alienated by the consequences of its avowed
intentions, produced by its product. The essential question remains: What is the anonymous project of an institutional order
really the project of? What is its meaning?

To begin with, Marx.

For Marx, there is the project's meaning in terms of fact, which
in the present situation (the bourgeois world) is an absurdity for
the bourgeois who conceal it from themselves; they are doing something other than what they think they are doing and, in so doing,
are digging their own graves. But there is also the project's meaning
in terms of right, which for Marx, a moralist and a Hegelian, is
that man's fundamental project must be the project of man, a
project to create man, so that the producer of the world can recognize himself in his product (Marx even dreamed that man can
coincide with his product, but here he was mistaken). This meaning of the project in terms of right is unfortunately only the ideal
and unrealized meaning of the project in terms of fact, which latter
alienates itself, and it is this alienation that man must become conscious of in order to work at transcending it by changing the world.

Thus Marx assumes an idealist point of view with regard to
reality—he judges and interprets it with an initial requirement that
alienation be suppressed and that man's relation to man be an
unmediated human relation, the production of a human world, a
human man. For Marx, man is what he makes, and it is essential
that he make what he is—that is, that he make man, that he be
able to recognize himself in what he makes. The categorical imperative of Marxist morality is: Make what you are—in order to

be what you make. And what man is, for Marx, is freedom at work. His projected disalienation is the possibility required for freedom to will itself through what it does, instead of doing things in which it is engulfed. The fundamental requirement of Marxist morality is that the human reality be totally overcome by freedom to the point of being total freedom, that it may realize itself and become its own goal on every level at once; the total man is the happy synthesis in action of the biological and the human, of the individual and the social, at the heart of the personal unity, the person created within the social project and the social project created within the person. The person totally creates himself and accedes to the universal means and reality of the recognition of all by each and of each by all. Perfect; as a matter of fact this is the requirement of moral freedom: a world which would be the means and the occasion of total accomplishment as an individual person and as a citizen, and vice versa. Is this possible? It doesn't matter; here is an absolute goal, the requirement of man-as-value. Starting here, it is possible to expose every alienation responsible for the fact that today as yesterday we are not what we produce and do not produce "ourselves," but only things which enslave us. The fundamental reason for our alienation is the present social and economic order, for in this world of ours, enmeshed in its praxis, we cannot, even with the best will in the world, desire in the name of freedom what we actually do, whatever our intention, simply because we have assumed, by merely choosing to live, the present social condition, the incarnation of a praxis in regard to which abstention is not possible. Man is impossible in this world of ours, therefore it is this world which must be changed; imperatively; it is the final and determinant reason for man's impossibility. Whatever my subjective conversions and psychotherapies may be, they will never be a solution, for the cause of all misfortunes is my real condition, and what I can best achieve is the consciousness of its contradictions and the resolution to change it.

He is quite content with these conclusions and quite in agreement with them; he wonders what he can add, now that he discovers himself a Marxist. Never, he feels, has he thought more lucidly, or been in possession of stronger evidence, and were he not condemned to write in order to feel he existed, he would announce that there was nothing more to say and would continue his meditations as a member of the Communist Party.

Now he tells himself, "Luckily I mentioned the C.P." Because the C.P. has always been a strong temptation, an impossible temptation which has nothing (or not much) to do with the reasons he has just revealed for the first time. The C.P. will always (?) be forbidden him because he is (1) a bourgeois, (2) a filthy intellectual, (3) a man belonging nowhere and objectively null who will never be "involved," from the others' point of view, (4) an opponent systematically dedicated to endless contestation by his very condition, which excludes him from subjective as well as objective integration, (5) an outsider, a foreigner who would be thrown out for meddling in politics. And what attracts him to the C.P. (in South America, in India, in Spain) is precisely the temptation of the impossible; condemned to do nothing at all, he is fatally obsessed by the total incarnation, the complete return to the positive, as by a forbidden thing—just as the husband is obsessed by the image of adultery, the lover by the idea of killing the object of his love, the miser by that of destroying his wealth, the soldier by that of desertion, the criminal by that of becoming a stool pigeon, the policeman by the image of crime, the respectable citizen by the notion of sexual crime, the believer by mortal sin or atheism, etc.—an acceptance or betrayal which not only his condition but the way in which he stabilizes it forbids him.

He has said a number of things at once here, and he must recapitulate in order to find himself again, still content, in the long run, with this method of investigation which consists of letting himself go as far as his own momentum will take him in order to examine afterward, objectively, what this controlled abandon has brought to light. Hence:

1. The C.P. is a temptation, but a temptation for bad reasons; it is likely that a Marxist analysis will prove inadequate to disalienate an individual and permit him to recover his unity. For if you change the world for bad reasons that have more to do with psychoanalysis and are unrealizable into the bargain, you risk having your new world turn out badly too—a world in which you will not find yourself again.

2. The C.P. is a temptation because it is forbidden him by an objective exclusion, but also, he has just admitted, by a subjective one, which relates to the stabilizing development of the former; he has made a vocation out of his condition and would feel he was perpetrating a betrayal by abandoning his vocation as an agent of contestation—and he is also incapable of doing so, knowing that he will not be able to integrate himself, that he will never even be a *condottiere* of the revolution (supposing that there were one) but, by temperament, a meticulous bureaucratic technician at best. Question: Is the temptation of the C.P. motivated by objective exclusion (temptation of the impossible) or subjective (temptation of betrayal)? By the latter, obviously. For the innocent man who is found guilty and condemned, escape is not a temptation but a task; if prohibition is imposed from the exterior, it is an obstacle. It is a temptation only if it is interiorized—the temptation to abolish a determination one has freely accepted (to be a husband, a lover, a believer, etc.), to betray. The temptation of the negative freedom which you are while at the same time you suppress it, the temptation of being the nonbeing of your being, the temptation of nothingness, of nullity. He returns to this.

But first it is 1 which must be developed. If the C.P. can be a temptation for bad reasons (mine: which are to abdicate oneself by integrating onself; to betray oneself while at the same time betraying one's class; to return to the positive while at the same time be-

ing the negation of what for him is positive and thereby detested—
the "Western world" which protects, nourishes, excludes, and has
raised him; to be, as both negation and betrayal, guaranteed by the
divinity of an orthodox order which believes itself infallible, an
orthodoxy which, even while he serves it, he will immediately contest), then Marxist action, the social action, the project to change
the world are not sufficient to disalienate and to recreate the unity
of the person, at least not in this world of ours. But what do we
know about someone else, how even imagine him without having
answered this question: Could the human reality ever become
social and public to the point where the citizen's labor will resolve
all the problems of the person and totally create him?

For us, in any case, and for the generation following ours, this
is not to be contemplated. Hence the legitimacy of this declaration:
Social and political action is not the solution of all our problems,
and though such action is absolutely necessary for that solution in
the last analysis, it is also necessary for us to free ourselves from
our subjective alienations (is this the right word?), which may warp
our sense of the facts and our action. Hence psychoanalysis retains
its privileges for us—and in saying "for us" he is perhaps exag-
geratedly timid, but he is not quite sure what he can rely on, and
he is also afraid of disapproval from the Marxists, at least immediately.

Psychoanalysis.

Having discussed Marx and the meaning he attached to the
human project, now he will try to determine what psychoanalysis
offers. For psychoanalysis—and this is what Marxists reproach it
for—a person's subjective misery is not a result of his being
alienated from fact by the social and economic world, or of the
impossibility of his developing that world's praxis without alienating himself still more, without entering into conflict with others and
himself, but it derives, above all and in particular, from an infan-

tile "complex" or—as he himself says—from a disgraceful choice turned against himself. He dismisses the Freudian interpretations, their way of basing man on the libido regarded as irreducible; besides, he does not know these interpretations in detail and does not want to risk discussing them. What interests him is that there is a frequently valid way of understanding a man starting from his childhood, from his first history, from his family situation, from the way in which, beginning with this situation, he has assumed his body, his natural life, his being-for-others. The Marxists, of course, can reply that the family is a bourgeois alienation and that the complexes it gives rise to will disappear with itself. He does not argue this point. But it is not at all certain that other complexes will not take their place, and after all, in his own case, he has had a family, and it would be of no use, it would even be a kind of speculative idealism, to claim he could resolve his infantile and family conflicts by explaining them away as bourgeois alienations resolved in spirit if not in fact by the postrevolutionary disappearance (after how many generations?) of the family.

In short, complexes surviving from childhood are neither explicable nor soluble by Marxist analysis as alienations like any others, because the original choice functions at a moment and at a period where there is still neither history nor conscious practice nor possibility of deliberate consciousness. And to take his case, Marxism would not help him understand his prepersonal choice of nullity and the way in which this choice was confirmed during the course of his subsequent history, on the occasion of the discovery of his mixed parentage and his exclusion. The Marxist explanation always supposes, as a matter of fact, that the world is the product of man. It implies a moral criticism applied from the point of view of an "ethic of action"; it starts from the highest requirement (that man be his own product and that he recognize himself in his product) and values the world's praxis in relation to that requirement; it *exposes* the objective alienations and starting from them explains the ideological alienations as superstructures, substitutes for action, metaphysics of consolation, hoaxes— Freedom that cannot recognize itself in its product and cannot know itself as free and productive is necessarily hoaxed and has not the means to expose the hoax; it is alien to itself, in fact. According to Marx our task is not so much to understand the hoaxes as to expose them as the pseudo truths of a world concealing its actual truth (work). In other words, Marx addresses himself to the producers, the workers, the men of praxis who create the world and who must be made aware of what they are doing; he legitimately ignores—and is not necessarily understood by—the intermediary consumers, capitalists, etc., who as men of money create nothing (save money) and upon whom an ethic of action can have no effect.

Now the man of praxis is necessarily an adult (he becomes adult as soon as he acts upon and is conscious of creating the world). But before becoming an adult, he has been a nonacting child, and it is as a child that he assumed certain habits, that his affectivity was formed, his feeling for life, things, other people, his "character"— that is, his original choice, which has therefore, necessarily, been first of all a choice *to be,* pertaining to psychoanalysis and radically incomprehensible from the point of view of an ethic of action. In the gravity of childhood, we have learned to consider the world not as the product of freedom at work, but as a theocratic order of which grownups were the gods. For the child, it was entirely a question of conforming to the laws, the norms and the uncomprehended, alien, absolute orders governing his existence from without; and though from the point of view of an ethic of action there are only problems of praxis (that is, problems to be resolved by action), from the child's point of view there are only "ontological" problems—for the child, it is a question of knowing what he is and what he must be. He receives *en bloc,* as a given value, the entire objective spirit of the society and is assigned the task of adapting himself to it (by apprenticeship, by training) even before he can have understood it, before he can establish himself within its reality as praxis. It is therefore legitimate to conclude that at this stage the child derives from the inculcated sociocultural heritage the only project he can be, a vital, subsequently religious project aiming at vital, subsequently mystical satisfactions, and that the social and cultural behavior to which he is limited has a strong tinge of affectivity and religiosity—that is, can be understood solely in the light of his infantile experiences and desires, starting from his affective and material dependence on his parents, from his desire for metaphysical security, from his craving for approval and comfort. Things, people, actions are charged for him with entirely irrational affective values in relation to his situation of dependence and passivity. And these magico-religious values, if they can be liquidated, can also be developed even during adult life—are all the more likely to be so if the occasion of a rupture has not been furnished by autonomous work becoming conscious of itself as such over and above its product. Women, idlers, intermediaries, bourgeois, members of the liberal professions, etc., will probably carry into their adult life the complexes and religious values of childhood for lack of occasions to liquidate them by the discovery that they make the world and that the world is the work of human beings. And this is particularly true of those societies which by their economic structure and their degree of technological evolution offer the human reality scarcely any opportunity to become conscious of itself as creating the social order and the world; in these societies, man therefore tends spontaneously to accord an ontological, religious, mystical value to the social order. The parallelism which Freud observed and mistakenly tried to base on genetic postulates is in reality based on analogous situations; the modern child, like the prehistoric adult, is dealing with a world and an objective spirit that are alien to him and which he stabilizes religiously for lack of consciousness of himself as its producer (having no effective technological and intellectual grasp of it).

Notice that the preceding discussion has been conducted from a Marxist viewpoint. Psychoanalysis is therefore accessible to Marxist criticism insofar as it is, in its classic forms, an accomplice of objective alienations; it interprets the human reality starting from an initial project *to be,* without explicitly providing it (save occasionally by manifesting its contradictions) the means of correcting and modifying this project, without demonstrating that the ultimate reason for subjective alienation is the objective alienation of freedom in a human world which, being estranged from freedom, must be changed. As a method of investigating the hoaxed consciousness, alienated in its freedom, psychoanalysis must confine itself to that delved consciousness, cannot account for the man of praxis. Therefore there can be a Marxist analysis of psychoanalysis, bringing to bear a true and moral historical point of view, but there cannot be a psychoanalysis of Marxism, although there can be a psychoanalysis of Marx and of Marxists insofar as their Marxism still carries religious values, has not yet completely liquidated the choice *to be* and is still tainted with naturalism, fanaticism, religiosity, etc. And Marxism is likely to remain impure as long as Marxist action and thought remain alienated—today and for a long time to come, as long as Marxism's ethical requirement remains idealist, as long as the Marxist himself, in this period of political struggle and the construction of socialism's foundations, is unable to recognize himself in his action, to resolve by action all his problems and all his contradictions. When he can authentically *be* what he will *do* (supposing that he ever can), then psychoanalysis will no longer concern him. It will not, however, be without a more general object; that could happen only if men were to be born adult, already engaged in the social order, already masters of its praxis and its techniques. Now, in even a postrevolutionary society, men will still be born as children, will still relate to the world by an original choice *to be,* and must liquidate this choice in order to realize themselves authentically. Psychoanalysis can and must furnish men the method for this liquidation. It will therefore retain its privileges.

Evidence: There is no effective psychoanalysis, no possible moral conversion not accompanied by a Marxist criticism, not oriented by the Marxist ethical requirement that man be what he makes, and that he make man. This fundamental requirement, common to existential psychoanalysis and to Marxism, must establish the effort of comprehension and the existential conversion of being-for-itself. The purpose of psychoanalysis must be to remove the psychological obstacles, to liquidate the choice-complexes of being which oppose both the consciousness of objective alienation (of which they are the accomplices) and the total realization of man in total action. Psychoanalysis, in other words, must lead to the comprehension of the necessity for freedom to change the world, to change its condition, to modify its situation, as it must also lead to the activation (or actualization—that is, to the recovery in the perspective of action) of every region of existence and dimension of being-for-itself as so many possibilities to make oneself free, to produce a human world.

Now he feels he has nothing more to say; he believes he has gone as far as he can on the theoretical level, and that if he is to advance further he must refer again to experience, to himself: examine the interference of praxis with the ontological in his case; examine that share of failure which, for him as for any being-for-itself, the impossibility of total activity represents, the impossibility of the moralization of all dimensions of existence at once within a single synthesizing action. The share of failure—that is, the share of solitude, of lived contradiction which cannot transcend itself in action and constitutes the "separating subjectivity."

Before dealing with himself, he takes a brief respite. The satisfied sense of having covered a good deal of ground—this is the advantage of the method he has adopted, which renounces systematic exposition, advances hesitantly and elaborates his thought, modulating it and moving it forward, pencil in hand (instead of claiming to set down thoughts already worked out but which, because they are always insufficiently elaborated, are only incomplete thoughts, truncated, systematized before they have reached their conclusion), battering down open doors and passing by those that are still closed. He wants to run to Morel now and tell him, "Don't judge me on the basis of that, I'm aware now of the inadequacies, the superficiality of what I gave you; I've made progress in three weeks, I think I'm on the right track now." He had flung himself into his new work (an autobiography?) without knowing where he was going, after four days of despair; he had been caught up in it and now, suddenly, he feels involved, feels he is doing something new which he cannot let go of without feeling beaten. And he becomes conscious of this: he is in the process of pleading an appeal. This self-analysis—which initially aimed only at freeing himself from his anxiety, at filling up an intolerably empty evening, at lessening the blow by anticipating how severe it was going to be— this self-analysis already amounted to more than fifteen hundred pages, written and rewritten over eight years. It has progressively become the proof—which he takes a dose of every day—that all is not lost; then his pledge of allegiance to his "vocation" as a writer; then the perspective which he assumed in regard to an anterior product and which, by running now to Morel, he would already claim to dominate. His betrayal complex, discovered in a new form: his horror of letting himself be identified by his acts or works, his need (not the Gidean strategy of taking the opposite point of view) to escape the image of himself his acts establish, by declaring himself beyond them, insisting upon himself as their transcendence. But is it not characteristic of the writer's project, of any project that claims to create, that it cannot install itself within its creation once it has become part of the outside world, once it exists, for it can exist only in action—and suffers this continual craving to explain in written words a fundamental silence, an original solitude from which the writer escapes only by the action of writing (a bridge he passes over only once, for it collapses behind him as he advances over the section he constructs ahead) and which he always finds forever intact? The writer who has written a book is a dead writer whose book is of no help to him and who can only begin again, with the feeling (*his* feeling, now) that everything is still to be said, that the problems to be resolved have grown merely more complicated, enriched by new aspects.

He might continue in this direction, declare (or repeat?) that writing is the only way he can make himself a man (because there is no other action in which he can recognize himself and make himself recognized, because writing is the only way to recover the irrecoverable, to reverse the signs of solitude, silence, nonbeing—the failure every action represents for him); but this is not what he meant. Rather this: that writing is for him a purifying *ascesis,* a way of abstracting himself from the real, of becoming pure mind, of appropriating a world which is alien to him and in which he plays no part, by denying it, by rendering it useless, arrogantly putting himself at its origin by the very act of explaining it, of dissolving it into ideas and words. Writing is a kind of Black Mass he celebrates every evening (before, when he did nothing else, he preferred writing late at night, between midnight and three in the morning) when, alone in a room he thinks of as a hole in the world, a room silhouetted against universal darkness by the single pool of light from his lamp that reveals a white page, he annihilates the world and himself merely by the corrosive work of his mind, constructs out of ink a universe which is drawn from—outlined against—the real and which, in a bundle of pages greedily accumulated and counted, is the only one which belongs to him: the Non-Universe, the annihilated universe.

There is this greedy labor of abstraction, and there is the image of the hole (he has discovered that one of his affective themes is

the image of the animal huddling in its lair, the oyster in its shell),
as well as the theme of destruction (for a long time he used to put
himself to sleep by imagining that he was firing a cannon out of
his window, or even through the walls; or else that he was besieged
and using a battery of machine guns to down people in the streets;
or again that he was in a car or even a tank and running down
great crowds of people) and his unconfessed claim to create abso-
lutes which he noticed the other evening when he was so annoyed
that Jacques wanted to discuss a passage he himself had insisted
Jacques read. Too impatient to listen to Jacques's remarks (impatient, in general, when other people talk; that's why he never
listens to what is said around him, preferring to read or to become
absorbed in himself; impatient again when Kay tells him something,
only half listening to her, actually outraged that she should dare
burst into his silent mental Non-Universe and trouble its geometry
by her real problems "of no importance" for him, everything that
comes from outside himself and bears the mark of the accidental
is of no importance; and when he simply cannot avoid it, when he
feels caught in reality, feels real himself—when someone shouts at
him, for instance, or gives him orders he cannot avoid by merely
going away—that is a catastrophe for him, a shake-up of his whole
being, creating a longing to escape, even by death, to find as soon
as possible that peace he is granted by the neutrality of a world
which his familiarity dismisses and whose asperities it attenuates;
and he hates having his habits questioned, his routines disturbed),
he waited until Jacques finally stopped talking, waited for him to
admire his own product instead of forcing him to come back down
to earth.

Here he has stumbled on a veritable gold mine: It is not the
theme of *ascesis,* of destruction or of mental abstraction which
proves so rich, but the theme of impatience, of the *behavior* of
abstraction which he has hitherto not noticed and which is his way
of *making himself* abstract, absent. As if he had touched a nerve

center, a swarm of instances of such behavior now come to mind, all motivated by his project of abstraction, of retreating into himself, so that he begins wondering if he is not dealing with what is really fundamental in his behavior, and with what explains (that is, makes intelligible as aspects of the same project) the following kinds of behavior:

His avarice, his way of preferring *specie* to the things he likes, choosing the abstract, universal equivalent of every possible possession and enjoyment; renouncing the enjoyment of life in favor of an abstract and disincarnated possibility, objectivized in money, of living and enjoying himself. By economizing on his pleasures and what others regard as need (to eat well, to live in comfortable rooms, to be decently dressed) he economizes his life, "sets it aside" as an abstract possibility quantified in money. And not only that; he has a tendency to hoard foodstuffs—he once dreamed of having enough to live on for a year—and to ration himself stringently when surrounded by mountains of supplies. Even as a child he was like that; when he was five his mother, before going out one morning, set in front of him a dish of cherries swimming in pink juice, and since there weren't many, even before he started eating, he began to regret the inevitable moment when there wouldn't be one left. So he ate very slowly, licking his spoon, and since his mother was in a hurry she asked, "Don't you like it?" And he answered, "Yes. I want to enjoy it." She thought that was very funny and told the story to everyone. Then when he was seven his grandmother gave him a big box of liqueur-filled bonbons for Christmas. And since he liked them, he locked the box in his drawer of the chest. He counted how many bonbons there were in the three-tiered box and decided that by eating only two a day, at four in the afternoon, he could make them last eighteen days. Eighteen days: an eternity. And every day he counted the number of days he had left for eating his two bonbons. And then, one day, he discovered that the second layer of his box was almost empty and the third already broached. He wanted to cry; they had robbed him—his sister and the maid—they had taken off the top drawer of the chest to get into his, and had stuffed themselves on the bon-bons. They had made fun of him, and he wondered how they could enjoy what they were eating at the very moment they ate it, and why everything was spoiled for him by the mere fact that it was transitory. Everything, really, was spoiled by this anticipated re-gret. At five, he was already regretting the fact that his grand-mother and his mother must die, and he would pray, "Dear God, let my mother and grandmother be immortal—and my sister and my father too," he would add conscientiously. And since he doubted that God would be willing to work this miracle, he prayed, "Dear God, let me die before my mother." That everyone around him was mortal obsessed him for a long time. Then he began to collect things, everything—his sister's old blotters, pieces of paper, pencil stubs, chalk, used erasers—refused to discard anything, hoping to preserve the period of time incarnated in this eraser, this pencil stub. Then at ten, when his father began giving them pocket money (a schilling each week), he put his own schilling in his bank and allowed himself only one ten-pfennig ice a week, and a ten-pfennig sandwich in winter (with some Liptauer and a caper) while his sister spent her schilling on ices in two days and came whimpering to her father for another. At the year's end he had a little fortune in his bank, so he bought Christmas presents for his mother, his heart heavy at having to spend his fortune. Then he ruined his vaca-tion counting every day how many days he had left and telling him-self, "Enjoy the day that's passing, you dumbbell," but he couldn't enjoy it, already he looked regretfully at this landscape, this house, these stairs that he would have to leave. And for some time now he was tempted—but he resisted the temptation—to count the years he had left to live, the years that still remained before he became impotent, senile, and if it had been possible he might have economized on his expenditure of energy in order to live longer.

He dreamed of being a *rentier* with a capital always preserved intact; he would live, meagerly enough, on the dividends alone. He had a horror of waste, of material generosity; when Kay used more gas than she needed to warm up the bottom of a pot, when she boiled more than enough water for their tea, he flew into a rage; when he was alone, he would measure three cups into the pot, just what he used; when Kay wanted to throw away stale bread, he would immediately gulp it down with hard cheese, so that nothing would be wasted.

His eccentricities. But already, probably because of his fundamental tendency toward escape, toward abstract and quintessentialized self-possession, this inventory begins to bore him. What importance, what interest can his real person have? Can he still progress, when the investigation suddenly loses all attraction for him? He hopes so, returns to his eccentricities; wonders for a moment what the imperious evidence was which several days ago made him think his eccentricities were so indicative; catches himself scratching at the skin around his nails. That's one. Others: Although he lives in disorder, his possessions have a secret arrangement for him, an order, a "me-ness" as Morel called it, by which he insists on being surrounded. He wants to be able to move, to orient himself comfortably in the world by virtue of calm and collected habits: invariable routines and schedules whose disturbance he reacts to with recriminatory bad humor; invariable topographical disposition of his universe, "everything in its place," and when it's elsewhere, as is often the case with his pen, he accuses Kay— "Where have you put my pen?" or, in a whimpering, panic-stricken tone, heavy with reproach, "You haven't seen my pen?" "I can't find my pen; I suppose it's disappeared." Kay watches this exhibition with incredulous scorn. Perhaps not scorn. His mother, yes— she found it despicable. "My toothbrush has disappeared!" "Look for it," she replied, "or I'll come and find it." And when she came, the toothbrush was "right under your nose."

This was an old impression: that the world was a hostile order full of traps and set in motion by the Enemy God. Even as a child he detested the world where you had to show yourself in broad daylight, naked, without a protecting shell, judged by your behavior. "Show what you can do." He didn't know how to do anything. He was paralyzed by invisible eyes, caught in snares he did not see; the world belonged to other people, was "the Other." He had never been good at gymnastics, at sports (except for swimming—in the water he was comfortable, it was the nonworld, the unorganized, he splashed about in it as in a liquid freedom). In the world, he was literally lost, dissolving into space, confiscated, seized with dizzy spells (he is always subject to vertigo), on the point of falling into the sky, into the hole gaping around him. Perhaps that's why he was always looking for hiding places under draperies, in dark holes—trying to plug up the world into which he leaked away by an agonizing hemorrhage of his being, to wrap himself in its protecting limits as if in a quilt. His eccentricities were an attempt to neutralize the world by making it a habit, an extension of the body, the basis of a familiar gesture. He always liked taking the same itineraries; he likes what he is used to. He realized this when, in relative prosperity, he continued eating the same food, oatmeal, that he had ordered during the years of dearth; when he was hungry, he was hungry for oatmeal. The center of his universe is his room, and as soon as he moves he arranges a corner with his familiar objects: fetishes to protect him against the irruption of the world and its open spaces. Once, in Switzerland, crossing the market square, he realized that he had never *seen* this city he had been living in for seven years; it was a familiar décor, as though painted on canvas, weightless, with neither density nor reality, and after eight years he was astonished to discover that the landscape was without a doubt the kind you could call "beautiful." It was Kay who after six months in the city made him take walks that would never have occurred to him. Walks bored him; everything

not related to the interminable labor of abstraction, which he incarnated in his manuscripts covered with his tiny handwriting, was
an intolerable loss of time. The slightest event in his draftproof
universe assumed gigantic proportions, was immediately digested,
neutralized, expelled from his life by the written account. His only
contacts with what is generally called life were (1) books, which
he sampled very slowly, rereading each paragraph until he had the
sense of having grasped the entire implicit meaning; (2) films,
which he permitted himself five times a week and where he lived
intensely the actions and situations rendered harmless by the reassuring limits the screen and the writers assigned them. Then he
came home to get rid of his existence by transfusing it into literature until three in the morning. His work, his room, were the
walls of the fortress he was raising against the world, and whoever
entered his life was an intruder he immediately put in irons; he
kept the intruder under observation until he came to rest, sitting
on the couch, then swiftly overcame him with a few questions, then
with silence, and finally bound him hand and foot by reading him
long passages. The intruder, thus anesthetized, was inserted by
force into his unreal universe, caught in his spider web of abstractions. As well as I can imagine him, the intruder probably finds
him a distant, inattentive creature, unapproachable, bringing each
conversation around to his curious intellectual speculations, dissecting every declaration in order to classify it in a category of
attitudes, rendering dialogue impossible by turning it into a medita-
tion *about* dialogue. An elusive man, certainly, who had cut himself
off from reality, including his own, by becoming the surgeon of the
awareness of all reality; an absent man.

But I've digressed. Safe only when he felt cut off from a reality
he could dismiss as a spectacle, outside himself, he was disabled as
soon as he had to turn and confront it. Once, having left for Italy
for two months, he returned after ten days, relieved to get back to
his den after having made himself miserable; overcome with bore-

dom, hunger (for he dared not eat in restaurants, the waiters terrified him), solitude, nullity in the streets of Milan, Venice, Bologna,
Florence, Rome; finally spending the days on his bed rereading
Man's Fate; crossing half of Venice (from the port, where he had
a room in a *pensione,* to the station) on foot (he would have had
to speak to take a *vaporetto*) to buy two *panettoni* and a tomato
stuffed with rice in the same *rosticceria* he had discovered the first
day and to which he subsequently returned in order not to have to
deal with a new set of people, already relying on habit. Appropriating the world by force of habit, concealing reality with routine,
abstracting himself from his own life and systematizing it into literature, in order not to have to live it any longer; tempted, finally,
by the invisible, nonproductive, nonfunctioning activity par excellence, theft, withdrawing some object in a shop from the concrete
richness of the real, annihilating it first by becoming the clandestine
owner of a clandestine object (that is, having become clandestine
for him and, for the former owner, absence of the object) and then
by reselling the object (sacred now because it belonged to a transcendent order) and by receiving currency in exchange. The ideal
essence of commerce, to steal is to transform concrete wealth into
abstract wealth without having done anything; it is to be the invisible agent—that is, altogether negative—of this abstractive destruction, conjuring away the real by an action which must conceal
itself, a null action which makes nothing happen except nothingness. Theft is poetry, the poetry of mercantile economy. And from
this point of view, Switzerland is certainly the most enjoyable
country to rob.

His cowardice (and timidity, of course). After everything I've
just said, it would be surprising if he weren't a coward too. I'm
coming to that. This notion of theft, however, goes further than I
thought. It is the concealment, the whisking away, the "out of
sight, out of mind"; and that reminds me how ten years ago, impotent with available women, he used to have necrophiliac day-

dreams and even started a story about a man who, in order to make love to a girl, first anesthetizes her with a wad of cotton soaked in chloroform and wrapped, so as not to burn his own skin, around the outside of a napkin ring: a horror of being seen, a craving to be the invisible voyeur; a sadistic temptation to kill or to anesthetize the Other to escape his (her) paralyzing gaze. The theme of abstraction, the project to interiorize his existence altogether, proves to be so fundamental that it seems to open all doors. This is why he must regard it with suspicion, look further: How was this project conceived? What else does it manifest? What conditions provoked it? That is still to come.

Avarice, hatred of the world and of self-realization, cowardice —it all belongs together. Cowardice: not exactly fear, but horror, the emotional refusal to exteriorize himself, to lose himself outside, to be conscious of himself in the world as a being of vulnerable flesh—vulnerable precisely because he refuses to exteriorize himself in actions and to exist by them alone. This is clearly shown by his demeanor; he appears to be a thin fellow with hollow cheeks and eyes, receding forehead and chin, a long neck poking forward over his slightly hunched back, with the gait of a heron and parsimonious gestures, as if he were trying to contain his being within himself. When he meets someone in a hallway, he stands aside awkwardly and murmurs an excuse which passes unnoticed, lowers his eyes as though caught doing something wrong. In the subway, he lets everyone get ahead of him, even if he himself has opened the door first, and stands in a corner to take up as little space as possible. If he talks, it is in a low, muffled voice, as though frightened by the vibrations his own throat creates in the surrounding air. He avoids the staircase or the elevator if he risks encountering there someone he knows even vaguely with whom he would have to speak and who might begin an "ordinary" conversation. A tendency to jumble his words together in his haste to finish what he has to say as quickly as possible, to fall back again into a rapt silence.

Great deference and formal politeness, always embarrassed, toward people with whom he has no personal connection—and often he has none, in fact, just because of this. This behavior gives him a preoccupied, abrupt manner (for in his concern to be brief, to reduce contact to the most impersonal level, he speaks in a tone of categorical declaration), a distant expression that intimidates interlocutors—they find him arrogant and assume he avoids them out of contempt. Furthermore, he always leaves others the initiative of setting the tone, of creating the atmosphere, of defining the relationship's nature, of formulating its rules and requirements, to which he immediately adapts himself, only too happy to so efface himself, adopting a different game with each interlocutor and, when involved in an argument, trying to show that each side is in the right.

I have emphasized "ordinary," for any personal conversation, especially when someone asks his advice, finds him receptive, even beaming, all too pleased to be consulted, to be regarded as worthy of a question. Overflowing with gratitude, he answers the man asking directions, astonished that *he* could give something, could pass for a member of the collectivity as good as the rest, could be integrated with the others rather than excluded, regarded as null. Matters grow more complicated here, and even before dealing with the clue the word "ordinary" provides, two others appear (on the one hand, his voluntary conformism with regard to all groups or representative individuals, never contradicting the man who takes him into his confidence or calls him to witness, even the worst kind of person; on the other, the gratitude he feels toward those who contemptuously regard him as a commonplace person when he is certain of not being one and revenges himself for such treatment by what he calls his betrayals, his affective prejudice for the group opposed to that which appeals to him) which we will soon have to deal with afterward.

Ordinary: The ordinary conversation about the weather terrifies him, paralyzes him; he never feels up to this interlocutor who expects him to be a man like any other and asks him to manifest himself as an ordinary member of the race. The exteriorization of these commonplaces is impossible for him. His terror is particularly intense when confronted with the tribe of salespeople, waiters, flunkies of any kind. This is important. There is a new key here. For a long time he thought his panic in the company of professional servitors was a moral disapproval, the horror of a system like capitalism which obliges some to sell and humiliate themselves for money. A noble explanation. What strikes me now is that he was panic-stricken before the very individuals whose job it was to satisfy his own requirements; these individuals wordlessly ask him to formulate desires, to state rules to which they will humbly adapt themselves, they precipitate him into a situation with no other rule than what he himself is willing to declare; they force him into autonomy. Yet he is horrified by autonomy; his fundamental attitude consists of scrupulously obeying a Rule forged by the Other (Has he not admitted as much with regard to Morel? Has he not just written that "he always leaves others the initiative of formulating the rules and requirements to which he immediately adapts himself, only too happy to efface himself," a notation whose importance had escaped him at the moment?), of formally, ritually performing the Other-requirement raised to the absolute—an absolute to such a degree, in fact, that he often rebels in order to feel its solidity and extent, his rebellions being violent recriminations (arguments with his superiors whom he rubs the wrong way and whose intransigence he magnifies on purpose; and his accusation that Kay leaves him no other alternative except to change himself radically or to "jump out the window," so imperative, he says, are her demands). But in dealing with flunkies there is no longer any Rule. At loose ends, defenseless, not knowing where to turn, he hesitates in order to oblige the flunky, gently, politely to manifest his requirements. He assumes the duty of serving this servant who asks only to serve him. He is tempted to push consideration to the point of buying the product the salesman extols, just to avoid having to ask for some other; tempted to order the dish the waiter likes; tempted, too, to leave immoderately large tips to reverse the roles: to be the waiter's servant instead of the person who has been served.

His gratitude to those who permit him to "give," to manifest himself as a man among men, is actually something different: he is grateful to anyone who inquires about something because the request can be satisfied according to a precise form and fixed rules, because within these rules he feels secure, comfortable, the instrument of a transcendent requirement into which he need only let himself flow as into a mold. And the other day, groping for a salient point by which to apprehend himself, he was complaining—significantly—that no rule, no law had been made for him, that he was rejected by society and nature alike. And some years before he wrote (but this is still valid) a sketch about a couple in which the wife is constantly asking, "What would you like?" and the husband answering, "I don't know, how about you?" and the wife replying, "I don't know, I asked you." And when Kay asks him what he wants to eat: "I don't know, you decide." Then there is his delight in filling out questionnaires that wrap him in their web of precise questions, permitting him, merely by obeying the printed requirements, to create an objective identity for himself that is perfectly adapted to an anonymous order, to flow into an impersonal world that is nevertheless prepared for him.

Here I am, at grips with characteristic psychoanalytic material. And in a better position to interpret this attitude of abstraction which just now seemed so fundamental to me. A second sounding of his grasp of his total reality would be approximately this: avarice, eccentricity, cowardice, systematizing intellectuality, all as a constant total means of existing as little as possible. Everything happens as if, since his earliest childhood, he were trying to suppress himself as a subject, stop living (*erleben*) in order to stop realizing his lived contradictions at the same time. He applies himself to neutralizing the world, his own existence and every signification, to replacing the lived project, the obligation to live, with rules, schedules, rigorous systematic tasks which are always gratuitous because stripped of any real and internal necessity—gratuitous, that is, without real motivation and having neither internal basis (in some urgency, desire, felt need) nor external basis (in the empirical reality of which they offer him no grasp, but to which they juxtapose themselves and which they conceal by theorizing about it)— rules by which he tries to mechanize his existence. His compulsive behavior, his attachment to habit, his avarice are all attempts to replace the activity of living and of realizing a human world by a mechanical activity affectively neuter (that is, without lived signification) arrived at by a coldly rational calculation (to eat the minimum amount necessary for survival, to calculate the daily rations in advance, to banish from his life all gratuitous enjoyments and expenses) and to perpetuate himself in existence by virtue of this mechanized, ritualized behavior perfected once and for all and thanks to which he would definitively complete his transactions with the world and with himself. To neutralize the world and himself (to "designify" it, in Hesnard's term) in order to replace it with the immutable universe of logical madness; to reduce to a minimum the lived contact with reality (he persists doggedly at this task in gaining his livelihood; as a journalist he puts the world into files, builds up interminable dossiers on every subject, claims to exhaust and petrify a country's reality by statistics, declares that by consulting his files he can give a view more exact than by an on-the-spot investigation; he has a weakness for world demographic problems, statistics on the world's resources, strategic theories, five-year plans; he would make a good official of the Planning Ministry or the Population Service), in order to avoid the conflicts, contradictions and anxieties which the slightest crack in his carapace of routines produces. Upon the death (sometimes imagined as an agreeable possibility) of his wife, who prevents his complete escape into autistic madness, he dreams of retiring to a tiny attic where he would lead a cloistered life still more isolated than his existence in Switzerland.

The impression all this leaves upon me: a schizoid personality whom Kay's constant, sometimes desperate struggle to rescue, to deflect from intellectual rumination, to invite into a human life has perhaps saved from madness.

Thus I am in possession of a compendious diagnostic which accords too large a share to psychoanalysis. I have defined the profound intention which organizes his behavior, I have shown that it is a matter of escape behavior, that he *is,* basically, a total escape mechanism. This is perhaps useful; it is still not much, and I am now going to try (how solemn it sounds to be writing in the first person) to ask, in order, the questions this first investigation raises.

1. What is he trying to escape—that is, what is the motivation of his escape? An entirely abstract answer which indicates an impasse to come: He is escaping the intolerable contradiction he would have to live if he assented to his profound situation; he is avoiding a contradictory situation by removing himself to a fabricated situation which, having no other profound purpose than to reject the first, remains artificial for him, threatened with collapse, marginal to his lived reality; therefore he never recognizes himself in what he does because his actions remain without any relation to what he is. What is it, then, that he is trying to escape?

2. To this question, psychoanalytic investigation alone cannot provide the answer.

It can explain, for instance, his inferiority complex or his sense of guilt as the nonliquidation of parental prohibitions and, as a consequence, his perseverance in an infantile attitude of affective dependence on the theological values of childhood; it can add that in relation to this infantile ethic his adult reality seems a sin, and

that he therefore attempts to avoid it by escaping into autistic behavior, an autistic universe. But why hasn't he liquidated the infantile behavior? Here two explanations are possible, which,
although they seem to complement each other, do not exhaust the
question:

a. because he has been powerfully traumatized during his childhood and has not had the necessary patience, courage and resolution to free himself;

b. because occasions propitious to this liquidation have not presented themselves, or, what comes to the same thing (and this
interpretation rather attracts me), because the liquidation, already
begun, of his infantile universe has again been thwarted by un-
favorable circumstances: by exile, exclusion, the impossibility of
working, isolation, circumstances which have reactivated an anterior situation, already partly overcome, and occasioned a regression.

This interpretation would account for the "miraculous coincidence" remarked on above. His situation of exile presents itself as
a particular fact—an intentional fact—miraculously foreseen by the
"nullity complex" of his earliest childhood, not because this nullity
situation was immediately chosen and stabilized by a fundamental
nullity complex, but (1) because the infantile nullity complex has
been developed and enriched by means of this situation; (2) because, having thus resumed the affective atmosphere of his childhood, he has also recovered the recollection of that atmosphere as
a kind of premonition; (3) the historical, Marxist explanation of
his attitude, starting from his objective condition as an exile
doomed to nullity, thus retains its validity; but it is complicated and
enriched by psychoanalytic significations which the lived experience of this objective condition has assumed, for on the occasion
of this objective condition he has reactivated certain infantile significations. Therefore, his attitude situating itself on two levels
which are historically distinct (on the level of objective necessity,

for it is true that his present situation is untenable, that he is doomed to alienation and can surmount it only by assuming his objective nullity in order to transcend it by intellectual effort; and on the level of the infantile nullity complex, which does not correspond to an objective necessity, has no further rational motivation, but reaches back to the prehistoric past of a choice of being), his liberation must be won on both these levels at once—as liquidation of the choice to be null and of the guilt complex (that is, as subjective conversion), and as the practical transcendence of his total situation, which instead of avoiding he must act upon and thereby transform.

This is not new (it has already been given some forty pages back), but it confirms me in my conviction that, after having acquired an approximative total view of the Marxist critique which can suitably be made of his mode of commitment to the world, he must begin not with that critique but with a psychoanalysis that would be circumspect as to its basic postulates. In fact, his "dialectical process" now looks as follows to me (and in tracing its historical development, perhaps I shall succeed in grasping the instruments in which his choice is incarnated and which have been furnished to him by events): There was a child who was marked in his early years by the disciplines of the bourgeois tradition and by the individual values with which his parents endowed that tradition. They gave him an inferiority complex, a guilt complex. Yes, "gave him." For an anxious moment, he wondered if he wasn't taking advantage of a determinist formula. Shouldn't he have said, more accurately, "He was urged by his surroundings to choose himself as inferior and guilty"? That was what he should say, of course, in principle. But the introduction of the notion of choice at this point would raise endless difficulties. It would assume that the two- or three-year-old child might have chosen himself differently under the same conditions; and if this were true, he would have to return to that age and relive it in recollection in order to seize once again the first

basis of the choice. Which is impossible in practice. I am quite willing to assume all responsibilities but not that of the child I was
made into. In practice, determinism (that is, the explanation of
behavior by external pressures) seems to me a process that must
apply to earliest childhood; under given conditions a child is necessarily the way he is, and anyone would be the same in his place, at
his age. The child is conditioned like a plant that is made to grow
straight or in a spiral; he is provided with certain instruments, all
others being excluded, by which to relate himself to others, to the
world, to himself. He is given a certain image of himself, of others,
of his value, his place in the world. It is in the frame of this first
conditioning that he will later choose himself. He is already marked,
already in gear with certain forms of fundamental behavior which,
whether he knows it or not, he has been obliged to adopt (not because discipline has forcibly imposed them upon him, but because
there is no other behavior available) and which constitute his mode
of initial contact with the world, the original structure of his behavior, on the basis of which his person will be established. The
child is an almost entirely fabricated being; his fundamental behavior is created for him. There is as yet no question of choice; the
child gets along with the means available, does his best to escape
punishment, to reconcile himself with the categorical and incomprehensible requirements of those around him. The behavior he
adopts to this end is a behavior of magical exorcism; it has no
meaning for him save that of magically making the grownups smile.
The child finds himself in a situation which is beyond his means;
obliged to play a game whose rules he does not know, he advances
hesitantly, exploring the path that will rouse the least reprobation.
Urged on by slaps and rewards to adopt attitudes which correspond
to what is incomprehensibly demanded of him, he alienates himself in a role, develops the possibilities which correspond to it,
assumes a "character."

What is created here is a mimetic adaptation to the requirements of the milieu, a montage of automatisms which, for the child, are devoid of all meaning. He is living beyond his means; his behavior, which he feels to be mysteriously significant for others, is not so for himself; his training affords him the means of manifesting these significations which escape him. And that is why he is doomed to act a part; he spends his time playing roles he does not understand though he sees they are understood by others; his resources as a deceiver are developed, and yet everyone is surprised to discover he employs these same resources either to hoax those around him or to play any role at all with equal ease. The fundamental role, further-more, the inculcated role, is in the image of the clothes and the boots he is given: they are too big for him, he doesn't manage to fill them, he swims in them, but that doesn't matter, "It'll fit you later on, when you get bigger." Like the sleeves, the laces, the trousers that are too long, the gestures go beyond him. This is just what the discipline intends; he is provided with cultural behavior whose cultural signification he is unaware of (who can boast of grasping it?), he swims in oversize manners; he will end up by filling them, like his clothes; he will end up by living the only sig-nifications he is given the means to signify; to the exclusion of all others, he owns in advance the means of the person he will be "when he gets bigger." He will become the character whose habits he has been obliged to develop; he will end up by producing the intention of his gestures, of the roles he has learned how to act; the objective will react upon the subjective; he will interiorize his role. At first he didn't know what he was doing or even that he was doing it; later he does what he knows how to do. At first he plays with words and speaks without knowing what he is saying; later he speaks and thinks only within the limits of his linguistic habits. Constituted language, the instrument of thought, is at first only a body that is too big for him, a body in which he swims; later he will assume this body and will make his own the intentions the latter permits him to produce—he will signify what he has the means of

signifying. The child becomes the subjective accomplice of a behavior structure which is objectively determined and which is his
familial, social, cultural role. To be otherwise, he would have to
invent different means from those he finds at his disposal. Normally
he does not invent them. The humble, obedient, obliging, polite behavior inculcated from the age of two reveals other people as terrors; producing intentions corresponding to this behavior (adopted
at first without express intention), he now is terrified. And he will
become still more profoundly terrified as his field of vision widens.
Starting from his conditioning and his basic possibilities, he transcends himself toward new possibilities. He is marked. There must
now be a crisis in his life, a rupture of continuity, a displacement in
order, for the child—incapable of coping with his arsenal of habits
and constituted means of perception—to be forced to modify his
infantile choice, to revoke it in rebellion. Adolescence may be this
occasion; but the occasion may also not present itself at all.

Whether or not it does, however, one never altogether rids oneself of one's childhood. It remains as the initial given situation. It
does not explain everything; it explains only the affective coloring
of the present. From another aspect, it must itself be explained,
first of all because it is a particular image of my social situation
(family, education, surroundings, etc.) and refers back to the
society and the entire world whose imprint it bears, later because a
man is explained just as much by his adult condition as by his
childhood.

His past conditions the way he formulates the world and situates
himself within it; his childhood qualifies the goals he assigns himself and the significations he perceives. But inversely, the real
world, with its perspectives and its possible objectives, conditions
and qualifies my relation to the past. The question now is to know
(1) if the past can be put to use and integrated with the present
possibilities so as to enlarge my grasp of reality—if the truth of the
past serves me to extend the objective truth of my actions and is

confirmed by it; or (2) if the past is a handicap, a conditioning which disadapts me in relation to my present condition—if the truth of the past contradicts the truth of my actions and introduces a moment of apparent irrationality into my behavior.

In the first case, the person will be simple; the totalization of his temporal dimensions will present itself as an immediately presented, available possibility. It will appear that "the first impulse is always the right one," that the past gives such a person certain rights over the world—and it will not appear that others affect his behavior (the citizen of Auteuil *never* goes to Aubervilliers).

In the second case, on the other hand, the person will be caught between contradictory significations and truths (proletariat and bourgeoisie, son and orphan, Jew and gentile, city and country), his past contests his present objectivity and, inversely, there is a halt in the gears, the person can be nothing wholly but must integrate incompatible structures by transcending them, feels alone because he never signifies himself when he employs the means of signification of a group to which he does not wholly belong, doomed to the contestation of whatever he does. For the person in this case, there is nothing "natural" or immediately evident; he must continually think, reflect, question; he must base his behavior on reasons that are universally admissible; he cannot make himself real (recover an objectivity that might be his own) save by inventing personal means of signification in order to perform his personal unity.

To understand a man you must therefore deal with him in terms both of his present condition and of his—for him—prehistoric past (that is, of a past anterior to *his* history). His way of dealing with events, organizing his world and putting it in perspective is realistic, rational, objectively conditioned (he formulates it according to the material and intellectual means he invents, at a moment's notice, starting with those which are already at one's disposal), but it is also and at the same time dense with a past, with passions, with

prejudices contracted in childhood, all of which qualify his behavior, give it a singular quality, an individual savor that is not
always fortunate.

The past conditions the present and the future, but present and
future act dialectically on the past and give it variable significations.
It is in any case unlikely that my childhood will survive in me as
such, as a raw determinant, that it will not receive from the present
a signification justifying the fact that I retain it within me; and the
justifications I find for it now cannot be pure make-believe: they
necessarily correspond (unless I go mad) to a present truth. It is
absurd to believe, as Hesnard does, that "infantile behavior can
continue to survive on its own account in later life," that "segments
of infantile life can occur separately in the existing adult" * as
"nonintegrated structures." If infantile behavior were merely this,
merely facts, fossils bequeathed by childhood, without present
meaning, how easy it would be to liquidate them! In reality, if infantile behavior has enduring life, it is because it has assumed, in
the present situation, significations no longer infantile. It is because
it is anything but alien to the person or automatic or accidental; it
is because it permits the organization of the present situation and,
confirmed by it at the same time, seems to be requisite to it. Such
behavior is "overdetermined"—conditioned by the past and the
present at the same time. Its infantile origin (the materialist-psy-
choanalytic explanation of the person by his past) cannot account
for the present motivating power of this past and of the value (or
antivalue) accorded it.

Yes, "segments of behavior" of infantile origin survive in us; but
their infantile motivation has been lost, an adult motivation has
replaced them, behavior originally accountable to an infantile intention is now accountable to a deeply personal intention, not at all
accidental, oblivious to the contingent condition of its reappear-
ance. An example: The sexually inhibited person who avoids con-

---

* *L'Univers Morbide de la Faute,* p. 308.

tact with women, laying down an ascetic and virtuous morality for himself, not only avoids his sexual existence but by doing so avoids existence itself; his bad faith is not confined to the sexual realm, it is complete; his inhibition, which originally was perhaps only the effect of training, without profound signification, has cancerously invaded his entire person, has been developed and individualized. It is now not only a sexual behavior, but a total behavior with ontological motivation; this man is afraid not only of his sexuality but of himself, his freedom in all its aspects. And it is impossible to distinguish the sexual motivations in this fear from the ontological ones, impossible to attribute a sexual signification rather than a moral one. The former is nothing more than a partial aspect of the latter, enveloped by it. And although there was originally an infantile motivation, you can never change a man only from the waist down; his morality now conditions and justifies his sexual behavior, although the latter originally conditioned the former. It is his entire person which he must now modify in order to modify his sexual behavior; his psychoanalytic treatment will succeed only insofar as it will incite him to this total modification, through his sexuality, for instance; it will be successful, in short, despite the psychiatrist's theoretical error, an error which all the same risks retarding his cure indefinitely.

Another example: A man has an antisexual complex, becomes a mystic, justifies his puritanism by his mysticism (a moral choice) and forgets its real conditioning. How can he demystify himself? By becoming conscious of the infantile conditioning of his choice— that is, of its accidental origin? But all choices are contingent and conditional, and if you tell me my Marxism is a result of my condition as a half-caste doomed to contest the existing order, you will not thereby deconvert me; for my convictions produce their own autonomous motivation (there is a specific cohesion of the "superstructure"), and I will not relinquish them if they account for my condition and afford me some grasp of it, if they strike an authentic balance between intention and action. Psychoanalysis finds its limit in authenticity. Making a moral choice relative by explaining its conditioning therefore proves nothing, either for or against that choice; I am a mystic "because" of the antisexual morality of my milieu. And then? And suppose this mysticism were, under the circumstances, in that milieu, the best possible attitude. But is it? Here is quite another question, to which the psychoanalytic dissection of my infantile conditioning furnishes no answer; the conditioning is a fact, a meditated fact which has become significant, an instrument of signification, indissociable from the way in which I assume it in order to situate myself in the world.

In conclusion: The infantile condition "survives" in us only insofar as our present condition confirms us in it, insofar as this behavior inherited from childhood permits the organization of a situation which seems to require it and thereby establishes us in a truth based on the facts. His nullity complex, to return to that, survives in him because an objective situation of nullity has caused it to revive—has permitted it to survive—just when it was being liquidated. He has not simply regressed to this infantile attitude, he has recovered it in a new light, with new significations, as his truth; and it is not by attacking the infantile origin of this "sentiment" that he can hope to rid himself of it. That "sentiment" does not exist; if it is not based on a lived reality which confirms it, it will vanish by itself. But on the other hand, if he had had a different childhood, he would doubtless not have assumed the events of his life in the same way, would not have accorded them the same signification.

The supposed conflict between the materialist explanation and psychoanalysis is therefore a false dilemma. Both, although they are on different levels, explain man by his condition (material, infantile). This explanation is always true, but that is also its weakness; if every choice is conditioned, you can always prove its condition-

ing was "given in advance" as a possibility or an objective probability, but you can never prove it was fatal or necessary, or foresee
it—you can foresee it only after the fact, by showing how and why
it was possible.

The psychological explanation, on the other hand, is always
false; feelings are not in the air, unmotivated or purely "subjective"; they always have an objective basis (the condition of fact)
which should not be considered as a neutral reality the "subject"
fits out with his subjective tastes, but as a network of significations
and potentialities from which we can retain and make effective only
some to the detriment of others. What is called the "subjective
side" has in fact nothing to do with subjectivity; it is merely the fact
that, in confronting an objective situation, we behave in a manner
which is not to be explained by this situation alone and which seems
to activate motivations that cannot be grasped objectively, irrational motivations. We always seem to be situated below the level
of objective reality; this is because at the moment we confront it,
we are already instruments of perception (habits, knowledge, apti-
tudes, mannerisms) acquired in the past, under different circumstances.

Up to this point, there has been no question of freedom; everything has been explicable by present or past conditioning. But what
is no longer explicable by conditioning alone is:

1. That we should cling to a past situation (to our past) when it
disadapts us for dealing with the present reality, and that the latter
has less reality for us than what we were in the past. If man were
merely the product of the circumstances which condition him, why
would present conditioning weigh less than past conditioning? The
difficulty of modifying the instruments of perception inherited from
the past does not suffice to explain the fact that we cling to attitudes
whose present value is exhausted; if we still cling to them, it is
because they incarnate significations and ethical values we adhere

to absolutely, values which are the norm by which we exist and without which we are afraid of going beyond our depth, of sinking into nothingness.

2. That we should be capable of modifying the instruments of perception we already are, of adjusting them to the circumstances, of transcending ourselves toward an enlarged grasp of the given. This perpetual modification, this power of initiative and transformation, is freedom.

The question now is one of knowing whether the total instrument of perception which we are (what he has elsewhere called the "original situation"), the way we situate ourselves in the present reality and establish its signification and truth, reveals the potentialities most valuable for us, affords us the widest possible grasp; or if it deceives us as to our condition, disguises the most important potentialities, raises obstacles to our grasp, abuses our assessment of our opportunities. In short, must the original situation be modified or is it a sufficient means to realize the real, to strike a balance between our intentions, our opportunities, and the objective signification of our actions? It is this question which is the first moment of moral conversion; and again he finds what he has said ten pages earlier: The subjective conversion must begin by an objective investigation. And this objective investigation (which applies to my total condition—that is, to the whole world as a tangle of possibilities and significations, constituted or potential) *is* the conversion at work. To know myself, to know what I am and can be, to understand if I am sufficiently equipped to do what, in my condition, is most effective and valuable, I must put in parentheses my habitual way of assuming my condition, I must suspend my original choice and its prejudices. But this contestation and suspension is not an instantaneous subjective operation; it is further work. You can suspend a commitment only by making another commitment; but in the present instance it is not a matter of another commitment but of taking stock of the contingency and the limitations of my means of perception, of contesting the tendencies incarnated in them—by elaborating various means, by interrogating the world about the opportunities which it offers and which I let pass because I have neither the means nor the heart to grasp them, by making myself "fidgety," by groping along until I find a new way of seeing this arbitrarily familiarized reality.

To learn how to see again. Because the solution of the problems of existence is outside (if it exists at all), freedom is outside, along with the instruments by which it can make itself free and without which it does not exist. (The unity of society and a civilization, à propos, is also outside, in the instruments of perception and action elaborated by and conditioning praxis. They furnish us the possibility of certain ethical programs to the exclusion of all the rest. Which does not mean that all ethical programs are of equal value; it is precisely because they are not that wanting to change the world has a meaning.) Being concerned with what is inside yourself, trying to find yourself within yourself is the surest means of not finding yourself at all, of futilely hashing over immutable psychological problems. You would be more likely to find yourself if you were concerned with the world, undertook something, forgot yourself—if you no longer craved a being-for-yourself that conformed to some norm.

He says this, but has still to prove it. "All the same," Jacques said, "you're looking for fame, aren't you?" "No," he answered quickly, "no—" with a tiny sense of superiority—"to be recognized by those I recognize." To be recognized by Morel and those who recognize Morel; no longer to be a nocturnal scribbler lost in the darkness between the Chemin Vert and the Rue Saint-Maur, covering sheets of paper with blue specks and producing nothing, like the thousands who hopelessly parade their mediocrity, filling their desk drawers with rejected manuscripts by which their human condition has been refused on paper as in other respects. "It comes down to the same thing," Jacques said. "Fame among a coterie of the elect means more to you than glory among the great mass of fools." This is not certain. He honestly believes that he is not in search of a coterie life. He believed in that in '47, imagining Paris was the center of the world, supposing he was exiled from truth because he was not in Paris, and dreaming he would be at the heart of the world and of truth if he could go to bistros and have discussions with Morel's circle. If he could do this, of course he would be admitted among the gods and acquire an absolute importance in all eyes, including his own. But he no longer believes this. He has known for some time that having a book published, even having it recognized by Morel's circle, is not a metaphysical revolution; that a book doesn't get you very far (just a little way), because afterward you have to begin again and keep abreast of where you were; and that merely not falling behind means you have to advance constantly, and constantly invent; and that there is nothing gained for good. Fame does not interest him (that is, fame for its own sake), perhaps because it has been offered to him anyway and because, measuring its mediocrity (pontificating bores him and he's no good at it), he has already refused it. If it still counts, as recognition, it is because of the possibilities of action, even the obligations to action it can provide; recognized, he would be in the world, it would no longer be a matter of indifference whether he did this, that, or the other thing; he would really exist as doing what he does, he would be obliged to continue under pain of abdication and betrayal. While if he abdicates, betrays, accepts money from the fascists or sells out to the Americans now, it matters to no one and he refuses to do so quite gratuitously, out of *amour-propre,* it will be said, out of love of austerity, without effect, since there are many in his position who sell out, and to whom his pure refusal— not opposition but merely refusal—simply leaves the field open. If he wants to be recognized, it is so that to write will some day become an action, not remain this futile and ascetic gesture of a man who works himself up every night and who, alone in conferring a staggering importance on what he says, is inevitably tempted to think that he is indulging in nothing more than spiritual exercises. How could he believe in his responsibility and his task, since what he thinks rouses no echo anywhere and produces no consequence, since, without a public, he has no possibility of action?

To things themselves. For weeks now he has postponed getting down "to things." Having grasped some fundamental attitudes, he is already tempted to think he is through, supposes he is cured of his abstract madness, enjoys the idle moments before getting down to work and tells himself, "You see, you're changing, you're enjoying things"; and he wonders if this euphoria isn't merely the stupid satisfaction of the schoolboy who thinks he knows everything because he's done his homework.

But try to find the signification of this kind of feeling—what is the right one? And where? Nowhere. Stupid satisfaction or awakening to life, engulfment or progress—this intermittent euphoria can be all these, but it is nothing of the kind for the moment; it will be one or the other according to the direction he takes. For the moment, he is heading nowhere; he is feeling his way. For fifteen days he wonders where to start, where to begin unraveling the skein. "Begin anywhere," Jacques said. "Once you've begun, it goes by itself."

"Yes," he answered, "but where is anywhere?" He thought he could penetrate himself by starting with some real event and proceeding backward from there, illuminating the signification which this event has for him by its historical density; then ridding the event of this individual signification, which perhaps obscures his assessment, in order to arrive at an interpretation of the facts which is not purely personal. Take Poujadism, for instance. His assessment of Poujadism is certainly emotional in part. He recognizes in the Poujadists the sluggish stupidity of big- and small-time profiteers who resent the society that keeps them from making out; he recognizes the drunken cowardice of his own (and, in itself, surprising) courage, as during a riot when the concierge, the grocer, the barber, and the newspaper vendor put out swastikas and dragged the Jewish woman and her daughter out of his building all the way to the S.A. car parked a hundred yards from a fireplug. (The crowd made a circle around them, spat on them. They were given buckets. "Wash!" shouted the S.A. man, and the women started dragging the buckets full of water from the fireplug to the car, the gray hair hanging over the old woman's forehead as she hobbled along, panting. "Faster!" the S.A. man screamed, and he tore the bucket out of the old woman's hands, flinging the water over the car in one great cascade; the car was a black Steyr 100; the crowd, frightened by its own audacity, watched in silence, and he himself, shaken by a kind of interior earthquake, felt only that he did not understand something that was happening, something that upset him deeply, something lodged in the inexplicable contradiction between, on the one hand, the silent, idle crowd, the motionless silhouette of the husky S.A. man, his boots and belt gleaming—the incarnation of arrogant power—and, on the other, the two panting, terrified women, their weakness straining beneath the scornful eyes of strength. It was his first image of the pogrom, decisive because from that day on, seized with a slight nausea at the sight of this gratuitous hatred, he realized that those in power, the masters of the world, were on the "other side," and that his own place, as a mute spectator sitting on his bicycle, was nowhere, that there was no way for him to pass into the camp of the violent and powerful, nor into the camp of the crowd, that complacent accomplice nervously enjoying its spectacle, nor into the camp of the victims, for whom he was not prepared to have sympathy—only a disgusted pity. Spectator: in the person of the two women, it was his father they were spitting on, his father whom he despised; in the person of the S.A. man was incarnated a virility he was beginning to hanker for; as for the crowd, its complicity was stealing his country from him, for he had no part in its silent communion. The world fell outside

him; again he was alone, weak, and null, the bastard taunted by
Strauss, kicked in the mud and not even fighting back, convinced
of his own irremediable impotence.) He was surely overestimating
the Poujadist danger and power, filtering out of the information he
gathered about the movement what confirmed his alarmist assessment of the situation and then, conscious that he was inclined toward alarmism (worse, toward defeatism when confronted with
the mounting strength of the new fascism; he could foresee opposition to it only as defensive), correcting this first assessment by a
second, which was calmer and more prudent and which boiled
down to an admission of ignorance: "It might become dangerous,
although it is not necessarily so at present." Aware of a certain real
aspect of Poujadism, he therefore feels that other aspects, just as
real, might well escape him. Rather than trust himself to the "first
impulse, which is always the right one," he should therefore undertake a scientific study of the phenomenon—that is, apply a method
so rigorous that his personal feelings would be put in parentheses
from the start. Fine. But what good would such a study do? What
if he learned everything about Poujadism, for instance? (Which
was impossible anyway, for such a movement would most likely be
altered or etiolated before he had succeeded in examining it thor-
oughly, just as he fears that a man's lifetime, his own in particular,
will be too short to permit him to grasp and change it.) Now he
has no particular desire to consecrate the years to come to the
scientific study of the contemporary neofascist movements in
France. That would be a false scent. He would do better to divide
his task into two phases: (1) to understand himself (and here the
study not of Poujadism but of the meaning he spontaneously accorded it can be precious, for his spontaneous reaction to this particular phenomenon is indicative of his total person, as is his attitude to women, friends, society, the bourgeoisie, money, Communism, etc.); (2) having reached an understanding of his original
choice and his original situation, to see what grasp of reality and

what possibilities of action this situation (which still remains to be explained) offers him in the world (which he must get to know better).

This much is beginning to be clear; and he now realizes that if he has been swimming so long to reach this conclusion, it is because he has momentarily relapsed into one of his most revealing failings: his taste for abstract and theoretic knowledge, the craving to conceive the world as a pure object entirely exterior to him thanks to an impersonal method of knowledge (his passion for statistics), instead of concerning himself for once with the place he himself takes in the world, with the way he himself can join it starting from his own situation—for it is understood that he will never rid himself of this situation (only modify it) or of the "prejudices" (idiosyncrasies) it necessarily inclines him to, that he will never be an anonymous, perfectly transparent, reasonable consciousness, but that he can only try to take advantage of the fact that his situation makes him sensitive to certain significations, makes him live intensely a certain truth, though one with many lacunae, of course, and one which he must complete by a reasoned understanding of those aspects that remain alien to him. He still has to assume himself in his individuality in order to transcend this individuality effectively and to *live* some positive undertaking which will make his truth explicit to himself, instead of trying (convinced that his situation exiles him forever from the world and from humanity) to participate in an undertaking by making every situation into an abstraction, systematically annihilating himself as a person in the articulation of austere and abstract generalities.

Now he sees where to begin (his second exile, at the age he began to integrate himself, with considerable effort; the chasm that appeared between himself and the society of men starting on a spring day in 1938), although beginning in the middle (almost arithmetically—he is twice as old now) is obviously not a beginning at all and must clarify itself by earlier experiences as it pro-

ceeds. He will call this chapter relating to his exclusion from the
world of men "They," and "We" what he has written up to this
point, since by using the first person plural he has shown that the
"we," the community of the living, comprises for him the ascetic
adherence of intellects to that anonymity of the generic, that abstract universality in which they can proliferate their theories and
lose themselves.

Then he will still have to take inventory of his reality as a person in relation to other persons; and he will call this chapter
"You." And finally, if he succeeds in his undertaking, he will have
the right to call the last chapter "I" and speak there in the first
person; he will grasp himself instead of his phantoms, the subject
at last of a situation developed on *his* account, a situation in which
he will see the totality of *his* means in order to make himself a man
and free—instead of being, as he is now, their sad dupe and complacent victim.

They

A. *Exclusion*

Covered with tarpaulins and full of soldiers, gray-green trucks with three axles, flat radiators and vertical windshields were rolling down the main avenue of the Thirteenth Bezirk at twilight. Standing with his forehead pressed against the window—the same window from which, four years before, he had seen two men with Socialist Party armbands shooting rifles in the street ("Get away from the window," the maid had said. "Why?" "Because of ricochets.")—he was admiring the interminable cavalcade of trucks, and then, seized by the excitement in the air, he took out his bicycle to go watch them on the highway.

Something crucial must be happening, but he couldn't have said what it was; all he knew for sure was his feverish desire to get nearer the trucks, to smell the gasoline and hear the rumble of their motors. The crowd formed a hedge along the highway; as each truck passed (bigger trucks now, uncovered, with the soldiers standing up), the crowd shouted, *"Heil!"* and raised their arms.

Pushing into the front row and raising his arm too, he shouted, *"Heil!"* with them, happy to be lost in the crowd and to see the soldiers laughing as they returned—somewhat weakly, he thought —the Nazi salute.

The next day, on his way to school, he went into the stationery store, where the thin, ill-tempered woman greeted him with *"Heil* Hitler!" *"Heil* Hitler!" he said. "I'd like a swastika." She took out some little boxes full of swastikas, he chose a large one—it cost thirty groschen—and pinned it on the green lapel of his Tyrolean jacket.

He wasn't quite sure how he felt about it. Two years before he had decided to be a Nazi because the Nazis were strong and noisy, arrogant, virile, and with a great power behind them that made nonsense out of this petty, putty Austria (Dollfuss, rustic idylls, patriotic songs no one believed in, good workmanship, honesty and thrift); because the Nazis saw things "big," talked loud, hated Jews and his father was a Jew. He would have liked to get rid of his father, with his business worries ("Your father has worries," "Business is bad"), his eternal reproaches ("You're such a dumbbell; you'd do better to learn your lessons; get something inside your head instead of worrying about your muscles; that boy will never come to anything; what can I do with a boy like you?"), his incomprehension, his narrow-mindedness, his Schaffhausen watch that gained five seconds a week according to a nightly check and that had to be regulated when it was more than fifteen seconds fast. He would have liked to get rid of such a father (even at six he preferred the garage mechanic), with his little potbelly, the vaseline he put in his nose every night, the liquid paraffin (*"Nujol tut wohl"*) he drank from the bottle, and the greasy old Jews he brought home to talk business with. But when he pinned the swastika on his lapel, he felt that something was wrong, and whenever he met anyone on the street, he felt as if he were at fault. He stared at other people's lapels, and other people stared at his, and he wondered if he had the right to wear a swastika, and if it showed on his face that his father was a Jew. And when he saw someone without a swastika, he was torn between the sense of his own superiority (here was someone in whose eyes he must be a redoubtable Nazi, in his leather breeches, his hobnail boots, his big swastika) and a hesitant admiration for someone who could defy the triumphant National Socialism.

In class that day, almost everyone wore swastikas, some even wore Hitlerjugend badges, but Felix wore the badge of the Dollfussjugend "because," he said, "I'm Austrian." The fact that Felix (an old Catholic family from the Vorarlberg), the boy who was first in math, Latin and gym, should claim to be Austrian left him openmouthed, and he wondered if it wasn't really more manful, after all, not to wear a swastika. Perhaps it was Felix who put the worm in the fruit that day (on the footbridge over the grade crossing— they had hoisted themselves up the beams while the father, redfaced and sputtering, had brandished his fist at them—it was Felix who had taught him the "Internationale" and the "Avanti Popolo," picked up God knows where; in the middle of class it was Felix who had put his behind on the desk and released an echoing fart which he fanned with a sheet of paper until protests rose from the back of the room against the stink, making him giggle hysterically and infuriating the German prof, a Monarchist with a distinguished Hapsburg face whose virility was accentuated by a scar at the corner of his mouth), making him suspect that not being a Nazi was not necessarily "less" than a Nazi but might mean "more." But what was possible for Felix was not possible for him; for Felix was a "whole" person with obvious rights to the world, with a Catholic father named Thomas who was a government official and a peasant grandmother who still baked her own bread. Whereas *he* was only half, a half man, half Jew, half Aryan—two halves that would never make a whole; he would have to get rid of one or the other.

The German prof with the saber cut on his chin, an arrogant patriot, Austria forever, love of one's country, duty and Chancellor Dollfuss always on his lips, had not come to class that day, and the man who did come, a tall, bombastic, gawky fellow, made them a little speech: "I was blind, the scales have fallen from my eyes, I confess the error of my ways, I believe in the Reich and in the Führer." But that didn't keep him from having his swastika taken away afterward. Some teachers came in wearing party badges, but the class didn't last long. They put bales of straw in the classrooms for the soldiers to sleep on. There was three weeks' vacation because the school had been requisitioned by the army.

He asked himself few questions during those three weeks. The universe had capsized into Nazism so quickly and so completely that, caught unawares, overcome by the facts, he tried only to make himself comfortable in it without attempting to understand or catch up with the gigantic head start the facts had just taken.

From one day to the next, Nazism had burst into bloom, had spread out over the city like a glue, had stuck to the walls, the fences, the sidewalk, painted huge swastikas and slogans: *"Wir kehren heim in's Reich," "Ein Volk ein Reich ein Führer."* The tentacles could be discerned in the questioning look of the stationery seller, the mealymouthed talk of big Klima with his Czech accent, his gold teeth, his hands folded over his belly, standing in front of his barbershop, the window full of little German flags, shouting *"Heil* Hitler!" as soon as he saw a familiar face. They had come out of their holes like rats, swastikas in their buttonholes, servile smiles on their lips—Klima, the baker, the dry-goods salesman, the tobacconist, the milkman with the Polish accent, they had to show themselves now, had to show how pleased they were. They vied to show their zeal, made calculations, for they mustn't let the occasion pass; after eight years of privation when they had had to bow to Herr Baron and Herr Major and Herr Kommerzienrat to sell barleysugar or a tube of paste or a shave, they changed their

approach, they were going to butter up the S.A. man on the corner,
smile knowingly at the major in the Heimwehr, glance greedily at
the Jew's shop across the street. *"Heim in's Reich";* they were going
to sell their linen sheets to the German businessmen who followed
close on the army's heels and who would give them synthetic fabrics
in return, buy up ten-year-old stocks; best of all, they were going
to share the cake of Jewish business—no, not share it, appropriate
it by signing up in the Nazi Party and looking for protectors. "Poor
lady, what will you do?" they would ask his mother with exag-
gerated solicitude, and between one *"Heil* Hitler!" and the next
they would lean over the counter to whisper some filth about the
Nazis and swear they opposed them, but if you let yourself be
taken in by their confidences they gave you a sly look that seemed
to say, "Turn about—after the *Juden,* we're the ones to make a
penny now." All except for big Frau Bachrach, monstrously fat,
disfigured by a tumor on her left cheek, with her Yiddish jargon
and her chlorotic, velvet-eyed daughter—Frau Bachrach sitting en-
throned among her dusty candies, destined for the cremation ovens,
greeting his father (how many customers did *he* have left?) with
a persecuted smile and moist lamentations, while the candy store
across the street sold out its ices every day.

They groveled, afraid someone would remember they had not
always been Nazis, afraid of missing their chance to get ahead, to
eat their slice of cake. And to spirit away their fear, they discovered
their Germanic souls; they listened to Germanic blood shrilling
through their veins; they said in voices like that of the pleasant
little minor official's wife, "There's nothing I can do, I simply
cannot *bear* breathing the same air as an Asiatic!"

For three weeks he took refuge in outdoor pleasures, riding his
bike around the school, watching the soldiers coming in and out
with cases of grenades, inspecting the 1930 trucks with their flat
radiators, asking the soldiers about the speeds they could make.
With Felix he climbed the Red Mountain, from the top of which

you could see most of the city, where suburban families went on
Saturday afternoons to fly kites (he had never had a kite) and to
ski or sled in winter. He took breakneck bike rides along the steep
paths of the Red Mountain with Felix, happy to keep up with this
"whole" man though he himself was only a half man, confident that
he had the muscles and the nerve of an Aryan, speaking the crudest
slang, the jargon of the toughs who lived on the other side of the
soccer field, a stretch of ground that even Bradovic, the team captain who was two years older than they, his eyes blue and insolent,
his chin covered with blond hair, would not cross at night unless he
was armed with a long key "to knock their teeth out with."

To be accepted by Felix and the big boys like Bradovic, Kalmar,
Urmann, Schoeps (whose father, a gigantic butcher, declared that
in his youth he could chin himself three times with one arm and
that even now he could do five chins on his butcher's hooks), he
had imposed a discipline on himself "whose severity deserved a
better cause," his father said. He had learned to spit considerable
distances (from the sidewalk to the other side of the first streetcar
track), and on his good days he could beat Felix. For months he
rode off every day, alone on his bicycle, clocking the time it took
him to cover a certain distance, pedaling as fast as he could, determined to beat his record, to beat the weakness he sensed within
himself, which he somehow identified with his Jewish blood. He
was determined to toughen himself, running uphill (he had been
teased once by a governess who had not liked him and who claimed,
when he was eleven, that he couldn't climb to the top of a tiny
grassy slope), trying to run a kilometer in less than three minutes,
carrying heavy stones, exercising every night by chinning on his
closet bar, then on a trapeze hung between two rooms. Despite his
weakness, his own fear, and the continual criticism of his parents,
he acquired skills which made him acceptable among the strongest
of the other boys, and to be accepted by them meant more to him
than to be accepted by his parents. He did not want to be the

prodigy his mother hoped would be the decoration of her family; just a boy like the rest, accepted by the rest; each triumph he won from them gave him a liberating revenge over his family.

Accepted, acceptable, not loved, admired, followed. Accepted by the groups that had formed at school according to the roads they all took to go home. Accepted by Bradovic ever since they had fought a duel with poles one evening and his own had broken and he had gone on with only a stump of wood, his hand bleeding; accepted by Felix ever since he had learned to throw snowballs far and hard and, hiding behind the rampart of shoveled snow, had aimed so well that his snowball had smashed against the windshield right in the driver's face, so that the furious driver had stopped his car and got out to look for them with his flashlight. Accepted, but without any friend or confidant; even Felix, whom he liked more than the rest, took sides against him when anyone began teasing him; even Felix, when he felt like it, called him "Jew, Jew, lick-my-ass Jew!" a chant that put an end to all possible discussion, a definitive statement which Felix considered of great subtlety and which he delighted in using instead of an answer or an explanation.

They, and Felix above all, were the way they were; they had their values and their obvious facts; they had something like a nature (strengths they utilized as it pleased them, muscles they didn't dream of increasing, a body they lived comfortably with). He, by nature, had none. What they were naturally he had become by having wanted to; he had chosen his models: to be tough, muscular, and severe like Andreas Hofer, the Tyrolean hero of the resistance against Napoleon, a man who was one with his rocky country, to the point of having dolomite in his head, probably; to be a piece of nature, united with it, insensible to everything except its own energies, participating in a cosmic force. He could become this model, the "whole" man, only by a patient *ascesis;* in other words, he would never become it at all, he wanted it because he wasn't it—and he could only want it because what he wanted was radically Other than himself. He wanted to become Other than himself, and because he was never this Other *for* himself, he attached the greatest importance to the exterior signs of his transformation, to his appearance-for-others. The limbs and muscles others had he made for himself, teaching himself to walk on the outer edges of his soles to make his legs bowed (the Tyrolean peasant, the "prolo," the football player are bowlegged), doing exercises to develop his thigh and calf muscles; rolling up his *Ledernhosen* so that these muscles were quite visible, and rolling down his socks or better still not wearing them so as not to break the curve of his leg. His pastimes were never gratuitous; bicycling, running, swimming, sun bathing were not activities with pleasure as their goal, but work he deliberately imposed on himself to increase his capital of muscles and tan. He did not choose his bicycle routes for pleasure or for the beauty of the landscape, but to add a fixed number of daily kilometers to his speedometer; during vacation with his grandparents, at thirteen or fourteen, he left the house every day after lunch, not to explore the countryside but to cover the same circuit ten times—a circuit including a steep hill, then a descent spoiled by big rocks and bogs which necessitated constant use of the brakes.

His only satisfaction was in overcoming himself, and he felt he defeated himself as soon as he indulged the slightest personal desire or preference. From his twelfth or thirteenth year, the beginning of his simultaneous conversion to Nazism and to a puritanical Catholicism, he had imposed a rigorous discipline upon himself, which consisted of systematically doing the opposite of whatever he was spontaneously inclined to do (taking the route to school he found most boring; not eating what he liked and eating what he didn't; praying for all humanity but not for himself or his parents, who, in the eyes of God, had no particular claim to grace, being only mortals like the rest) and offering to God the pleasures he refused himself, though without feeling exonerated even so. For to have any claim on the grace of God, he should be deep in prayer all the time and not only in the morning, in the toilet (the only place where he was certain not to be seen, where he said three paters and three Aves in Latin until his father, suspecting God knows what practices, got in the habit of pounding on the toilet door as soon as he had taken refuge inside and shouting furiously, "He's in there again like a hen laying eggs!"—a habit which provoked him to hide, when he wanted to pray, behind the dressing-room wardrobe, then, doubting the effectiveness of his prayers, to say them once more on the way to school), and at night, kneeling under his covers, to make sure he wouldn't be caught. At any moment he might wake up guiltily and remind himself, "I'm not praying," so that instead of a prayer, for which he lacked serenity, he could offer God some expiatory act, like not looking at the cars in the street, keeping his eyes fixed on his feet.

Yet he loved God no more than his physical exercises. It was impossible for him to conceive God, who remained a terrifying and jealous abstraction (in short, the God of the Jews), and nothing he learned in catechism class established Him as a clement and smiling savior. "God sees all, knows all, judges all." He was living transfixed by this judge's stare with its terrible and unknown requirements; before God he felt always guilty and about to be punished, unless he was imposing some privation on himself and overcoming his desires.

A religious *ascesis* (though not a mystical one—not loving himself, he felt despised by God and could therefore neither love nor communicate with God but only exorcise Him), a physical *ascesis,* the feeling of his own minimal value and the attribution of value to what was most alien to him; aspects of a fundamental attitude of refusal, as if, incapable of accepting himself for what he was (incapable of establishing his value in his real situation), he could reach salvation only by conforming to alien norms and rules, wait-

ing for an impossible transfiguration; as if he had either to efface
himself (as he did before God) or make himself radically Other in
order to accede to some dignity, even a minor one, as if the fact of
remaining himself despite these exercises were a failure, a kind of
inner corruption.

So I was wrong to think I could say that in 1938, at the age of
fifteen, he was on the verge of integrating himself, and that the
Anschluss *again* flung him into exile. The truth is that the events of
the period made him conscious of an exile from which in fact he
had never emerged, obliged him to admit that the bridges between
himself and the others were cut, to assume this separation which
he was making such heroic efforts to overcome. That these efforts
were futile precisely because of their voluntary nature he had
always, deep down, suspected. He knew he could feel some people,
imitate a prolo and, by the slang formulas, the guttural noises, the
careless and sometimes shabby clothes, magically invoke a pro-
letarian universe (that is, a universe exempt from bourgeois artifices
and familial complications, a universe he would enter as an orphan,
a child without known origins, therefore without a Jewish father and
without an Aryan mother, therefore simply a man judged by his
merits and strength alone), but he also felt he lacked something
essential in order to deceive the prolos and himself: the boldness,
the conviction, the confidence in the solidity of his role—that is,
in himself. That a fault subsisted at the heart of his being, under-
mining the whole structure, he had realized whenever it was a
question of employing physical force and the acquired slang formulas. He knew that in relation to his weight his strength was at least
equal to that of the huskiest of his schoolfellows, and his agility,
maintained by daily exercises, was probably hard to beat; he outstripped them all when it came to climbing poles of ropes without
using his legs; he was fifth, and first in his school, in the school
swimming championships; he could throw a stone or a ball as far
as anyone; and yet he was among the worst handball players in his

class, completely worthless in any team sport. (The most popular
of these consisted of throwing the ball at a member of the opposite
side; if you hit him, he was "killed," eliminated, unless he caught
the ball in the air. This brutal game terrified him; he made no effort
to catch the ball and tried to take refuge in the crowd that huddled
against the radiator pipes or to conceal himself behind good
catchers. The ball frightened him; so much so that several times it
hit him in the face, and, his eyes smarting with dust, his face burning, he felt on the verge of tears. It hit him several times in the
genitals too; he ran from it like a rabbit from the hunter, feared it
so much that often he was the only "survivor" and had to go
through another torture: trying to avoid a "death" he knew was
ultimately fatal. Lacking confidence in his aim, he felt embarrassed
by the ball when he managed to get hold of it, and he thought only
of getting rid of it as soon as possible, throwing it in no particular
direction.) He was worst still in any exercise that demanded boldness. Brutal and cynical prolos like Bradovic or Kalmar were particularly good at the saddle jump—raised one notch each time the
"horse" was to be cleared by a kind of scaring flight, clapping of
both hands on the cold leather, landing on the "animal" itself. It
was all right at the beginning, but as soon as the horse was several
notches up, his fear of hurting himself (it had happened once)
made his knees buckle and he leaped without conviction, landing
on the horse beneath the contemptuous gaze of the gym teacher.
Failing where those weaker than he succeeded, he knew that only
his cowardice was responsible. And he was so cowardly that his
other performances passed unnoticed; he was classified as a bad
athlete. Only in the spring of 1939 did the gym teacher discover his
resources, the occasion an exercise of pure strength: hanging from
the bar, they were to chin themselves as often as possible—six for
Bradovic, seven for Kalmar and only five for Felix. "Try for five,"
the gym teacher said to him, probably suspecting his ambition.
Then, under the astonished eyes of the whole class, starting slowly

in order to save his strength, while the gym teacher counted, he chinned himself thirteen times. He was in ecstasy. Leutner, who came after him, beat his record with fourteen. But he knew he could have beaten Leutner if *he* had come afterward. The instructor's remarks soon annihilated his triumph. He didn't say, "First Leutner with fourteen, second G with thirteen." He said, "The big surprise today is that G chinned thirteen times." The big surprise. They hadn't expected so many from him; he was not particularly admired for his prowess and more was not asked of him later on. It was really surprising that someone as mediocre should have given such a performance. And he knew that the contempt such surprise implied was justified. He had the strength but not the courage, the matter but not the spirit of a good athlete; his athlete's body was paradoxically inhibited by a timid soul. His strength could only *be,* apply itself reflexively to his own body, in exercises without danger; it could not act; it was turned in on itself, narcissistically, but without a basis in the world, without a hold on it. A strength turned back on itself, ascetic and voluntary, perfectly summing up the fundamental sterility of his person. Rootless strength, abstract as his thoughts were to be later; what he lacked was transcendence, or, if you prefer, life. Such strength could function only by holding the world at a distance (like his intellect later on) but could not embrace the world.

He was tempted to say then, and again recently, that this deep inconsistency, this cowardice consisting of a lack of courage rather than any real fear, was inherent and inevitable in his situation. Caught between a mother and a father incompatible not only because of their origins, their religion, their "race," but particularly because of their temperaments and values, he had no foundation anywhere, no point of view he could adopt as profoundly his own; he was tempted by all the roles the world offered, while at the same time being unable to commit himself to any of them. In this false situation, false from every point of view, he was condemned to invent an individual truth at the same time that he was incapable of inventing one. This is the explanation of his inconsistency, but not his excuse. For others in an analogous situation (Mauthner, Weiss, Hoffman, later on) were, on the contrary, noisy, combative, energetic, and therefore cynical, but they overcame their contradiction by ambitions (social ambitions—to "arrive" and impress others—in Weiss and Mauthner, ambition to be a better Nazi than the Aryans in Hoffman, who was killed in 1941 on the Russian front) which, though they resolved nothing, provided them with a façade, a solidity, a surface which he lacked. And before searching, by means of a deeper analysis, for the origin of this lack of surface, I want to describe the events after which he finally renounced all attempts to acquire one.

The summer of 1938 had been quite agreeably spent. And he had not had the eyes to see what was going badly. His father had worries and his mother referred to them, said business was bad, but that was usual enough. Someone with the badge of an old party member began coming to the house at night for conferences with his father, whose "partner" he was going to be to keep the business from being "Aryanized" (that is, appropriated by an Aryan). He went swimming in the public pool with K, a little red-headed boy who wore a Hitlerjugend uniform and who, of modest family, had developed a crush on him ever since he had seen their living room. With motives that were doubtless ulterior, his mother had one evening asked K, in his velvet shorts and Hitlerjugend belt, to sit in one of the deep salon armchairs, had offered him a glass of something and begun making conversation. K was disturbed and, Hitlerjugend though he was, began saying that the racial laws should be taken with a grain of salt. With K, Felix and others, he swam two hundred yards in the pool one day, after which he made a bet, out of breath as he was, that he could do a certain number of deep-knee bends right afterward. They took him up on it, he won the bet, and K told him he was a good guy and it was too bad he couldn't join the Hitlerjugend.

Just before the vacation, the Conservatory student who gave him piano lessons showed up one afternoon in an S.A. uniform. He spoke to his mother, gave him his harmony lesson and told him this would be their last session. After the lesson they went out into the street together. The young S.A. teacher seemed uneasy, and as they passed a fence he said, "In here," and pushed him through an opening into a sunny empty lot. It was warm, and the young teacher (his name was Opitz or something of the kind) put his hand on his shoulder and said, his pale forehead dripping with sweat, "I'd like to go on teaching you—you're a talented boy. I think you could become a good musician. I'd like to teach you counterpoint. But you have to understand, I'm in the S.A., I can't let myself be caught giving lessons to a half-caste. I'm really awfully sorry. And promise you'll go on working at your music. You promise?"

Keeping his hand on his shoulder, he made him promise. They shook hands, "between men," in silence. "Go out first and walk ahead," Opitz said. "We shouldn't be seen together. Goodbye."

On the way home, he really felt sorry for that nice Opitz who had looked so embarrassed. And he decided he should try to become a great musician. Because there would be no more lessons, he began practicing quite regularly for a few weeks; his piano had acquired the signification of a challenge. He played (badly—he never acquired the minimal agility to interpret in the true sense of the word) during a few warm afternoons instead of going swimming, and the music he wrung from the instrument, staring at the maple leaves that shimmered in the sunshine outside the window, was like a triumphant affirmation against the world. Afterward he stopped playing; vacation came, and after the vacation, no more piano.

He spent that vacation in the village where their maid had been born, in the house of some farmers. A tiny village some twenty kilometers from Salzburg; when you came out of a woods there was a road, and on each side of the road some low brick houses, a few fields, and some peat bogs that were no longer worked. The farmer had a clubfoot (a war wound), a squint-eyed wife, a senile mother, three children, a one-story house, a little barn, six hens, two hogs, perhaps an acre of peat bog, two of poor wheat, and a pasture. He arrived on the farm just as they were bringing in the wheat (cut by sickle) and the next day he offered to help thresh it. For three days, he threshed the wheat with a flail, an astonishing tool that turned in his hand and over his head and made his palms smooth and calloused. Three days of threshing, one of winnowing. Then a week of transporting peat in a wheelbarrow over ditches full of water bridged by trembling planks. The first time, he dumped the whole barrow into the ditch; later it went better, the farmer was pleased with him, and he happy because of it. After the peat, there was the hay which he cut with a scythe, careful not to nick the legs of the man cutting beside him. A few kilometers away there was a little lake to which he bicycled to swim, some woods, some abandoned peat works, wagons that had once been used to carry the peat and on which, after pushing them up their still intact rails, he could coast down with amazing speed. For a long time he remembered such things with great happiness; he had virtually forgotten himself and by manual work exteriorized himself in a product (wheat, hay, peat: ailment, fuel, wealth) whose indisputable value would permit him to re-enter the society of men in the simplest, most direct way.

I know, this dream of simplicity was sheer romanticism and his "great happiness" of the period was not unalloyed. He could have escaped into field labor only if he had been born a farmer, and the uncertain joy he derived from it was more nostalgia than anything else. Threshing the wheat and carrying blocks of peat, he discovered the elementary needs which make all men alike; it was a way of

returning to a human generality exempt from morality. He wanted
to be the servant of elementary man in his generality, a work force
producing indisputable vital wealth, a power unquestioned as to
its origins or its destination because all men are equal before fire
and bread, equally cold in winter, and hungry without food; to
work toward the satisfaction of elemental needs. (A temptation he
has not dismissed to this day, since he often dreams of working as
a farmer, as a bricklayer in a Communist country, since he can
fascinate himself with the statistics of national and world production, of five-year plans, trade blockades and the problems of American surplus; since the least quantity of food is something sacred
for him, an image of wealth connected with an incident that crystal-
lized whole visions of the world: At the age of nine or so he had
made a little ball of bread crumbs and flicked it off the table after
a meal. "What's the matter with you?" his father had shouted.
"Food is not to be played with! There are millions of men dying
of hunger all over the world!" He didn't play with bread after that,
and when he saw American films where people broke eggs over
each other's head and threw pies in each other's face, he grew furious with the film and the stupidity of the laughing audience, his
heart pounding with indignation at all that food wasted, with all
the millions of men dying of hunger all over the world.) Starting
from humanity's elementary needs, starting from the naked body,
emaciated or gleaming with sweat, starting from the body's labor,
its power and its wretchedness, without decoration or clothing (for
with them begin the differences and the hierarchies, the myths,
mystiques and exclusivities, the rules and social values), directly at
grips with *things,* stripping men with his eyes and wondering what
they would look like naked and judging them consequently ("Did
he have a potbelly?" he asked his mother when she came home
from a lecture by Amundsen. "A little." "What do you mean, a
little—like Papa?" "A little less," she said, "just a little stomach."
He couldn't respect a man, no matter how great his prestige, if he

had a potbelly, and his admiration for Alexander of Macedonia was due to the powerful musculature of his statue), his was a way of putting in parentheses the whole social and cultural nexus, the origin of his complications and his exclusion, getting rid, through the naturalist or materialist perspective, of the social, racial and religious moralities, the sources of his alienation, his laceration and his guilt feelings.

Elemental needs, elemental works: a way of making a *tabula rasa* of history and the distinctions between man and man; hunger, sweat and toil: means of access to a forbidden fraternity, the nostalgia for which ultimately led him to the extreme left. But even then he already felt that the elemental humanity whose destitution he would share—being destitute of any sociocultural roots himself —existed nowhere, that the wretchedest members of the proletariat were more imbued with culture than he (that the ideal proletariat existed no more than the man of perfect simplicity, Gide's quest for whom was to appeal to him so greatly), that the farmers of Salzburg judged him and scorned him by norms he would never satisfy —out of scorn for "city people" and especially for people from Vienna, because of his very excess of good will, and because of his education. He could do a farmer's work as well as he liked, but in the farmer's eyes it wasn't *his* work, and because he hadn't been born here in this village, didn't have it in his blood, didn't love it in the same way as the natives, he could never be one of them.

He felt this, and when there was no more work to do he began imposing tasks upon himself again: to bicycle to the next village every morning and then back up the steep hillside without putting his feet on the ground; to read five pages of Nietzsche every night (*The Birth of Tragedy*) without understanding a word and getting through one English lesson of the Langenscheidt method, which consisted of learning a chapter of Dickens by heart. In short, every task he accomplished was changed into an escape, became a struggle to attain a result that was entirely objective (muscles, impersonal knowledge, elemental wealth), whose objectivity became a source of separation, since he no longer recognized himself in his work and could protect himself in it only by virtue of a rational will hardened against itself.

"Should I get a divorce?" his mother asked, when they were back in Vienna. She embarked on a long explanation: that the business could be put in her name if she got a divorce; that she could keep the apartment; that she could even declare her husband not to be the father of her children if she could find an accomplice. "I wouldn't want you to reproach me some day for having stayed with your father and not having tried everything to save the Business." Of course he and his sister had said, "Stay with Father." The Business meant nothing to them except endless boredom and bother, and they were quite incapable of imagining the future. Their father had grown thinner; one night the man with the old party member's badge came to the house; there was a long discussion; the man had decided to take over the Business for himself, and their father, his face gray, had collapsed on the sofa, gasping for breath, on the verge of a syncope. A week later, they were evicted from the apartment; a party official coveted it, and since a non-Aryan couple was living there, he had priority.

His father's illness and expulsion did not particularly affect him. He watched it all as a series of events that didn't concern him. He was incapable of taking sides with the weak or the strong because, wanting to be strong, he despised the weak and, rejected by the strong into the camp of the weak, he detached himself from the latter in order not to feel weak and lost and secretly allowed himself the chance to change camps, in spite of everything, by the force of his perseverance. He had still not broken with the Nazis (this rupture was a late one and occurred under conditions which hardly had the value of a choice), he maintained a troubled complicity with them whenever it was a question of taking sides, as if putting himself verbally on their side could free him from being, in fact, in the opposite camp, as if his subjective complicity magically kept open a path toward "salvation" or at least maintained an escape from his true condition. He was pleased to see his uncle on his mother's side wearing the swastika of the *Reichskulturkammer* in his capacity as director of a theatrical agency that procured engagements for performers, and by this avuncular badge he contested the Jewishness he inherited on his paternal side.

This one-way contestation (for he never dreamed of contesting the maternal Aryanness by the paternal Jewishness, thus choosing to endure this Jewishness as an external curse which was often identified with the misfortune of having this particular father) requires a commentary already too long postponed. This odd family, which was divided against itself and whose divisions he had had to interiorize, must be described. Described objectively. Having told himself this for some time already, he is struck by the egocentric character of his account, each impulse toward description breaking off or dissolving at once into considerations about himself, as if he were quite incapable of extending his consciousness outside the magic circle in which it confined itself, incapable of coming to grips with empirical reality. This is quite significant; his memory provides him only vague, pale recollections, not that he has a bad memory (quite the contrary), but because he has never been able to live events without intellectual mediation. He has always watched himself living; he has never taken things for what they were. The reason I have just offered for this (or one of the reasons, for there are certainly others) is his need to contest: to contest his father by his mother, his Jewishness by his Catholicity, his Catholicity by his Jewishness. There was nothing simple or immediate for him, each moment always referred to its opposite, nothing was what it was but remained divided from itself by an elsewhere he had to shift into in order to be facing whatever it was. He lived events by his interrogative mediation on the attitude he was to adopt toward them, as when he watched Hitler's triumphant entry into the city from the balcony of his father's office, seized by the fever of the hysterical crowd he would have liked to join, at the same time infected by the anguish of his father, who already felt like a stranger in his own office and stared at the big safe as if his enemies were about to empty it; as when he watched the Jewish woman forced to wash the S.A. man's car, hesitating to feel sorry for her and hesitating to hate her torturers, wondering if his pity wouldn't make him into the cowardly and weak "Yid" he refused to become, and if his hatred wouldn't prove he lacked the power to be strong.

I don't know precisely what occurred between the mother and the maternal grandfather at this period. But the latter, surnamed Yaroslav because of his adoration for Czechoslovakia and Prague ("Learn Czech, my boy! Wherever you go, when you say, 'Nazdar!' there will be people to answer, 'Nazdar pane,' and you'll be accepted"), had urged her to get rid of her Jewish husband. "Think of your children," he had said. "What will you gain by hanging on to your scruples about Jacob? Jacob's ruined. Take my advice, believe me, or you'll regret it."

Yaroslav had never liked Jacob much, and he fought a series of epic battles with Maria. He was full of resentment against this proud daughter who claimed to "raise" herself above the family milieu, and Maria, in order not to have to blush for her father, always claimed he was endowed with fathomless wisdom. "There's no one better than Yaroslav. Remember what our papa told us— if you find something that doesn't belong to you, even if it's only a pin, don't touch it!" "Just as my Yaroslav says, don't worry, one way or another things always manage to come out all right." These commonplaces were offered as though they were the pinnacle of wisdom and ended in Grandfather being called "Saint Yaroslav." He had been born in some village of Bohemia and with his tiny, chubby wife to whom he had given four children (one had died in infancy) he had led the most ordinary *vie de bohème*. He had been a singer ("an opera singer," his mother said), a third-rate one to judge from his continual wanderings between Dresden, Leipzig, Nuremberg, and provincial engagements, often living with his whole family in one room that sometimes had a ceiling so low they could reach up and swat the cockroaches swarming across it, sometimes was near a railroad viaduct under which his mother had played in the stream.

Yaroslav had settled in Vienna in 1918 as "director of a theatrical agency," for, having made his debut as a tenor and retired as a bass, he had finally lost his voice. "I went to work as a secretary," his mother had told him, "and God knows I was a dutiful daughter. I brought home every penny I earned, and even in winter I walked to the office to save the ten groschen the streetcar would have cost." She had been a pretty, dark girl, with good legs and severe glances despite the inviting smile that revealed two rows of regular white teeth. She must have had her fill of not taking the streetcar and of eating bad food, and she certainly had a devouring ambition to rise above her modest station in life. In short, she married her boss, fifteen years older than she (she was twenty-four), after violent scenes with her Yaroslav, who shouted, "You can't marry that Jew!" Maria was a stubborn girl. Not only did she marry that Jew, a timid man with few social gifts, a niggling, scrupulous "agent" in his rich brother-in-law's crate-and-barrel business, but she even persuaded her Jewish husband, despised by his Aryan in-laws, to put money in Yaroslav's "theatrical agency"; the Jew owed them that to deserve Maria.

Convinced she had bridged the gulf, had entered a superior social order, Maria began by getting some culture: she read many of the books people talked about and studied works on art as well; she took piano lessons in order to be able to play for her guests. And she refused to see her horrible Jewish in-laws (especially fat Anna, who had a partnership in the business), who on their side spoke bitterly of this pretentious *Goyin* who was glad enough to take their money but who put on her contemptuous airs before the *Juden*

("Jacob, why are you still hanging around with those *Juden*?").
Jacob must have soon realized that he would regret this marriage.
Youngest son (or almost) of a numerous family of Moravian landowners (property, houses, trucking), he had been sacrificed to his
brothers. He would not inherit the property because it was being
given to the oldest brother; he would not be allowed to study because Oscar was more talented; he would not go into the trucking
business because Bruno wanted to. Finally, to be got rid of, he was
sent to Sister Anna (rich, fat, beringed, covered with pearls and
lace, brooding over her wealth amid her flabby flesh like a mollusk
in its shell, married to a tiny, sickly, wizened man the war had
apparently made rich. Weak, unsure of himself, conscious of his
limitations and his ignorance, Jacob needed to be protected, respected, and tenderly encouraged as well. It was probably the
advice giver, the counselor in Maria that attracted him; in this
young and energetic woman who never hesitated and seemed ready
to swallow the whole world, he must have sought a moral support.
And she probably saw in him an instrument of her ambitions to
rise socially.

Spineless, dedicated to his routine out of fear of the unknown
("I don't care about what I don't understand," a saying magnificent
for its naïveté and its complacent timidity, characteristic of the
man Jacob, resigned to his mediocrity, making it into a virtue by
claiming it was modesty and defiantly opposing it to the too urgent
or intelligent interlocutor before whom, in reality, he desperately
tried to put on a good front, especially with regard to his son), vulnerable, having decided once and for all that greatness and ambition were other people's business (so much so that he believed the
great and the ambitious were of a different essence, professed his
respect for the old nobility, remained attached to the Emperor and
the Empire, addressed nobles by their titles and bowed before
them, distinguished the ranks of the Army and humbly admired his
"intellectual" brother, Oscar, an intolerably arrogant man), Jacob

probably dreamed of some quiet corner and a life without incident
when, at thirty-nine, he happened to meet this young woman who
won him by guile.

I shall elsewhere describe what their relations were or might have
been on the personal level. I'm not sure I can explain their behavior
in detail, particularly the motivation of Maria's icy ambition, always
tricked out in excessive bursts of sentiment. Having known her
only after he was grown up and receiving only from her what he
knows of his childhood, he sees her as an iceberg of which the
greatest and heaviest portion remains below the surface, while that
which shows gives an impression of a density, an opacity difficult
to comprehend. Maria was convinced that her place was at the top
of the social pyramid and that consequently the world owed her
such a place. During the first years of her marriage, she insisted on
dazzling her parents and her brothers and sisters with her opulence
every Sunday, as if by exhibiting this wealth, exaggerating it, she
took revenge upon the "ordinary" family she had come from, the
family which had begrudged her streetcar tickets. It was from a
need to feel "superior," a member of the same race as the ancient
nobility whose values must have dominated her childhood, that
she too respected titles, ranks and manners, invented a grandfather
who was a count, perpetuated her father's anti-Semitism (fundamentally a resentment, the wretched singer Yaroslav being convinced that his career had been spoiled by the Jewish conspiracy)
and persuaded her husband to quarrel with his own family in order
to take over and enlarge the Business.

Annoyed by twenty years of boasting and by the arrogance
which, from the pinnacle of her "success," Maria paraded before
her family, the latter probably took its long-delayed revenge in
1938 when it retorted, "Now you see what you get for marrying a
Jew. Get out of it by yourself." It was doubtless out of pride that
Maria failed to ask for a divorce, in order not to confess her defeat
to her family. But all the same she requested a legal separation, and

while she took her children to live in her sister's apartment, Jacob
was relegated to a verminous rented room where she visited him
one hour a day.

Humiliated, confused, stubborn, Jacob felt that he was being
done an absolute and undeserved wrong; consequently, since he
was within his rights, he would not budge. To defend himself, become an exile—such actions would have been beneath his dignity;
he had no taste for adventure, spoke no foreign language, was terrified by novelty, preferred to be a wreck "at home" rather than an
arriviste abroad. To Maria's months and months of pressure to
make him go to Brazil, Jacob opposed a child's stubborn refusal.
In his hierarchized and formalist universe, Right was on his side
("I have done nothing I cannot answer for"); therefore he would
wait with lowered head ("with your Jewish stiffness," Maria called
it) for whatever blows were to fall, blows he could scarcely credit,
moreover, for the changes occurring around him were so incomprehensible to him that after the war, in 1951, he was still saying,
"I have nothing against this Hitler, and if it weren't for his anti-
Semitism, I'd probably vote for him tomorrow. The man restored
order, did something for his country." Respect for titles and ranks,
love of order, the necessary basis of the hierarchy in which Jacob
and Maria sought a place their whole life long, made their daughter
a neurotic girl as convinced as they were that success consists in
cutting a figure among "respectable people" and prompted her (at
the price of unknown humiliations and agonies) to frequent
throughout the war Nazi leaders, dignitaries and diplomats, from
whom she begged impossible jobs.

Even as late as November 1938, they were still living from day
to day without believing in the catastrophes occurring all around
them. Not that they doubted the perversity and the administrative
effectiveness of the persecutors of the Jews (the Dachau concentration camp was already sending little boxes of ashes to wives of Jews
seized in their own homes); rather, like the persecutors themselves,

they were convinced that "this sort of thing couldn't happen to me." And why? Well, because when your name is G, when you have "connections," when you're "respectable people," you aren't treated like some *Juden* from Galicia; because, when you think the world owes you something and you've always been on the side of order, then you can't be persecuted by a regime of order; because the Nazi persecutors were among those "little people" who always tipped their hats to you and with whom you could always settle things by a tip (and Maria was particularly good at impressing her successive concierges by condescending kindnesses and coins pressed into their palms); because, finally, if the rank-and-file Nazis made trouble for you, you could always speak to the directors of the regime who were not "of the people" but belonged (or were ambitious to belong) to that same level of "respectable people" with whom Maria excelled in establishing a flattering class complicity. (*"Entre nous,* Herr Doktor, I know you don't think the way all those hysterics do.")

All the same, by November things began to look bad. At school one day, classes were dismissed at ten o'clock in the morning. Kalmar ran to get wooden poles from the gym and gave them to Urmann, Bradovic, Kamleitner and others. Accompanied by a gang of boys who guessed something was up, they left school and headed toward a crossroads five hundred yards away. Here stood a low yellow house that looked like a farmhouse, and an apartment building put up around 1900, with a dry-goods shop on the ground floor. In the house was a knife grinder's shop run by a man with the interesting name Amadeo Amadei, but it was toward the Oser dry-goods shop that they were headed. It was at the corner. They hesitated for a long moment, then Kalmar rushed forward and broke the window with his pole. It refused to fall into splinters. Bradovic and Urmann entered the shop and came out armed with the kind of rods used to pull down the metal shutters at night. Kalmar dashed forward, banging his rod against the glass, fell flat on his back, quickly got up, furious now, and began smashing the shop window with great whacks. They were starting on the second window when the shopkeeper, his face pale, appeared on the doorstep. "Shut up or you'll get hurt," Kalmar said in a threatening tone. Two sales-girls came out and lowered the shutters over the ruined displays. It was only as they were leaving that he began to suspect that Oser must be a Jew.

It was early, it was snowing, and he decided to walk to Yaro-slav's, where he had been having his lunch ever since they had temporarily moved to Uncle Oscar's—the latter was leaving for Boston. As he came down the Mariahilferstrasse, he saw a column of smoke on the right, and he headed toward it. In a little square with low, dirty, peeling façades (looking like the entire neighbor-hood and four fifths of Vienna, stuck here for no good reason, smelling of poverty, fleas, leaking gas and futility, with suspicious faces, motheaten coats, uneven sidewalks, a look of failure and indolence), a building with a cupola was burning. It was a funny-looking building with a big portico in which only one little door was open. Smoky flames were coming out of the roof and licking the cupola, against which a short steeple appeared to be leaning. There were some twenty idlers, no firemen (what was the Fire Department waiting for, he asked, but no one answered), and a policeman who said, "Stand back, the steeple's going to fall!" but no one moved. He waited a long time for the steeple to fall; it was only when he got bored and decided to leave that he noticed two S.A. men with tanks of gasoline and suspected that the building was a synagogue and that they had set it on fire themselves.

The next day he heard that synagogues all over the Reich had been destroyed, Jewish shop windows broken, Jews rounded up and made to scrub sidewalks, and that Yankel (his maternal aunt's boy friend, an antique dealer who wrote pornographic stories) had been forced to scrub too, and that many Jews had been arrested and deported. He also heard people talking about the Nuremberg laws, according to which his father had a vaguely privileged status as a baptized Jew and the husband of an Aryan mother of Christian children, who, from the fact of their religion, were half-castes of the first class (the second class included individuals with only one Jewish grandparent), whereas they would be classed as Jews altogether had they not been baptized. His mother took steps to obtain new birth certificates for her children, for their father had been baptized in 1930 (upon Maria's insistence; she had even forced Jacob to change his name so that his Jewishness should become less apparent), and paid the sum of one hundred schillings for this service, a considerable amount since they had argued for months on end before paying sixty for a secondhand radio and since he had had to wait years before they bought him a bicycle costing a hundred and ten, and they had to forge documents on which his father figured as a "Roman Catholic."

Jews deported never came back, wives had received little boxes full of ashes and marked with their husbands' names; he no longer had any contact, in class, with Bradovic's gang or with the others, since he now had to put over eight kilometers on his speedometer to reach school, and he began to regard the militant Nazis as a hostile race capable of breaking his head for him because of his two Jewish grandparents. The Nazis were on the other side, the bridges were cut; he was tolerated at school, but grudgingly, and the English prof, an old party member, "impartially" asked him sticklers in order not to have to give him the good marks he would otherwise deserve. He began to suspect that the injustices of the history and geography prof (this dated back two or three years; his face showed that he called him to the blackboard only to send him back to his seat with a furious look of scorn) had had racial reasons too, and with the teachers changing every week he began to realize that his inadequacy in so many subjects (physics, chemistry, history, geography) was doubtless due in large measure to the ignorance and the mental confusion of his instructors.

A puny wretch, furious and pathetic, regularly bombarded by erasers, chalk, explosions of cherry pits, stink bombs and sneezing powder, until, on the verge of tears, he begged them to listen to him, gave them a course in racial education (*Rassenkunde*), showing them dolichocephalic, brachycephalic types, Nordic, Frisian, Baltic, Alpine and Latin races (in hierarchic order), and explaining that Hannibal, since he had proved to be a great general, must have been a blond, blue-eyed Druse; similarly that Christ, since he had blue eyes and blond hair (in German paintings), was Aryan; and so forth. The rural, Alpine, artisanal, peasant and family values of the Catholic regime (the so-called New Era of Dollfuss) gave way to the heroic values of Germanic mythology, blood, force, the clan, the Wagnerian grandeur, the cult of the leader, discipline, and the hierarchy, the "useful" (and not Promethean) sacrifice to a nation whose superhuman greatness was reflected upon the sons it was devouring; the hollow, exalted style (*à la* Goebbels) became obligatory, and the composition richest in pompous commonplaces passed for the best.

Only the Greek professor, Sacher, a graying, clubfooted giant with a jagged nose, resisted this inflation of words and sentiments; his severe gray eyes showed what seemed to be a secret benevolence when, sitting on the edge of his desk, he made G conjugate irregular verbs or translate a passage from *The Iliad*. The incarnation of justice, inaccessible to persuasion, imperturbably advancing through his Homer, more methodical and demanding than any other prof (he insisted they know every verb and vocable learned during three years), Sacher was the man he liked most without ever having exchanged a word with him; he dreamed of calling for him as he left school if he ever was rich enough to have a car when he grew up. But he already doubted that a man like Sacher could stay in school for long, opposing his equitable rigor to the prejudicial treatment the leaders of the Hitlerjugend enjoyed, being excused from classes when it served the "responsibilities of their charge" and given good marks by the other profs.

He felt the world closing over him and, alone now, absorbed himself in three activities: his bicycle, music and reading. The bicycle had become his chief instrument of penetration and domination. Astride it every morning at seven-twenty with the same delight, he was alone and victorious, dividing the city in two for over eight kilometers and at a speed he never let fall below twenty-five kilometers an hour, absorbing the jolts from the bad paving by inflating his tires to something less than capacity, and reaching school at seven-forty, intoxicated by the speed and the risks taken at the crossroads, at the red lights and on the snowy highway where the motorcycles and the military trucks made the laws. These solitary rides were a revenge on the city, on the shiny chromium of the Luftwaffe daggers, on the black S.S. daggers and the shiny, echoing boots, the fearful elegance of men Aryan to the seventh generation, invested with a right to regard the business of all humanity as their own; the masking of their flesh (and therefore their humanity and their consciousness) entirely in black made them into unforeseeable and sacred instruments of a secret and supreme power. The earth which they arrogantly strode across he barely brushed over with his tires; and unlike the Wehrmacht motorcycles and cars, he overcame the least ruggedness by the work of his muscles, realizing in their effort the configuration of a city they did not possess save at a distance and on the surface. The *ascesis* of his own recreation changed its meaning. It was no longer a victory over himself and the voluntary construction of a new being with neither race nor origin on the ruins of the old; it was also a challenge to and a victory over other people, a conquest of this city which, crossing it so often, he began to love, an establishment in the very soil that was being morally alienated from him, an acquisition of a carnal citizenship constituting a kind of antidote to the Jewishness that he knew circulated in his veins and that he imagined as an invading germ swelling his flesh, sprouting black hairs and fat at the joints, thickening the noble parts of the body. Jewishness, for him, was essentially passive, the dead weight of artificiality—that cancerous proliferation—paralyzing his transcendence. He did not imagine that a Jew could be slim, agile, graceful, athletic; he identified Aryan values with the highest vital values, with the nobility of the body charged with energy—not because he had ever met a single Aryan who incarnated all the values of this ideal type (they sometimes approached it, and even when they were far from it they possessed these qualities by the mere fact that they could invoke their Aryanness against him), but because he had learned to assimilate Jewishness to unredeemable artificiality (and this by virtue of his refusal of his own Jewishness, a pure obstacle, a dimension of being he could in no way put to advantage) and Aryanness to vital value. It seemed to him that everything he refused in himself was besmirched with Jewishness and everything to which he aspired was aureoled with Aryanness. He had permitted a dichotomy to establish itself within him, where the Aryan crossed swords with the Jew like God with the powers of darkness. It is tempting, of course, to explain starting here his puritanical and cold-blooded aspects: Refusing Jewishness, an aspect of his artificiality impossible to assume, he would have to refuse his entire artificiality, since you cannot refuse yourself halfway—rot cannot remain only partial, but necessarily pervades the whole being and must be hunted out in all its dimensions. Though tempting, this explanation cannot be a final one; the discovery of his Jewishness as an original stain might not have corrupted him altogether and motivated an *ascesis* dedicated to overcome it if, at the very moment this discovery occurred, he had not already placed himself in a situation of inferiority and vital nonvalue. Rather than as an original motivation, the discovery of his Jewishness through the derision of others complicated and confirmed a choice of inferiority

and culpability already made, a choice which rendered him receptive to that derision—he felt it was well founded. So his drama had
to be as follows: Derided for his Jewishness because of his real
weaknesses, and derided for his weaknesses because of his Jewishness, he chose to impute the weaknesses to his Jewishness and
thereby to give them a substratum that was both biological and
metaphysical. He decided that at a certain period (probably around
twelve, an age when he began seeing a good deal of a Nazi pederast
who provoked in him an ambition for virile values and made him
regard his own weaknesses with horror) he could shed his inconsistency, his cowardice and the inferiority in which he had established himself only on condition that he suppress his Jewishness
at the same time. This was to render the conversion impossible
from the start and to bar all paths toward salvation; it was to
postulate that he could change only by becoming Other, that his
aspiration to a metaphysical metamorphosis was pursued by an
ascetic will which did not affect the profound basis of his choice
and therefore remained exterior to him, in no way capable of
accomplishment, condemning him forever to renew the experiment
of his failure. Rather than the determining motive of his isolation
and his weaknesses, his Jewishness thus became their alibi; he had
done everything under the sun to get rid of them, without success.
The very manner—quite voluntary—which he had adopted from
the outset rendered success impossible. And it was no good wondering if he could have integrated and declared himself under different historical conditions, with a different racial origin. Would
he have even tried to change himself in the direction of self-affirmation if his bastardy had not guaranteed the failure of his undertaking and assured him that he would always be inferior and subject? Supposing he had been Aryan, would he not have found
other biological obstacles to his emancipation? An idle question,
but one which illuminates the meaning of my remarks: Jewishness
and the experience of Nazism were occasions which confirmed him

in an original attitude and which he exploited to the latter's benefit. Historical objectivity was deflected to the advantage of a prehistoric choice in which its truth * was reflected, his individual signification accounting, so far as he was concerned, for his objective signification. All the same, he was not a victim of the event. The event was the occasion for him to victimize himself.

A reactionary theory? It is no theory; this time, it is a certainty. And to prove that the truth is never reactionary, I shall add this: "Objectively, a wrong was done him; but he had chosen to deserve

---

* Morel later suggested this idea to me: The first infantile attitude ("the constituted," as Morel puts it) might be the "cloudy reflection" of the bastard condition. And would that not be why this first attitude, motivated by the situation of objective bastardy, confirmed itself upon the discovery of this situation—even more, seized upon the situation as the objective truth of an attitude which had hitherto seemed quite individual and contingent? This would constitute the explanation of the feeling of "miraculous coincidence."

In fact, until the age of seven, he had felt null and inferior and guilty without quite knowing why (because, in particular, of his mother's exorbitant requirements). Then, with his Jewishness, he found a solid basis for this feeling. But if this reason suddenly seemed determinant, it is because it was certainly the real one even before he knew it.

—His mother had married a Jew whom she did not forgive for being Jewish;

—the fact of having married a Jew opposed her aristocratic ambitions while at the same time it permitted her to satisfy them in part;

—this Jewish father was, in his own family and in his own house, the "poor relation" despite his relative wealth, continually harangued, shoved, nagged at;

—the law, at home, was his mother's law, and his father represented failure and forfeiture.

And for those reasons:

—His mother monopolized her son to make of him a virile aristocratic super-Aryan whose handsome bearing would satisfy her own social ambitions and relieve her of the compromise she had had to accept;

—the son, incapable of satisfying his mother's requirements, felt guilty and null;

—he spontaneously identified his nullity and his guilt with his racial impurity—that is, with his father's share in himself.

His mother's attitude was therefore motivated by the conflict between her aristocratic ambition and the fact that she had married a Jew. And it was the way his mother tried, through her son, by her attitude toward him, to surmount this contradiction, which conditioned her son's original complex.

this wrong subjectively. The reactionary is not an individual who recognizes that he has been thus and so; the reactionary is an individual who believes he deserves injustice and who goes about deserving it in fact. In order to combat injustice effectively and to recognize its arbitrary quality, he must not have been its accomplice. Yet he *was* its accomplice. Effectiveness in combat preserves belief in the possibility of victory; he did not believe in this possibility; he was beaten before he ever began to fight.

This truth, of which the above is the subjective aspect, has also, however, an historical aspect. I have said that his revolt against his weaknesses was made in bad faith, because it was a revolt against an ineffaceable Jewishness. I have said he was beaten in advance, by himself in the first place, because he had chosen the very victory which was, of all those possible, the one victory forbidden him. But what other victory could he have chosen? Vienna between 1934 and 1938 was a city heading for catastrophe, first amputated from its empire, then from faith in its own possibilities of survival, finally from its democratic liberties—therefore from the possibility of giving the present a meaning. Feeling itself sliding toward the abyss, toward nullity and oblivion, it tried to keep itself from living, as if that could also keep it from falling in ruins. It clung to its own remains and desperately tried to warm its corpse by the cult of memory, by the simulacra of a time gone by. That was Dollfuss—a bourgeoisie clinging to privileges it knew to be ephemeral, renouncing life in order to survive, crying, *"Peccavi."* Work, Family, Nation, Church. In this context, Nazism was like a great wind of regenerative barbarism, the emanation of a country which declared itself facing the future, facing expansion; it offered him both a way of revolting against the chauvinist and clerical asphyxia and a means of freeing himself from the maternal conformism and from the narrow-mindedness of a detested father. To become a Nazi was to rise up against his situation as a mediocre student in a condemned country and against that of a spoiled son, dishonor of his family, of whom it was predicted that he would "come to nothing." No other instrument of liberation was available to him at the time. But here historical objectivity made his revolt into an abortive attempt. His only instrument of liberation was rotten, and by having tried to employ it he had thrust his nose in his own filth; he learned that salvation was impossible. There was no way toward himself, even with the best will in the world; he had no choice save a choice between false situations, and by proletarianizing and Nazifying himself he had at least chosen the way which best attested to his desire for autonomy. What could henceforth be surprising in the fact that this desire, stripped of all means of realizing itself, remained purely *voluntary* and that his actions never resulted from his own conviction, that he remained inconsistent, weak and vulnerable even in his attempt to change himself? There was no place for him in the world or in his family (unless he resigned himself to joining with his father and accepting a future as a box manufacturer with money and business worries), nor outside it (unless he succeeded in shedding his Jewishness, to which he futilely applied himself). His condition was one of exclusion and weakness, it inevitably maintained him in the attitude that had been his since his earliest childhood; and he could not even regard this as abnormal.

Events had therefore furnished him only so many occasions to confirm his original attitude; he exploited them in the direction of the latter, but no other was offered to him. His condition had an objective meaning of weakness, inconsistency, self-division, against which the best intentions of unification, or self-affirmation and of strength remained necessarily inoperative—subjective and voluntary good intentions deflected, by the logic of his objective situation, in the very direction he was trying to avoid. It was this condition he would have to change in order to correct his weaknesses. But he had no control over his condition; he could merely struggle against himself, against his way of living his contradictions, leaving those contradictions themselves intact. His attempts to make himself a man were doomed to sterility and bad faith; they amounted to an agonized revolt against a condition which, seizing him from behind, became a destiny submitted to, a destiny whose permanence he discovered in himself because of his dread of the inconsistency and the inauthenticity of his own efforts.

His attempts at self-affirmation and integration were doomed, since, even supposing that the possibility of suppressing his Jewishness existed, they could succeed only by changing him into someone else. But this bad faith of his escape project concealed an objective truth: The entire man, in accord with himself and with others, was Other, and no way could lead to him. The defeatism, cowardice and masochism he accused himself of as subjective weaknesses (his conviction that no one loved him, his readiness to feel dismissed and insulted, his way of regarding other people as necessarily stronger and more valuable than himself and of submitting to their exclusivities) had an objective basis, accounted for a situation of fact to which his infantile choice had made him sensitive and against whose meaning (that he was insignificant, had no future and no place in the world) he could not protect himself without bad faith. Doubtless there were other possible ways of living this truth. But were they better? His own was tinged with masochism; he interiorized his exclusion as a biological fault at the same time that he saw it as the deserved punishment of his cowardice and his sins. Mauthner and Weiss made aggressive choices; resolved to compensate for their racial blemish, they made themselves noisy, greedy and scornful, ambitious to gain their revenge by social success—wealth, the power wealth confers, and the respect it imposes upon the Aryan bourgeoisie. As for Hoffman, he had made himself a fanatic Nazi to beat the anti-Semites on their own ground. *Arrivisme* and fanaticism were the only other ways immediately open to the half-caste. I contend they were worse still; avoiding their contradiction without transcending it, repressing it but conserving it (as an incurable wound), fanaticism and *arrivisme* led these half-castes to alienate themselves in roles that conformed to bourgeois norms and requirements, that "collaborated" with the hoaxes this class secreted. More conformist, more avid of honors than even those of whom they wished to become the equals, they were all the more insatiably eager for victories of prestige which no victory could convince them they had really won. Doubtless they were combative, but their values, phony positives, were merely the reverse of the nothingness that fissured their arrogance and whose corrosion they vainly attempted to conceal. They were excessively positive and rigid, while he was excessively negative and flabby. The inauthentic half-caste seems doomed to excesses by which he tries to end his laceration, to repudiate one of the terms of his contradiction. If I choose an excessive negativism, it is not because I dream of giving him any credit for it; he was brought to it by his infantile masochism—*arrivisme* and fanaticism were not within his range. It was by virtue of the contingent choice developed since his childhood, and not by some moral option, that he had cut himself off from the possibility of an excessive positivism. If I contend that he made the better choice thereby, it is because the consciousness that continues to reflect on its contradictions in humiliation and suffering remains better armed to assume its condition and someday to attempt a liberating synthesis than the consciousness which claims fulfillment by alienating itself among the fetishes of its time.

B. *Persecution and Treason*

Objectively based on his half-caste condition, the conviction that he could become a "whole" man only by becoming Other and that consequently man was Other and a failure as "himself"—this conviction is rooted so far back in his childhood that its objective signification does not suffice to account for it. I can doubtless say that for any child adults are fearful divinities legislating in the absolute, and that any child is imprisoned by the prestige emanating from the Other; yet for me the Other has the metaphysical superiority of seeming exempt (because seen from outside) from the secret inconsistency and doubt which every subject bears deep inside himself. I could doubtless add that because of his half-caste condition, he simply overenlarged the prestige originally attaching to the Other, and that this condition therefore extended longer than is customary the inferiority feelings characteristic of infantile dependence, delaying their liquidation. However, this explanation does not satisfy me, because it explains too well; it describes as a necessary and therefore immutable effect an attitude which was not really so necessary (for instance, had he not found himself continually at fault with regard to parents, the discovery of his Jewishness would have assumed a less serious and less definitive signification for him) and for which he believes he can find a remedy.

One of the aspects of this attitude is the constant attribution of value, throughout his life, to the types of humanity who are most remote from himself and whom he admires in proportion as they differ from the people around him. Man, for him, was always the Other, not only Other than himself, but Other than those whose situation he shared and whom he might have called his peers. At the age of nine or ten, he wanted so much to become Chinese that he prayed for weeks that God would change him into a Chinese boy, even for only a few days. At seven he convinced Halama, the tailor's idiot son and obviously a hereditary syphilitic, that he was a Jew and that instead of leaving the catechism class he was going to stay on as a spy. He was quite ignorant, at the time, of his Jewish origins and their possible signification. He was merely trying to deceive Halama and distinguish himself in other people's eyes. "Sir," Halama screamed as the father came into the classroom, "G's staying in class even though he's a Jew." "Who said so?" the father asked. "He did," Halama answered. "Is that true?" the father asked, turning to G. "No," he said. "Then why did you say so?" "It was a joke to make him think so," he said. "You must not play jokes like that," the father said gravely. And when he came home that day, he found out his father was a Jew who had converted to Catholicism.

To be a Jew, a Chinese, a Negro, a Nazi—he had always wanted to incarnate the negation of what he was, merely another undifferentiated self. He wanted to be someone disturbing, scandalous, and admirable too. To be Other than himself while remaining himself; to be himself and his opposite; to be a girl for a day while continuing to be a boy (a favor he had also asked God for at ten, after inventing at five an imaginary playmate he pursued among the roses of the wallpaper during his afternoon naps—the androgyne "Rini," a little girl with a penis).

Perhaps this tendency toward contradictory singularization, acquired long before his consciousness of the Jewish-Aryan dichotomy, dates back to the period of Ninon Vilmorin, a servant girl from Nice with Negroid features, her cheeks pitted with smallpox, her black hair oiled and braided, repulsively ugly according to most people but beautiful in his eyes. Back to the period of Ninon (who, when he was five, told him frightening and fantastic adventure stories), because she was at the origin of a misunderstanding: Vacationing on one of the Carinthian lakes, he had acquired so dark a tan that he was taken for a Negro child. Since, thanks to Ninon, he also spoke French better than German, he was assumed to be her son and people went into ecstasies when they learned he was his own mother's son. To be admired because he seemed to be what he was not may have made a deep impression on him; for the moment I can see no other origin for this tendency toward difference which subsequently became one of the dominant themes of his life.

This taste, moreover, was not stamped with vanity, dandyism, or that mania for "distinction" he so loathes in the bourgeoisie. It was simply a question of escaping the common measure and also of protecting himself against the persecuting forces of reification. By wanting to be a Negro, a Chinese, a hermaphrodite, a squirrel, a lemur (or some other animal, as when he hid under the sheets, under a sofa, in a closet, or walked on all fours barking or mewing), he was trying to escape human supremacy and its coercion. This coercion proved so strong that he acquired the sense of systematic persecution quite early and preferred identifying himself with persecuted animals (tiny creatures cowering in cages, Bambi pursued by hateful hunters), sympathizing with anything that crawls and risks being stepped on, to the point where at even the age of three or four he was picking up beetles, slugs and caterpillars from the sidewalk and tenderly setting them down where they would be safe (his mother: "Leave those nasty bugs alone!" he: "Why? God made them too!") from human wickedness. Men were on one side, animals on the other; he was on the animals' side. He burst into tears when his sister threw his Teddy bear against the wall; it hurt him. He played for hours on end with his painted-plaster menagerie; but he stubbornly refused to put his animals in their cages. He had them parading across the whole room, except for the monkey. This monkey, hanging his one arm from a tree, his pink mouth open, provoked a stubborn antagonism in him; the monkey not only looked mean (he was not the only one) but gave evidence of an all too obvious human presence—because he walked upright, because he was hung from a branch and couldn't move around the room, because this green branch introduced a vegetal dissonance into the animal harmony.

The correct interpretation of his tendency toward difference is surely this: to exchange the human world for another in order to protect himself against the constraints and norms of the people around him, and, thanks to this desertion, to take refuge from various persecutions and judgments. This is the key to that treason complex whose history he wanted to recount: his attempt to abandon all collectivities which applied their constraints to him, beginning with the human race.

There are two possible reactions to disproportionate coercion:

revolt and masochism. But a child of three has no means of rebelling; he feels guilty and in danger of abandonment. I am not sure what "disproportionate coercion" is and whether a more combative child would have reacted differently to the pressures brought to bear upon him. I am sure that Maria's requirements were such that no child could have satisfied them. His sister, moreover, also became masochistic. Maria wanted to be perfect; just as she had passionately committed herself, after her marriage, to her household, to culture and "Society," so, after the birth of her first child, she decided to be a perfect mother with the luckiest child in the world. This child, a girl named Helena, was a golden-haired "treasure." Maria nursed her herself, determined to sacrifice the beauty of her breasts (a relatively easy sacrifice: Maria was frigid; her ambitions with regard to respectability, her passion to be a great lady demanded that she be a good and faithful wife, well informed, orderly and energetic—it did not require her to love her husband). She decided that this daughter satisfied her every wish, that she was the happiest mother in the world. To prove it to herself, she devoted a huge notebook to Helena in which she set down her happiness every day. Her daughter was the "ray of sunshine in her life," "a radiant creature." After this daughter, Maria decided she wanted a son. I can see her calculating the most opportune date for his birth and deciding that of his conception in consequence. Helena was born in June, summer being the most comfortable season for maternity; but a second child within twelve months was bad for the health and an interval of two years between children was too great for familial equilibrium. So she decided that her son would be born eighteen months after her daughter, that his virile strength would be as perfect as the girl's feminine charm, and that he would be named after an actor she admired for his virility. From the moment of her son's birth, Maria's maternal passion began to slacken; it fell off still further when she discovered that instead of the radiant being his name seemed to require, her son was ugly, hateful and dark-haired ("You had black hair growing down to the bridge of your nose and when Yaroslav saw you he screamed, 'But what's all that black stuff?' "), and that Helena's sun miracle had not been repeated in his case. Probably less loved than his sister, the son felt inferior to her and incapable of competing with her for parental favors. They left his black curls, they said he looked like a girl, they thought he seemed a little soft—except for his nurse, whom he hammered with his fists because it made her laugh until he hurt her and she became angry. He wanted to be a girl because everyone found his sister prettier and more interesting than he was. Then, at about four, his curls were cut off; they told him that he was a boy now and that he should behave like one. He wept for his curls and refused to be a boy. They discovered that he squinted and lisped, and they took him to doctors. They gave him glasses and made him do *s* exercises with his tongue held in a kind of tiny metal brace. They decided he was not growing fast enough and he was given cod-liver oil and brains every morning. But, perched on a high chair, the tray that was lowered over his head holding him prisoner, a bib tied around his neck, he would not eat, and every meal was an interminable tantrum his mother and sister finally refused to sit through.

He felt he was being persecuted, asked to be what he didn't want to be, or couldn't be: to be "a man," "a big brave boy," to eat, not to drink, to defecate at fixed hours, to wet neither his pants nor his bed, not to touch his *pipi* ("or it'll get inflamed," and when it was inflamed because he had phimosis, his mother said, "That's because you've been playing with your *pipi* again"; she sent for the doctor, they spread him out on the big table in front of everybody, and the doctor "pushed back" his *pipi,* which hurt a lot and he thought it was a punishment for playing with it), not to dirty the white gloves he was to wear even in summer, not to walk in puddles, not to soil his clothes, not to pick his nose, not to run on all fours, not to tease his sister, not to play with scissors, not to play in the living room, etc. "Put your hand on the table, close your mouth, don't stare at the lady, it's not polite, say hello to the gentleman, say thank you to the lady"; then he had to kiss Mme. Martel's hand (Mme. Martel was an old Frenchwoman who gave his mother lessons and whose false teeth fascinated him), speak to people at his mother's parties to show off how much he knew, to greet them one by one when he came in and when he left, not forgetting to kiss the ladies' hands, so that they could see how well brought up he was at the age of four. And to bow to the gentlemen, clicking his heels, and to take off his cap when he met someone in the street, and not to unbutton his gloves or his coat ("What will people think, they'll think Frau G's little boy is badly brought up, Frau G's little boy doesn't even have white gloves, I'm ashamed of you, I don't deserve it after everything I've done for you, after all the money we've spent"). In the evening, when his father came home, he asked, "Has the boy been good?" or "What has the boy done now?" and then, according to the answer, he held out his rough cheek which smelled of tobacco or said, "Go away, good-for-nothing." When he was bad (once he broke a windowpane in the vestibule with a tennis ball, that was one of his worst crimes), his father gave him two slaps, one with each hand, called him an imbecile and a good-for-nothing, shouted wonderingly, "How can anyone be so stupid?", told him that he would have to pay the damages out of his pocket money (one schilling a week), and declared he wouldn't talk to him for three days; he kept his word. The child would have welcomed all the slaps and punishments in the world, would have punished himself if that would have helped expiate his crimes. But there was no immediate expiation possible; tears and pardon humbly begged from a man pretending to be unaware of his existence were no good whatever; he had to purge his guilt and for days on end endure a silent moral condemnation.

For him such moral condemnation—a hard, silent, arrogant reprobation focusing on his guilt, which, since it was inexpiable, was absolute—constituted the worst punishment of all. There was no possible atonement. He was guilty, which meant that no one loved him any more, that he had no place in his family, nor any rights to existence. It was as if he no longer existed, since he wasn't the son he was supposed to be and what he was they no longer wanted. Guilty without appeal—that is, not conforming to his being-for-others, to that image of himself which alone had any right to tenderness and protection; not conforming, deprived of being, reduced to his inner shadows, he experienced a kind of catastrophic earthquake—the universe collapsed, he fell into an abyss; his body was being stripped of his conforming and protecting identity, reducing itself to a heap of guilty flesh; self-conscious, virtually annihilated by his failure, he retired into a corner and longed for death.

He was perhaps three years old when, having broken a light bulb with one of his building blocks, he first thought of avoiding moral condemnation by punishing himself; to annihilate his guilt in anticipation of his condemnation, he lay down and knocked his head against the floor. His mother ran in, picked him up and asked what had got into him. She supposed it had been a tantrum and, annoyed by his attitude, forgot about the bulb. After that, he punished himself secretly: biting himself, pulling out his hair, kneeling in the corner of his own accord after he had been exiled there several times ("Go kneel in the corner!"), or, when he was sent into the dark vestibule at night ("Stand in front of the door"), throwing himself at the door head first, until he saw stars and could hear terrible cracks. Since the expiation of his guilt was refused, since even after punishment he continued to be subject to universal reprobation, there was nothing to do but invent his own expiations in the hope of simultaneously destroying his badness and of proving, by his struggle against himself, that he was perhaps not so bad after all. But no sign indicated that he had obtained this proof.

He felt he always had to deserve parental favor and that he lived in the continued postponement of condemnation and abandonment. It soon became clear to him that the role of son was perhaps beyond his ability; that his mother had wanted a son, but perhaps not the child that he himself was. She would say, "I want to be proud of you," and she encouraged him to dream of a heroic future: explorer, aviator, captain. "Will you take me up in your plane?" she asked. "Oh, yes," he answered, "and when I'm grown up I'll marry you." Then she laughed and told her guests what he had said. She called him into the living room and asked him in front of everyone what he wanted to be when he was grown up. "And you'll leave me all alone?" He knew she was asking him to play his role and obediently recited it. When she took him visiting or saw someone she knew coming down the street, she would indoctrinate him: "Stand up straight. Don't forget to take off your cap. Don't look self-conscious. Look people in the eyes when you talk to them. Don't mumble, open your mouth. Look like a little man." He was convinced that all grownups were judges; each meeting was a test he had to pass; he had to behave with others according to a host of rules she reminded him of each time. Human relationships were regulated by a complicated ritual and he felt he would never be equal to all the requirements of Good Behavior. Maria chattered loudly with other people, and he noticed she described him, to them, as quite different from what he was for himself—as intelligent, good-humored, brave and inquisitive. "Only he's a little shy," she added. "And naughty." He discovered that naughtiness was set down to his credit for other people (probably as a sign of virility) and that shyness excused his silence and awkwardness. To cure him of it, she forced him to answer the telephone, whose ringing terrified him (behind the black instrument someone was waiting, he was spied on from afar without seeing anything, and by picking up the receiver he would have to become someone, a voice able to inform the invisible interlocutor, would have to fill a role defined by strict and mysterious rules). The first time, he had merely picked up the receiver and then run away, trembling with fear, to call his mother. She had insisted that he say in the future, "Hello. This is A.G. Who's calling?"

When he was five years old he asked her, "Why did you want a little boy?"

"So I could love him."

"But you couldn't tell that your little boy would be me, so how could you be sure you would love him?"

"A mother always loves her children."

"Even when they're bad?"

"Even when they're bad," she said. "Mothers have big hearts. They suffer even when they can't help loving their children. They're like the Virgin Mary. The Good Lord gives them children only when they have warm hearts."

So he decided she loved him, although he was himself, because she had a warm heart and couldn't help herself. But he still wanted to find out if it was himself or only her son she loved, and if she wouldn't have preferred another kind of son, and if she would have had him for her son if she had married another man; or if, in that case, there would be another boy to call her "Mama" whom she would love as much as him; or whether she might love him more; or whether she would simply love him without noticing that he wasn't himself.

The impression that he had been brought into the world for a specific purpose ("Why do people have children?" "To have someone to love," they told him first; and later: "To have someone to lean on when we're old," or even: "You'll see, when I'm an old woman you'll abandon me for some girl"), that he owed his parents a debt and that he was an ingrate for not giving them more satisfaction, was consolidated by his second year at school. At the age of seven, his semester report card showed a 2 in drawing (1 being excellent, 2 good, 3 adequate, and 4 poor), and at the end of the year a 2 in arithmetic. These "failures" assume catastrophic proportions for his mother. Not only was he not the first in his class, he was bringing home Bad Grades. "God knows I spare nothing on your education! When I think of all the money we've spent on your governesses, your French lessons, your music. . . . And Frau G's son is a mediocre student! Look at R's son! He has no governesses, he hasn't learned French, his father is an ordinary engineer, but he's first in everything! And my son brings home twos on his report card!" At nine he had a third 2—in deportment. It was just before his birthday. Beside herself, his mother announced she would send him to a boarding school where they'd teach him how to work, and she rushed to the telephone, where she pretended to speak to the head of the school. "Yes, Herr Direktor, and be sure to pound something into his head." "With a hammer, if you have to," his father added. It was only after he tearfully promised to try much harder and begged forgiveness several times that his mother agreed to let him stay at home. Reprieved. The threat of boarding school remained hanging over his head.

In a situation of insecurity and guilt, he loved and feared his mother as the dog loves and fears his master, quivering with joy when she caressed him, overwhelmed when she rebuffed him, dreaming of some law he could permanently obey which would guarantee him against her reprobation, and discovering that such a law, if it existed, was capricious and required not only obedience but initiative, audacity and ambition, which he became still more incapable of as the certainty of his mediocrity and inadequacy grew. Continually at fault in a universe swarming with rules and imperatives none of which was within his power, he felt illegitimate, and to make a place for himself within legitimacy he labored long and hard, doomed to failure by his very attitude of submission. Having lost faith in his chances of success (if he had ever had such faith), he struggled without conviction. He was doomed to mediocrity because he believed in a formula for success, and he believed in this formula because he was convinced of his mediocrity—that there was nothing in him on which to base success, and that this success could therefore have only an exterior basis. To improve, he would have to become Other and regulate his behavior according to alien criteria. But the more he forced himself to do so, the more mediocre he became, feeling that he would never equal those who set these criteria and of whom he could be merely the pale and servile imitator.

When an individual respects legitimacy yet cannot come to terms with the world and succeed according to its norms, mysticism offers a tempting solution: By God he can raise himself above all particular rules without contesting their legitimacy; he merely transfers himself to another level, that of the absolute Law, in regard to which all particular rules reveal their contingency. He exchanges his relative illegitimacy for an absolute illegitimacy; absolutely guilty and inadequate, he rediscovers a relative peace in the conviction that success is impossible and, in any case, does not depend on him. The judgment of God, even if it is terrible, protects him against the judgment of men. Persecuted by the latter, he betrays them all; by praying for them, by invoking, for him and them alike, a divine pity without discriminations, he makes all men equal in the nullity common to them in God's eyes. But he, praying for them twice a day as for himself (because, he says, he has no particular claim to divine pity), *he* knows this nullity; and from this particular knowledge he becomes conscious of an absolute superiority. He is superior because he understands what others conceal from themselves, he is nearer to God because he knows himself irremediably and absolutely separated from Him, while the others, who think they can touch Him with their little individual misfortunes, are ignorant of this separation.

Progressively, he has learned to see the world upside down, from the Eternal point of view. He began quite simply, one day when he had been scolded, by praying while he was still crying—praying without conviction, merely to ease his conscience, telling himself that God, if He existed, would give him the intelligence and the courage he lacked and that in any case he could lose nothing by asking for them. This lukewarm prayer by which he tried to come to terms with God, lacking the ability to come to terms with men, developed, in the space of several weeks, into an instrument for the total annihilation of all humanity. He had been told that God sees all and is all-powerful, judges each moment according to intentions, not deeds. Feeling absolutely guilty and devoid of the qualities that might have saved him, he needed a miraculous transfiguration. But how could he approach this God of miracles who saw further into him than he himself, who perhaps discerned some basely egotistic motive in his prayers, such as the fear of blows and blame? He could imagine only neutral and ritual means; God was the distant absolute, and only formulas consecrated by Him could reach Him. Therefore he chose the most neutral prayers to invoke Him, the Pater and the Ave, prayers in which there was no place for any personal, i.e., any suspect solicitation. He did not believe the problems of a mediocre child could move the Eternal, who had the entire creation to worry about, especially since this child was probably mediocre because the Eternal was revolted by his sins and his lack of fervor. "Pray, faith will come after," he was taught. He prayed in German first, then in Latin, for he was told that God, though he understood all languages, had chosen Latin in which to be glorified. "Make me improve and forgive my presumption; it's for my parents' sake and not my own that I ask it," he added at the end of his prayer. But he decided later that his parents were merely individuals with no special claims to divine grace, and he modified his formula: three Paters, three Aves, and at the end a "Help us, my parents and myself, as well as all men."

Thus, with the help of religious logic, he began to see humanity upside down, from the Eternal viewpoint, as a heap of wretchedness and nullity, an ash falling back into ashes, its cares and agitations merely the mask of nothingness. Moving from spontaneous to reasoned humility, he discovered the pride of knowing his nullity better than others and therefore being superior to them by the fact that he was inferior to them. Such pride had nothing exalting about it; its only benefit, a dubious one at that, was the stern discipline imposed on him. To please God, he must permanently abase himself, for everything he refused himself in this world would be set down to his credit in the next; the finitude of the creature is what separates him from God (the nondivine in him, his nonbeing with regard to the Eternal), while the negation of his finitude (by mortification and *ascesis*) is what brings him closer to God and, diminishing him on earth, increases him in heaven. The less is more, the more less, pain is good and pleasure bad, true faith is infinite remorse, loving God is suffering for life. But he did not love God; he wondered how saints dared love God; who was he to give God his love? The creature, before God, was merely a heap of offal whose love could only stink in heaven's nostrils. For him, faith was abjection, fear and trembling; love of God was systematic hatred of himself. At about twelve he therefore descended into hell, blaming on himself as so many sins and weaknesses the desires he surrendered to, systematically opposing his spontaneous tastes. Achieving a kind of drought and vacuum after several months of such exercises, accomplishing the agreeable and the disagreeable with equal facility, inured to the point where everything became indifferent (where cold showers no longer made him cold, where dry bread no longer seemed dry, nor tea without sugar bitter, nor lukewarm water stale), he reached the limit of mortification, devoid of inclinations to oppose. Having no pronounced tastes, finding nothing repugnant, he had only his routine prayers to offer God, spoken with a dry heart and an empty mind. All he might have sacrificed to Him was annihilated. He had vanquished his pleasures along with his faculty for suffering; his victory—indifference—was a defeat which left him emptyhanded.

Empty is too much to say, for from this very defeat he derived a kind of pride. Like the women lining up in front of the Laennec Clinic, each bidding for the glory of having suffered more than the others, he silently prided himself on his ability to endure, his capacity for sacrifice; he had stripped himself of everything others clung to, he had conquered in himself the humanity by which they remained enslaved. (Something like the pride he felt at the age of three, sitting beside his sister on the commode where his mother washed them, being cited as an example to his whimpering sister. "When she says 'Ow' I don't flinch, and when she screams and cries I say 'Ow.'" He had been the first to venture jumping down from the commode, and he stared scornfully at his sister, thinking, She's afraid. At the same age he proved his resistance to pain by pulling out handfuls of his own hair.) A prisoner of his masochism from the start, his faith had dialectically led him to the experience of humility, and from there to resentment and pride. Starting with the intention of improving by divine favor, the logic of his original attitude led him to abase himself still further; and once conscious of his greater and irremediable abasement, he had claimed it as his dignity. The humanity that trampled upon him was the instrument of his abasement; but he was the only one to know that this abasement was deserved (and deserved for reasons known to God and himself alone), and that his executioners were fundamentally worth no more than he; therefore he suffered for them all, experiencing a wretchedness they should have felt; he let himself be crucified and indeed crucified himself, praying for his executioners. He exiled himself from the human world, passing imperceptibly into the Lord's camp, as seven years before he had passed into that of the animals. He was seeking in imposed exile a religious signification, and in so doing went himself one better, tried to make a virtue out of it as if he had chosen it; he felt he had raised himself because he had achieved being the lowest.

The world had already become external to him at this period. The religious *ascesis* had taught him to accept it as an instrument of mortification. But mortification has a logic which dialectically leads you where you had not dreamed of going. Used as arbitrary baffles to facilitate self-mortification, rules became alien objects; he discovered that they were contingent and therefore contestable. Mysticism was therefore a machine for contestation; it made him see his companions from the outside, his unbelieving parents who sinned and who would also die, their imperatives and their scarcely holy preoccupations. These parents who did not go to mass, did not take communion and did not pray—he was no longer sure that their will was identified with the will of God. Religion provided him a discipline more demanding than the family discipline and therefore liberated him from it.

What I like about this mystical period is that it illustrates the complexity of the dialectical process. He had not chosen himself as a mystic (and in fact he never found faith) any more than he had chosen himself as inferior. He had found himself in a situation of inferiority and in order to escape persecution he had asked religion for a miracle, a ready-made structure consisting of an ensemble of rites and magical practices. It was in its ritual and objective rigidity that he tried to incorporate religion into himself. And it was only then that religious objectivity assumed significations for him, significations which were, moreover, extrinsic to that religion (his "faith" being Judaic or Puritan rather than Catholic). The objective spirit of religion was based on a prereligious attitude of inferiority and despair which now animated a faith of dogmatic dryness. It was his infantile complexes which made him accessible to the religious experience and deflected the latter from its ordinary meaning; but subsequently, the religious experience deflected the attitude with which he had addressed himself to God from *its* original meaning (masochistic submission)—it furnished him an instrument of contestation and opened a way toward possible liberation.

What strikes me in this dialectic is the archcrime of a structure of objective behavior charged with a certain historical signification (obscure for the individual who adopts it) in an attitude whose motivations are extrinsic to this "superstructure." Is this not always the process when the superstructure is an aspect of man's alienation? Marxism teaches us to see the superstructure in its causal relation to praxis, as if religious mystification, for instance, were deliberately instituted by the ruling class to conceal from the oppressed their alienation and to help them endure it. Actually, of course, there is no question of a deliberate stratagem, of an explicit intention. Marxism imputes to the oppressors intentions corresponding to the objective signification of their behavior, in which it is properly cathartic: it describes men in their involuntary actions and thereby requires them to assume actions which they have not willed and cannot justify, it requires them to deny themselves or to become cynics; it holds up the cynical image of themselves which they conceal from themselves. Yet the resistance to Marxism's demystification process does not derive only from the material interests and the socioeconomic structure which the superstructure sublimates as far as it can; such resistance also derives from the anchoring of this superstructure in the individual complexes. Without psychological basis, the superstructure would be much more fragile than it is; yet it owes a part of its solidity to the fact that it can satisfy psychological needs which are not entirely determined by the existing society and which call into play an infinite diversity of contingent circumstances and individual choices. This is why it is always possible to explain an attitude such as anti-Semitism or religiosity by the objective situation which it necessarily accounts for, since it rises out of it and is motivated by it; possible to say, for instance, that anti-Semitism results from the obstruction of opportunities for social ascension among thousands of *petits bourgeois* who, unable to grow rich, to rise socially in a recession economy, compensate their desire for ascension by putting a group of the citizens under society's condemnation, appropriating the wealth of Jews and "foreigners," and "raising themselves" by the contempt they show for them. Yet this explanation, if it illuminates the objective implications of anti-Semitism, does not account for it altogether; it fails notably in explaining its emotional basis in some people while others remain exempt from it, though willing to profit by it. Appearing at a certain economic juncture, with a precise objective signification (as a means of palliating the contradictions of capitalist society), the fact is that anti-Semitism is also based, emotionally, on sexual repression—for instance, permitting the frustrated Aryan woman to believe herself in danger of rape, permitting the inhibited Aryan man to feed his images of violence and lubricity—therefore flourishing by preference in societies or milieus that are repressed and puritanical, and unable to achieve its most virulent form where sex is not a problematical activity. Economic motives are therefore not enough to account for it; in fact, anti-Semitism subsists independently of them in a latent state and does not disappear with them. The economic juncture occasions the appearance of attitudes which precede it in latency, furnishing them with a positive content; but the attitude itself, although it is of course conditioned by the social praxis, is rooted beneath the latter, in the penumbra of vital prehistoric motivations (called "psychological"), and is thematized only when the state of affairs offers it a signification and a social application justifying by an appearance of rationality what originates in the irrational, etc.

For him, who needed a miracle without believing in one, religion became interesting only from the moment he discovered it was a way of canceling out other people—of considering guilty those who made him guilty, of considering inessential an existence that was scarcely endurable, of considering essential its obverse, the side God sees. I shall return to these sophisms of faith only to say this: that faith betrays the society of men, that the believer, like the traitor, is a man who, while you think you are dealing with him and seeing him in his reality, treacherously escapes into a superreality and deals with the now from the alien perspective of the Eternal, judging those men who regard him as their equal by norms unknown to all men and to himself. Socially excluded or maladjusted, he bails out of "his" society and takes his revenge by symbolically destroying it.

It makes little difference whether this symbolic destruction functions through mysticism (a means of regarding the real as illusory with regard to the superreal Being of God and his Kingdom), through materialism (a means of regarding human significations as the illusory man-made nothingness shimmering on the surface of an unqualified Matter) or through treason properly speaking (a means of denying the society to which one actually belongs for another, opposed society which one prefers to it because it contests one's own society and with which one mentally allies oneself because this mental integration in the alien society need never submit to the test of reality—one is not *in* that alien society—and permits the contestation of one's own society without any positive rejoinder); mysticism, materialism and treason are the three possible forms of a single fundamental attitude, the escape from and negation of reality in favor of an abstract, absolute reality acceptable only insofar as it permits affective reality to be regarded as inessential. And to these three forms a fourth should be added, which he is to discern later on: the activity of writing, which abolishes reality in favor of an abstract and merely signified reality to which the writer sacrifices his life, continually annihilating in thoughts and words the reality of his existence in the world.

Not to be here; to be only a transparent, ineffable and therefore invulnerable presence, a transcendent scrutiny sliding over the surfaces of events without taking hold, impervious to reproaches, disengaged from all commitments toward others because absolutely committed toward the absolutely Other—this is how he began to be toward his twelfth year, this is how he still is today. To exchange religiosity for Nazism after a year's *ascesis* was an easy matter. Like religion, Nazism permitted him to integrate himself mentally in another realm, that of the Reich, which would never be the realm of his fellow beings, which denied them, which he himself could never achieve, and which permitted him to disdain the world around him.

And he just said reality was an entanglement of significations! Here is the third interpretation I have given of his conversion to Nazism, and it is as valid as the preceding two. Virile protest; desire to be Other (that is, Aryan) and to exterminate in himself the Jewish "weakness"; religion of Strength, Race and the Reich, by virtue of which he could transfer himself to a Germanic Elsewhere from which he would scornfully contest men and events as a lesser reality—Nazism was all that for him, and this too: a Rule like a religious discipline, similarly intransigent, which no one had tried to impose upon him. A Rule by which no one would have dreamed of gauging him, and which he had chosen for just that reason—precisely because this Rule (as religion before it, but to a greater extent) was not made for him; because no one asked him to excel according to its norms; because even the least obedience to it was a supererogatory act; because, even if he were last among the Nazis, he was still first, for the virtues which were supposedly inherent in the "Germanic race" were lacking in him, and to possess even the slightest trace of them was already a victory over his abjection.

Perhaps this interpretation contains all the others: Unable to excel by the family rule, unable to be what he should have been, he chose to conform to alien rules, to do what no one expected of him, to answer for requirements not personally intended for him in order to conceal his failure to satisfy those which were. The good Catholic no one asked him to be, the good Nazi no one could have expected, later the good Frenchman when France no longer existed nor did any real Frenchman within four hundred kilometers—so that was it: to disguise himself in a borrowed being which made no attempt to fool anyone, to mask his nullity by an Otherness which frankly admitted itself as such, to overcome his fellow beings, absolutely this time, on grounds completely alien to them (as to himself), and also to impose these grounds upon the strangers who would say of him, "This Jew is a good Catholic, a good Nazi; this Austrian speaks French perfectly; this Frenchman knows more about Germany, England, the U.S.A. and India, than the Germans, English, Americans and Indians." To be what he is not, though not in order to stay that way and accomplish something positive, but only to deny what he is (incompletely), what he cannot entirely be, and therefore compensate for his infirmity by an excellence no one would contest, for there was no God, there were no Nazis, no Frenchmen, no Germans, English, Americans or Indians to put him to the test. A choice, therefore, of grounds on which he was unbeatable because no one dreamed of competing with him, a way of astounding other people by showing himself to be so different from the sort of person they were expecting—injecting into his relations with others a corrosive dose of negativity, presenting himself as the negation of the world he ought to have in common with them, therefore of them and of himself.

I am going to try to trace the genesis of this negativism, but before that I should like to clarify the above theoretically (a praiseworthy ambition, of course, but how characteristic of the attitude he has just described, for, having spoken of himself, having allowed the reader to think for a moment that he can finally come to grips with him, here he is, rushing to confound the reader already; creating the theory for his own interpretations of himself, he presents himself as the pure theorizing mind of a "himself" he suddenly abandons like an empty skin, leaving it in the reader's hands, overpowering the reader with abstract digressions that will prove, according to the perspective taken with regard to their object, that he is who he isn't, that he is the undefinable and ineffable scrutiny focused on all things, himself included).

Starting from a child feeling persecuted and trying to escape the constraints of the human world, I have reached an adolescent feeling, if not continually persecuted, at least excluded and the object of contempt. The original inferiority situation has subsisted, hence also the conviction that he is inferior; but this original attitude of inferiority and alienation has been complicated, as it has developed, by a negativist attitude of resentment, pride and treason which will remain dominant for a long time. He has chosen this attitude no more deliberately than he has chosen inferiority; he has fallen into it by a dialectic whose basis cannot be found in his conscious intentions, but in the instruments of perception and behavior which circumstances have offered him and which, set in motion to the advantage of his original attitude, have reacted upon it by their inherent logic—a logic which can reveal itself only in this situation. I mean that the law of the process is not in events any more than in the intention which makes use of them; but then, utilizing certain instruments of behavior (systems of thought, beliefs, stock attitudes), the original intention was led beyond itself, discovering significations and reasons which were entirely alien to it at the start and which it nevertheless finished by assuming as its own. He came to religion, for instance, out of despair, and to Nazism out of virile protest, and continued with them for quite different reasons (to raise himself above deriding humanity and to reject it in favor of an absolute Otherness). Has he been the plaything of some logic immanent in these beliefs and in his situation? That would be too much to say. But the original intention had to assume the condition of fact and articulate itself against it by a certain (finite) number of possibilities thematically unforeseen—by certain "objective possibilities." So being-for-itself, having adopted this attitude for reasons it is soon to forget, finds itself actually living by these objective possibilities, first unconsciously, then gradually discovering them as its own—that is, discovering in its attitude new possible significations (discovering "temptations," unforeseen possibilities, significations to which it will attribute value and which it will choose as subjectively determinant when it chooses itself, by thematizing them, as the subject of behavior which was at first its own only objectively, and as if in spite of itself).

This is to say, in fact and historically, that we merely choose to be what we can already be without having chosen it (or, as Marx said, that humanity asks itself only the questions it can answer), that the choice assumes, thematizes, and attributes value to significations which offer themselves to being-for-itself without its having wanted or foreseen them, but which it begins to live in secretly as the objective significations attaching themselves to its behavior intact with the empirical world and other people. The most reassuring thing that can happen to a man is that the behavior by which he rationally deals with events allows of only one signification and that his freedom can choose itself through the attribution of value to this signifying behavior. To be the man of a single signification and a single intention—that is what we are all nostalgic for, because this condition is refused us and because, intellectuals or not, we live in contradiction, incapable of summing up our existence in one clear, positive, effective action, gnawed by bad conscience or guilty of bad faith when we claim to do so against all the evidence. Today our behavior always signifies more than we would like it to signify in order to live in peace with ourselves and with others; peace can be achieved only at the price of deceptions, abusive simplifications, and amputations of ourselves. Honesty would require us to assume the contradictions in which we live, but we can do this only by agreeing to confess the dark, negative, ineffective side of our action; and this confession itself cannot be an action, since it affects the share of failure which action implies. This confession, an attempt to recover the share of ourselves which cannot be realized in action, which action reduces to silence, which, as our irremediable solitude, separates us from our positive image, this confession can be only literary—that is, simultaneously individual, public and uninfluential in terms of action (though not necessarily inoperative).

Nostalgia for a simple and effective action is something I understand very well, for everyone wants to escape contradiction and solitude; but at the same time I am ashamed of it, for it is impossible to escape these conditions (and that is why I regard his case as significant of the common condition). This nostalgia, if we yield to it, is cowardice, for it desires a world where objective signification (attaching in the first place to behavior which seems the only possible and rational behavior) would impose itself with a clarity so imperative that we could stop choosing it without our behavior being modified by it; we would be inside truth "by the force of events," protected by the laws of a historical process (which would no longer deserve the qualification of "dialectical"—it would be a providential "way of the world"), sure of making real the human world whether we chose it or not; we would *be chosen* ("elected") *by* history and would go "in the right direction" even without wanting to. Saved from the start, we would be condemned to being and doing what we would do, as the Swedes are condemned to happiness—as the gods, if they existed, would be condemned to perpetual life. But that is not possible, and that is why I refer to a cowardly nostalgia secreted by each being-for-itself whose historical good fortune, despite and because of its agonies, is this: It is condemned to thought, to doubt, to contestation, condemned to freedom, to the certainty that man can be nothing. Torn by the contradictory significations of its behavior, protected against itself by no grace of state, each being-for-itself feels riveted to the necessity of choosing; and because this condition so weighs upon it, it engages in occasional crusades with such eagerness, dogmatizing anti-Communism or Communism, rendering absolute the opposition between East and West, between formal democracy and socialism. It projects outside, upon the other camp, one term of its contradiction which it identifies as absolute Evil, claims to be proof against its temptations and thereby reassures others like itself. And they have great need of reassurance; as bourgeois infected with Marxism and haunted by the decline of their class, they rattle their swords against it, predict the great catastrophe, preach the great purification, because for them the annihilation of the Marxist devil haunting them is the only hope of being able to endure their bourgeois being without shame or remorse; as Marxists infected with *bourgeoisism* because they come from the bourgeoisie and must live side by side with it, they try, unable to destroy it or to eradicate it from themselves, to cut themselves off from it by religious dogma which humiliates their bourgeois intelligence, exorcises the temptations of their origins, raises them to the dignity of the elect, the heralds of history (a role all the more tempting because history, for the last ten years, has been made without them and because their impotence to make it and to live according to its ideas encourages ideological absolutism).

But he does not want to talk about this now, for fear that several precocious generalizations might cast doubt on the methodical examination he promises himself to make later on. His intention, for the moment, is to show how his original condition, in the course of various "prefabricated" attitudes, has assumed various objective significations; how each of these significations permits a true interpretation of his existence, for each has been a temptation for him; but how each of these interpretations offers only a partial truth, for the total truth, accessible only to historical description, is this: that he could not unify himself by any one of the contradictory objective significations which were offered to him, that he spent his life seeking a signification which would permit him to subsume them all, that the choice of this signification has never been able to avoid the consciousness of its revocability, the evidence that it was only one possibility among others equally tempting, and that what was fundamental in him, his ultimate truth, was this necessity always to be seeking the activity capable of passing beyond the objective significations offered to him to their synthesis. Yes, his truth is that he must seek, must invent an activity which unites his individual "Diaspora" and leads its scattered members into a new country, a conquest over which his rights would remain precarious. But for this activity to become even conceivable has taken a long time—he has discovered that country only after already committing himself to it. It is another activity, an undertaking begun for other reasons, in the dark, which has progressively assumed an unforeseen signification, afterward discovered to be perhaps his only possibility of salvation. For at the start this undertaking aimed only at showing that there was no undertaking, no salvation possible, that he could only crucify himself upon the double impossibility of being and of being nothing, of choosing a single signification for himself and of choosing all that were offered to him. But that will come later.

The train on July 20, 1939 ("Date of entry into Switzerland: July 21, 1939," question and answer which have recurred over ten years on dozens of questionnaires and forms), boarded at the West Station, his father pale, thin, exceptionally upset and saying, "This may be the last time we'll see each other!"; but he wasn't thinking so far ahead, they were going to spend the vacation in Montreux. They stayed at the Pension Beau Séjour, which cost eight Swiss francs a day, a strangely empty Byzantine villa with too many servants and a casino he had to take his sister to in the afternoons so that a handsome Chilean could dance with her between cups of chocolate. Departure for Zurich fifteen days later, staying first at a hotel, later at a pension, then in the same pension but with the three of them in one room and with one meal a day, then only breakfast. The miserly prosperity of Zurich, overabundance, stinginess, antialcohol self-righteousness, League of Women, Protection of Young Girls, Zwingli, clean blue streetcars, cabarets and bars hidden in the Old Town where gusts of tobacco smoke and the smell of beer suggested vice, prostitution, Forbidden Pleasures. A

complacent opulence assuming the expression of modest content-
ment, poverty (regarded as shameful) relieved with scornful pity,
as one might treat a disease. For him, his mother and his sister, the
apprenticeship of hunger before shop windows full of food while
the past fell from them like scales, and with it the future. The Nazi-
Soviet Pact, the invasion of Poland, his mother's feverish maneuvers
to "settle" them in Switzerland, a letter to the Pope, interminable
financial calculations, the discovery of a German-Swiss boarding
school up in the mountains approved by the German ambassador
and costing 650 Swiss francs a month—a fortune. For Maria, who
had spent three months deciding to get him a bicycle that cost 110
schillings, who bought a radio only in 1936, and secondhand at
that, who had every month struggled to set aside two hundred
schillings for French lessons and piano lessons which Jacob dis-
approved of—for Maria, finding 650 Swiss francs a month to "save
the boy" ("By saving you I lost you, and I knew it") was a challenge. The kind of challenge which the thrifty bourgeois who has
been saving for twenty years in hopes that his stinginess will permit
him to "improve his position" accepts only on very great occasions,
when he feels that all is lost already because the opulent future
he dreamed of has fallen away and the meager remains suddenly
burn his fingers—"Let's take advantage of it while we still have
something." Jewels sold, secret funds changed into dollars at a
wretched exchange in bars where she met suspicious characters (an
old American woman with a Polish gigolo); purchase of his first
suit with long trousers, which he wore for three years, having no
other; arrival in Graubünden, where his mother confided to the
head of the school that her son was half Jewish, that she wanted
to save him, that she could not pay the entire tuition (which would
be sent regularly, each month, from Germany) and that she hoped
he would give her a reduced rate; she obtained it (a cut of fifty
francs) thanks to her power of making people feel it would be
unworthy of her high opinion of them not to yield to her, but she

did not guess that the director whose Swiss patriotism she appealed to was a Nazi drunkard who enjoyed taking his revenge for her victory over him.

Institut Montana: a huge yellow building towering over a little village in a narrow valley, fifty thousand feet above sea level; tiny separate rooms whose windows overlooked the granitic mass of a gray mountain that crushed him beneath its immutability. At first the mountain thrilled him, then it weighed on him; he dreamed of the sea because the sea inspires dreams, while the mountain, unchanging, daunts imagination. Men crawl in its shadow, their thoughts short as the horizon, narrow as the valley, greedy as the rocky soil; because human activity does not affect it, the mountain is discouraging, nourishes introversion, conservatism. History washes over its feet without affecting it, and men of the mountain do not believe in history; for them there is only a lunar eternity, boredom articulated by the barber, tobacco and wine.

As an exile, it was a success. Some sixty children, rich Dutch, German and Swiss boys banded together in vague cliques secreting the snob values (jazz, movie stars, exotic cigarettes, whisky) of spoiled and abandoned adolescents, bored with their own emancipation. It was as if he had landed on a new planet, accustomed as he was to virile values (vigor, sobriety, contempt for decadent artifices), armed with a Bruckner symphony (which infatuated him by its repetitive length and its polyphonic elaborations) and records of Ravel (chosen because of their relative hermeticism for an untrained ear), a bicycle and one rough gray suit. They made fun of his Viennese accent, his ignorance of jazz, alcohol, tobacco and racing cars, as well as of his naïve seriousness. There were eighteen months to get through until graduation. Shut into his cell of six square yards, where he was permitted to play music only on Saturday and Sunday afternoons, he began to realize he was terribly alone.

Winter '39–'40. His window steamed over, his brass lamp casting its yellow circle on the raw wood table. His mother was working at Yaroslav's to pay his tuition and Yaroslav dealt with her unkindly, taking his revenge on this stubborn daughter. Sitting at his table, he stuck his nails into the raw wood and stared at nothing for whole evenings at a time. The nothingness gradually rose from his stomach, then filled his whole chest. He wanted to lay his head on the desk and sob, but the master prowled the corridors on crepe soles and might walk in without knocking. He said, "My God, let me die," but he didn't believe in God any more. Then he put his forehead against the steamy glass and stared out into the darkness. There was nothing to do. Nothing to hope for. The world was like the great granite mountain; he could only look at its mass, he was nothing but this looking on the surface of an alien world which had no use for him. That was when he began feeling that life is insupportable; that man is a wound in which the world turns like a knife; and that between man and the world there was one term too many.

Wondering later what this terrible desire to cry meant, this impulse to huddle in a corner in his own body's warmth, what name to give this blankness, which he had experienced before (the first time, at the age of five or six, when he had fallen in love with a pale, silent little girl with long brown hair; later, listening to a Chopin waltz; still later, when he fell in love again—this time with two girls; and after that, whenever he encountered the specific atmosphere of loving), he discovered that "sadness is self-pity." Self-pity: nostalgia for a world whose textures and limits are identified with those of the body, because the body becomes the only home, both Promised Land and Paradise Lost, when it is the only endurable thing left; desire to wrap his arms around his own body, last refuge of life's sweetness, last barrier against a hostile world; and after this desire, the appeal to another body to make him conscious of his own, a body he would love and press himself against as against his own sweetness objectified.

For the man confined in an alien and hostile world, there are three possibilities: to attempt to escape, to resign himself to his lot and escape in dreams, and to adopt the imprisoning order, to conform to its requirements, even at the price of self-distortion. Among these three possibilities, I have elsewhere set up an absolute hierarchy: I have attributed to the first (the effort of liberation) a moral significance, to the second (the creation of an imaginary world to live in because the real world is inaccessible) an aesthetic significance, and to the third (a behavior of conformist heteronomy) a vital significance. Now, since these three possibilities are the three objective meanings of the confined man's situation, it is more than likely that he will discover each of them, one day or another, as a temptation. If the word "alienation" is to have a meaning, this alienated man cannot live in either the third or the second attitude without suffering, at least secretly, from their contradictions and their inauthenticity, and therefore without being tempted to escape them by the first (his success is another question). It is this dialectic that *his* history seems to me to illustrate.

To attempt to escape. . . . There could be no question of escape in the winter of 1939–40. For outside his cell his prison was the whole world. This world was at war; the camp he belonged to according to his origins repudiated him because of his Jewishness, suspected him because of this repudiation, and rejected him into the other camp; but the other camp repudiated him in its turn, first of all because he had a German passport (brown, with a black swastika; it revealed his half-caste nature only to the initiated by underlining the first name once, the last name twice), then because he was not Jewish enough for his hostility to the Reich to be trusted. As for Switzerland, its citizens mistrusted him as a German, and the authorities (anxious not to offend Germany) suspected he was not German enough. So there was no effective escape possible, nor any way of conforming to the local order, which set up unrealizable requirements: that he be Swiss and "think Swiss"; that he be German (he wasn't German enough; after 1943 he would be too German); that he be a carefree lover of jazz, cigarettes and American film stars. There remained the second way.

This way, escape into imagination, was imposed upon him in fact, without his having to choose it. But precisely for this reason he followed it at first against his will, without recognizing it as his own. He could do nothing but dream of the possibility of living which had been refused him; but dreaming had to be learned, too, and he had still not discovered (invented) this possibility which, objectively, was the only one he had. I want to emphasize this possible gap between objective and subjective possibilities, for it shows a limitation of the Marxist explanation. As a matter of fact, it is only historically that men always choose their objective possibilities; not because the history of collectivities deals with huge numbers that verify statistical probability, but because it deals with long periods. Shrink history to a few days or months and it will evaporate into the diversity and indecision of collective as well as individual behavior, the ways which upon methodical examination reveal themselves (and therefore exist objectively) as the only possible ones rarely being the ones chosen from the start; collective behavior acts, first, the meaning of its situation; when, subjectively, it is not prepared for its objective possibilities, then what happens to it is the same thing that happens to the individual in the same case: it goes mad. It disguises reality, preferring its chimeras, it yields itself up to a terror that aims at expelling reality from its heart; it pursues this reality which it refuses to know, in the persons of the "traitors." Society must have traitors to pursue, for it feels betrayed, since history confers upon its behavior an objective meaning which robs it of its intentions, weakens its meaning in order to substitute another meaning for it. Traitors, for this mad society, are quite simply those who recognize what it does not want to see: the inavoidable toward which it is advancing, walking backward. This refusal of reality, and therefore of the "only way objectively possible," can last days or years. If it lasts a long time, society's schizophrenic behavior secretes a kind of secondary reality; the world of madness tends to objectify itself, the notion of what is really possible and of what is not is lost, the meaning of history fades, and groups of lunatics appear preaching that truth is violent (of course, since such "truth" must repudiate reality), that atomic bombs must be dropped on the forests of Dien-Bien Phu, that the Algerians must be slaughtered and M. Duclos hanged.

All this to say that in 1939 he was not subjectively ready to choose and therefore to make his own the only objective possibility available, and that he advanced toward it backward, unawares, only to discover that after many long months he had in fact adopted it while he was looking for—and thought he was doing—something entirely different. That he had discovered it I nevertheless set down to his credit; others, in the same situation, continued to avoid their effective possibilities. The individual, like Marx's proletariat, appropriates his vocation, the objective meaning of his existence, only if he chooses it, attributes value to it, makes himself its responsible subject; he can miss it indefinitely.

And he began by missing it. The radical solitude which excludes us from humanity, which obliges us to invent our own values because other people's are irremediably alien to us—this was the solitude he was not prepared for. At sixteen he was not inclined to dreaming, nor to philosophical contestation, nor to creating his own way. Discovering his solitude, he decided he must be guilty, for you must have a strong mind to believe you are right when everyone around you says you are wrong. He decided he was wrong to be a Jew; he decided he was wrong not to enjoy jazz, cigarettes, film stars (lovingly drawn on big sheets of paper by Kunz, to the applause of his confederates), and, with his pathetic good will, began to make it his duty to understand these infatuations. Only there was nothing to understand (except that this infatuation was the manifestation of an intellectual vacuity masking its boredom by snob distractions, parochial squabbles as to the superiority of the paternal Buick or Chevrolet), which is why, instead of producing edifying answers to his ingenuous questions, they suspected he patronized their "values" and, incapable of justifying them, made them into a superiority system: derision of his incomprehension; incomprehensible allusions or silence as soon as he came into their rooms; and, despite this boycott, Kunz every Saturday borrowing his phonograph ("Pierre wants to know if you'll lend us your victrola"), which was better than theirs and which he would not see again until Monday, when he couldn't use it again until the following week.

His nails thrust into the raw wood of his desk where the brass lamp projected its circle of light, the nothingness swelled within him—the feeling of being nothing. And just to hold on to something, he began to pay attention to his studies for the first time in his life. He had two terms to make up, and private lessons to help him to do so; a challenge the chemistry prof (a German Nazi who intrigued him, with whom he engaged in a sporting rivalry) flung him: to learn the courses he had missed in fewer lessons than had been set for him. How entertaining was the aridity of the natural sciences which fill the mind and by their apparent rigor protect it against anxiety and doubt; how reassuring was the precision of laws, figures and theories which, once learned, permitted you to annihilate the contingent diversity of the real; the world could be spirited away by an intellectual gymnastic which, occupying the mind, maintained your being in hibernation. To see the world scientifically: to kill off its significations, to detach yourself from the concrete, to stop living and feeling, to intellectualize your affective contact with life, to mechanize it in obedience to a Rule, no longer anything but impersonal Reason. Scientific discipline replaced religious discipline; the *ascesis* was almost the same. He played dead. It was the only kind of conformism accessible to him—conforming to scientific discipline since he could not conform to the norms of those around him. But this conformism was also a treason. Against the human world he took sides this time with the mineral world; man was chemistry.

This was not enough. The rudiments of science taught in his school were not sufficient for mechanizing the whole world. And then, it is not true that the sciences are exact. Perhaps he would have excelled in them if intellectual gymnastics, limited by rigorous rules, were the last word of the scientific spirit. This was not the case. Mathematics in particular, detested from the start, demanded a high-wire boldness (insisted that the reasoner release the thread of his linear logic, seize the multiple aspects of the question at a glance in order to choose a different thread) of which his mind, fearing the void and seeking security, was incapable. None of the scholarly disciplines provided a law he could submit to in servile obedience, a means for him to die to himself, entirely defined by exterior requirements.

Then he invented something else. He decided that the "whole man" was French, that the body of true thought and reason was the French language, that the country where life was still and par excellence possible was France. France, which was the Other of all that he was and knew, the Unknown par excellence, since it was a forbidden country where not one of his ancestors had set foot; but an *existing* Unknown (unlike Brazil or Africa or China, so absolutely alien that they couldn't even be Other; lacking any relation with them, he couldn't even reject himself in their favor) whose Otherness he could explore, by means of the language, in order to lose himself in it.

A passionate, disciplined, ascetic attempt: One day during the winter of 1939–40 he resolved to make himself French and to expel from himself everything by which he was Other than the Other. From that winter day on, he read only French books—at night, on the raw wood desk, in the circle of the brass lamp, marking in the margin each line of text containing a new word and after some thirty pages jotting in his yellow notebook all these words, each in a phrase to indicate its meaning; discovering that thirty pages were enough to appropriate an author's vocabulary (with the exception of Giraudoux and his fireworks of exotic words). His yellow notebook swelled from week to week, amassing the French substance, which he swallowed with methodical patience; methodically he read his way through all the French authors of any interest at all in the school library, quickly discarding the members of the Académie Française and other bores (Bordeaux, Estaunie, Cherbuliez, Bourget) for Marcel Arland, Proust (proud of following his meanders but with no enjoyment), Giraudoux (who disconcerted him; did his "profundity" mean anything?), Malraux (misunderstood at the time), Maurois, Baudelaire, Valéry, scorning the classics, convinced that thought had progressed since, that what was most recent was most valuable.

He assimilated the French substance as, before, he had prayed and developed his muscles, with the same voluntary insistence, but this time with the sense of total involvement, compelling himself, in this German school where no one spoke French (except the prof, in class) to think only in French; speaking to himself in French, making up dialogues, poring over the dictionary whenever he came up against an obstacle, discovering the nonequivalence of languages —the fact that by knowing one you can no longer refer to another; moving within French, as in a closed system (his jubilation when he began to dream in French, then his weakness for sprinkling his German compositions with Gallicisms). He was totally engaged in this work, for the first time in his life; this undertaking gathered up all the significations of his previous behavior, realized all his complexes, contradictions and possibilities, starting with his masochism.

For at the start his "French *ascesis*" was a masochistic project, and only accessorily an attempt to escape. He postulated that man was French as he had previously admitted that man was Aryan. But he gained by the exchange; he was no more French than he was

Aryan, but in relation to France he was only one foreigner among others, while in relation to the Aryans he was an individual essentially inferior. He had no possibility of appropriating Aryanness, which was denied him as the very basis of human dignity; but he could at least try to appropriate French thought, since to do so it was enough that he think in French. He did not think of it as the thought of a particular race or people (carrying within it, like German, clots of mystery and irrationality, its very vocabulary corrupted by value judgments: *Blut, Volk, Deutsch, Führer,* blond Siegfried against black Hagen, *Reich, Rasse, Volksfremd, Kraft, Reinheit,* the "destructive" Jewish mentality, *Wein, Weib, Gesang*), but as thought itself, the exercise of reason, transparent and universal. To become French, for him, was to abandon the swamps of Teutonism for universal reason; the universal was French. But French was Other.

Which is to say that he converted to French as you convert to a religion—the religion of the French language which required a totalitarian discipline, the renunciation of his entire past, of everything which had been himself, and the mystical submission to an alien Rule which (like the exercises of religious mortification) permitted him to enter into communion with the universal. A discipline more radical than all those he had hitherto imposed on himself, because it required that he refuse everything (including the present—his school, his mountain, his profs, his fellow students) and because it promised him everything (the abstract universal) if he succeeded in this autodestructive abstraction.

So here he is praying again, as four years before. But instead of saying three Paters and three Aves morning and night and doing the opposite of what he likes the rest of the time, he prays all day long; he humbles himself before French thought, his prayer is the linguistic control to which he subjects his own spontaneity, a constantly surveyed reading, a laborious accumulation of a vocabulary, the isolation that his refusal of the surrounding Germanness plunges him into. Once again he has an absolute Rule which he wants to define him entirely, to relieve him of facing his own existence, to protect him against other people's requirements. He has dedicated himself to French as the mystic dedicates himself to God; and in relation to his secret French reality (absolute as the mystic's reality for God), his reality as a miserable schoolboy, snubbed and despised, is merely inessential.

At the start, his conversion to French was therefore only a means of regression to the old habit of his original masochism. Unable to satisfy others' requirements, unable to be the good little fellow he wanted to be (if someone called him "good little fellow" and stroked his head, saying, "You did that very well, that's just the way everyone should do it," he would wriggle with delight like the "good dog" who had been his favorite hero as a child and whom he had wanted to be like), he withdrew from all requirements, isolated himself, imposed upon himself a rule which, alien to the rules around him, permitted him to contest them and, though he was the last, made him the first. How surprising he should not have noticed this sooner—his original choice was the "original masochism" he has just described. Starting here, everything grows clear: his need for an absolute Rule, which might also be called absolute "value," something by which everything can be measured and by which an absolute hierarchy of things would be established (his anxiety, for instance, during his eleventh year, to know which animal was the strongest, the biggest or the fastest, who was the oldest man, the greatest genius humanity had produced, the greatest composer, writer or explorer, the best athlete, etc., and no sooner had he found the answer than he set up a cult of this "greatest," devalued everything that was "less"); his need for a discipline whose observation would assure him of being good and deserving; his collector's mania (as soon as something seemed good or valuable to him, it was the good, the valuable in itself which he tried to constitute by collecting all its contingent fragments); his confu-

sion when his value was contested by other people's, and his eagerness to convert to their values once they were expounded to him
with sufficient seriousness; his readiness to betray these values for
new ones, to change "loyalties" provided his new master demanded
total submission—for he himself had backed no value and, all
value being denied him, turned himself inside out to accept other
people's, condemning himself to seeing them remain alien to him;
his taste for systematization, rationalization—masochistic submission to the Law; and his desire to "jump out the window" when
he was scolded—a way of making others' reprobation into an absolute and obeying its real demands, that he no longer exist. The
same thing was true of his conversion to French. French was the
absolute good and value, therefore everything else was rubbish,
therefore he would despise everything else and accomplish what
the French value required of him; to the degree that he was not
French he no longer existed.

The first—the first among the last. The conversion to French
had the same moral structure as the mystical crisis of three years
before. Faced with the French absolute, he was nothing, a little fool
struggling in the shadows (who lacked the grace of being French as
he had lacked divine grace, and who, during his first trip in French-
speaking Switzerland, religiously listened to the railwaymen talking
in their singsong Vaudois accent, telling himself, "I'd give half my
life to *possess* French like the stupidest man there"), doomed to
contemplate from a distance, respectfully, the French *lumière,* convinced that such light was not for him, that he was condemned to
remain alien to the society of French men. Absolutely inferior since
he was irremediably non-French; but in the very frame of this inferiority, the first among the non-French, since he knew the inferiority the others were unaware of and considered it with horror.
How reassuring this religious universe was that he created for himself out of nothing, really, not even the excuse of a catechism class
this time. His French theology reveals his original choice in all its

nakedness; it reveals that this choice was masochism. How reassuring, in fact, *to be* inferior by birth (for that was what he had chosen to be; if not, why convert to French, which he knew only too well that he could not become?), surrounded on all sides, utterly enclosed within a condition of inferiority for which he is not responsible (it isn't his fault if he wasn't born French) and from which he thinks he can never escape (how could a Viennese-Jewish subman become French?). Inferior, therefore irresponsible, impotent "in essence" and therefore innocent, he chooses to be the man who can do nothing—save scrupulously and slavishly imitate the masters he gives himself (the French). They are God and His Law for him; he has only to submit to them. The alien Law which he observes as the condition of his mystical accession to being relieves him of the responsibility of coming to grips with existence. All his contradictions are spirited away by this religious postulate: "When you have made your way into the Law of French, you will become a Man, all your problems will be miraculously resolved." A Man, Someone Else. Yet you can never become Someone Else. He has chosen perpetual servitude. A servitude which (as always) had its "good side"; to adore French as an absolute good permitted him to feel disgust and hatred for the world around him with a clear conscience. *With a clear conscience:* he was no longer responsible for the hatred and the disgust to which he was spontaneously inclined, he made the divine French stand surety for him; he felt hatred and disgust under protection, by virtue of the absolute superiority of the god he adored. Here he resembled the Moslem or the Nazi who also lets the absolute superiority of his faith and his race stand surety for his resentment; his resentment is legitimate since it is addressed solely against "infidels" and "human refuse."

From his example, I perceive two things: (1) that the victim of the totalitarian ideologies is infected by them to the point where he is spontaneously inclined to transpose them to a different level and to direct them against others who become his own victims (this

is the mechanism of anti-Semitism, of caste superiority, of all resentment feelings); (2) that he had assumed (i.e., chosen) his
condition of inferiority to such a degree that he spontaneously reinvented it when (for he was rid, now, of the surrounding anti-
Semitism) it was tending to modify itself. Accustomed to live with
a ceiling over his head (the ceiling of anti-Semitism and parental
condemnation, a ceiling which protected him against the dizziness
of altitudes, against the anxiety of being able to make himself into
what he was not, a ceiling which gave him security in his inferiority,
persuading him that the world belonged to and was made by superior men essentially different from himself, and that he could do
nothing against its course), he reinvented a new ceiling for himself
when the old one collapsed. The victim's condition offers at least
this moral comfort: The victim counts for nothing in the order
oppressing him, he is not responsible for the wrong done him; he
cannot, materially, realize his freedom; he can desire it and dream
of it without danger. Oppression protects him against responsibility.
And I also perceive this from his example: The victim is the accomplice of his condition. That is the best definition one can give of
him. The man who feels and believes himself a victim is the man
convinced that They are doing him a wrong against which he is
helpless. As soon as he opposes oppression by action (by action,
not by plaintive rebellion and protests in the name of the Rights
of Man), as soon as he refuses it effectively, he ceases to behave as
a victim. Rejecting, along with the order which oppresses him, all
legality, no longer appealing in the name of the Law, assuming his
claims as the basis of a justice which he means to obtain for himself (and not to receive from on high—from whom?), he makes
himself the supreme legislator; no longer a victim, but an avenger
and therefore already a man. But this transition from the victim's
state to that of revolutionary legislative will can only be accomplished by the dialectic of action. And the victim is in fact convinced, by his long servitude, that he can do nothing. To be liber-

ated, he must be flung into action first, in self-defense. If you merely get rid of oppression (that is, if oppression disappears of its own accord) without the victim's being actively apprenticed to freedom, the same thing happens all over again—the victim flings himself into a new slavery. How can he behave as a free man, if he has neither subjectively nor objectively apprenticed himself to such behavior? Liberated, in his new surroundings, from his racial stigma, he soon invented a new stigma for himself: that of not being French. Accustomed by his infantile situation to conceive of man as essentially Other than himself, he has not, in the shadow of his Swiss mountain, claimed humanity for himself, but projected it upon a France which at the time seemed to him the antithesis of Germany and, by the same token, of himself.

Such, at least, seems to me to be the profound motivation of his conversion to French. The course of events will now enrich that conversion with new significations unforeseen by him, objective significations which he will finally assume and which will lead him to discover supplementary motivations in his choice. This had begun at the time of the fall of France. He had established himself in the war as if it were going to last forever, as if the armed Franco-German opposition expressed an immutable reality. He had converted to a strong France which he believed to be Germany's equal. And now it was collapsing. The Belgian frontier, the Marne, Paris, pincers closing in, "successful bombardments," barrage battles of which one heard no mention the next day, "The Marseillaise" and nasal, bombastic voices that were evidently lying coming out of the radio in the rat-faced Dutch boy's room where he sipped his Dole, the only drinkable Swiss red wine. "The Marseillaise" meant a speech was coming, military marches meant no speech. "He's giving it to his girl," said Rat-Face. "No kidding," he said. "They do that all the time," Rat-Face said. "It's to calm their nerves." "You think so?" he asked. "Now he's beginning to wash his hands," said Rat-Face, "he's pulling on his pants, his chauffeur is waiting downstairs." An eloquent and emotional voice: "We shall fight to the end, behind the Pyrenees, in Africa," or something like that, and then they knew it was over. The machine ran on, the wheels turned, the gears ground together, the machine was well oiled, well regulated now, Germany was a great machine eating into bucolic, dreamy, cultivated France, the France of poplars, streams, Michèle Morgan, and Giraudoux, Secretary of State for Propaganda, mobilizing his Juliet, his Pacific, and his armadillos against the Nazi tanks. Again the fever, the triumphal marches, the air thickening, time clotting for days on end into a motionless Moment, something stops existing, something crucial begins (as when two hundred thousand Germans on the Austrian front wait while Schuschnigg, with his pinched, Jesuitical face, waits for Chamberlain's answer, and it was no, for the answer from Paris, where there is no government, and it was no, while Miklas waits for Schuschnigg to give the order to fire, and it was no, and Miklas resigns, and Schuschnigg resigns, and Globocnik, in his S.A. uniform, comes out on the balcony over-looking the Ring, *Sieg Heil, wir kehren Heim in's Reich,* the Führer commands we obey, Seyss-Inquart and his murderer's face), the machine triumphs, France falls; it was no. No, man will not win. He understands this suddenly. *Man is defeated.* Man exists only in defeat because the triumph belongs to the machines. And what he has not dared to do before he does now: he begins to hate Germany, its S.A. men, its language with its links of silence, murder and mystery, its mystique of machines and motorized power, its blood consciousness, its complacent citizens' so-called patriotism. And he understands this too: that man does not exist, to love the French is to love what does not exist, is to affirm nonbeing against being, is to oppose the imaginary to the real. Then his conversion to the French suddenly takes on a meaning. He, who does not exist, who is only a nullity rejected by the world and without any possibility save to reject the world in return, suddenly has a brother, and this brother is a whole people, a nation annihilated like himself, existing no more than the dream by which he declares himself against the real machine. France is suddenly a brother in whom he recognizes himself, a nation of bistros and *flâneurs,* of dreamers never at grips with events, men who ask only to live reflectively, composing verses, books, music, and whom he loves because of the drubbing they have received, instead of being angry with them for not being able to defend themselves. He is convinced that the French are like him, that they are his own adventure transposed to the scale of history, men defeated, trampled on, exiled on their own land, atomized into forty million solitudes, each man weeping before his circle of light on a desk of raw wood and secretly re-creating man and France in his imagination, dreaming over a book. To speak, to read, to think in French becomes a means of defying history. In opposition to being, he perpetuates the France which no longer exists, and by the same token creates, in opposition to reality, a world where man is possible. This possibility (the dream) which I said was the only one accessible to him, in default of a real liberation or conformism, he now found himself swept into by the unforeseen interrelation of facts; it became, after the fact, the objective signification of his conversion to French, he had only to develop it now—a lived signification identical with his personal situation.

C. *"The Impossible Nullity"* *

To assimilate, to incorporate French, to create France, to create man from day to day, when neither existed, in opposition to reality —perhaps I'm exaggerating, perhaps he wasn't thinking in terms this extreme; but he must have been living a signification of this kind already when, still alienated in his religious submission, he worshiped defunct man by worshiping French, resuscitated him at night in masses celebrated to his glory. Masses by which defunct man was temporarily reincarnated by reciting the magic words,

---

* Cf. Jean-Paul Sartre, *Saint Genêt.*

murmured prayers by which he himself, who was dead, revived, touched by grace. By speaking the language of man to himself he hoped to become man. He began writing—in a blue notebook, with a mechanical pencil. He did not think of becoming a writer, he was not writing to be someone; for him writing was a way of praying, of borrowing from the language of men the magical means of acceding to that truth which he found neither in himself nor around him. A truth alien in itself, like the believer's God, like Him not to be interiorized, a truth he would have felt presumptuous trying to produce, before which he religiously bowed his head and merely learned his ritual formulas; he made up sentences out of borrowed words and turns of phrase in the hope that true thought would spring from the series of syllables, as true faith was said to spring from prayer.

This was probably why Valéry and his essays on rigor infatuated him so. Here was a man who (in *Variété III*) declared that beauty obeys rigorous laws and that genius, consciously or not, merely chooses the variables of a universal equation (that of aesthetics, which is also that of the universe). What was this equation? To understand it, he took special courses in mathematics; one day, thanks to the universal equation, he too would create beauty and truth. Meanwhile he studied the style of the great authors and imitated Proust in his compositions. Imitated; everything he wrote during the school year '40–'41 was imitation, an attempt to conjure up on paper the thoughts and feelings of French authors, to acquire the technique of this invocation. He did not write what he felt or thought, for he was convinced it was foolish and worthless; he wrote to learn the linguistic substance of other people's truth, in the hope that at the end of this apprenticeship, by speaking as they did, he too would have true thoughts and feelings— theirs. Patiently, with his yellow word book and his blue notebook, he forged himself a soul according to the alien norms he believed absolute and eternal. He wrote to be Other, to get rid of himself.

He became true for himself only by transposing himself in writing. Therefore he will never be through writing, forging himself a truth.

It was on this imitation, fabricated day after day, that he built his life. The conversion to French was a desperate escape from the Austro-German–Judaeo-Christian contradiction, petrified by exile. Of course, if he had been twenty-five he might have assumed his contradiction instead of running away from it. There were many possible alternatives: He might have transcended it by a philosophical or historical synthesis; he might have established himself in exile, gone into business or politics, written books, had children, or merely made love and a living as well as he could, feeling lucky to be in Switzerland. Only he wasn't seventeen yet, and, as a *petit-bourgeois* adolescent, he knew nothing of the world; along with his country, his school and his family, the point of view had vanished from which he might have seen the world in perspective, discerned the contours of a future, found his niche. He had never found it because he was too much of a child (the world was the realm of grownups) and because he loathed his father's life; he imagined no future because the war's end would have restored nothing he might have hoped to have back (he had had nothing, being only a child). And then (for these same reasons) he didn't imagine the war *could* end; in how many years? He who was nothing couldn't plan years ahead; you must already be something in order to hope for something. He didn't know who he was; he was nothing but a tangle of objective contradictions which came to him from outside and of which he wasn't even clearly aware. On the one hand there was his nullity and on the other, outside, an alien humanity furiously exploding into the incomprehensible quarrels of the grownups. He was in the camp of both the victors and the vanquished, and equally rejected by both. He loathed the victors, but for reasons as null as himself. He hoped for their defeat, but there was no one to oppose them; and if there had been someone (which he didn't conceive of) he would have had nothing in com-

mon with him. He was a witness of a ridiculous history which took
so long to transpire that its perspectives outstripped his own; he
did not know who he would be when the history took a different
turn (if it did); he foresaw nothing because his despair was absolute, and his despair was absolute because the world remained
alien for him, an absurd world of despair. And he would have to
live with that. He had installed himself in despair; and because he
refused his individual condition (because he fled the Austro-German–Judaeo-Christian contradiction for the myth of the French
absolute), he deprived himself of the means of transcending it. I
understood this only much later, six years later. Because I was incapable of thinking my condition, of situating my despair in its
historical relativity, of grasping its concrete motivations, I lived it
absolutely, as the immutably true vision of an immutably despairing world, as a metaphysical truth against which the historical
truth, supposing it even countenanced hope, remained impotent.

I know, most adolescents pass through this metaphysical stage.
Because they are no longer children protected against consciousness
of themselves and the world by their parents' values and interces-
sion; because (particularly when they are bourgeois) they discover the world (which they still have no means of making or
knowing) as an alien reality, made without consulting them, in
which they are told to find a place while at the same time they are
refused the capacity to take one, they begin a revolt against the
world's order and norms which they have no reason to accept, for,
not making them, they need not answer for them. Parasites while
their parents pay for their education, they hate the benefactor who
puts them under obligation and slyly waits for them on the day they
receive their diplomas, anxious to teach them that "you have to
grow up" and to bury them alive in a career continuing the old
order; pariahs when they must wring their own educations from a
society which considers them slugs and which, after having mul-
tiplied the difficulties on their road, attempts to win them back by

conceding a diploma on condition—"on condition that you understand it is this society which has allowed you to grow up and that you undertake nothing to disturb the existing order." Parasites, then, or pariahs, always nonintegrated, oppressed by society or family, they are inclined by their theoretic equipment, having no grasp of reality, to judge the world in the abstract, to contest it by values no society (in essence) realizes (and particularly not theirs), to contest the world by virtue of the infinite number of opportunities of which they dream and in relation to which the finitude of the possible is always, as Bataille puts it, a fall from grace (*déchéance*).

This is the "despair of youth" (bourgeois youth)—to know it can only decline; to know that the infinity of the possible, of which it can dream precisely because it is nothing as yet, will collapse; to know that its requirements will be necessarily disappointed when it "becomes something," but *only* this "something" ("I was like you once, but now I have responsibilities; you can't always do what you want in life"); to know it will end up by accepting the world it now rejects because it has not created it, knows the world will open its sympathetic arms and say paternally, "What's the use of revolt? We've all gone through it. We're offering you a Splendid Position. You're only hurting yourself by rejecting it." Then youth accepts the "splendid position," swearing to keep its soul unsullied. But what good is an unsullied soul when you have a splendid position? Telling yourself you're worth more than what you are, more than the world, distinguishing man from his actions, collaborating with an inhuman society by reading Malraux or *Les Temps Modernes* and hanging reproductions of abstract paintings on the walls.

Feeling this, even if he doesn't think it; about to enter a world which prescribes a role he has not chosen; conscious that the possibility of playing this role is a hereditary privilege guaranteed by and preserving the social order, the (bourgeois) adolescent sees his life already worked out (a fine career) and, because he has not yet lived it, because he still *sees* it as a destiny without glory, he wonders what this world and this life are worth. Not much. And he is right. Only the discovery of this metaphysical truth (the absurdity of the world and of life) remains a sterile one; metaphysical consciousness cannot reach beyond itself toward a morality because it is rootless, an abstract protest, incapable of inserting itself into history by an action for which it does not possess the means. And insofar as he does not create his means, but leaps from the metaphysical adolescence into a ready-made adult career, the bourgeois adolescent continues his despair into man's estate. He is a full-fledged nihilist, a man who "plays the game" quite cynically and who (remember, my friends?) after a day of honorable work and before returning to a respectable home, trots out, in some bar or other, his agonizingly lucid thoughts.

All this to say that his despair had nothing exceptional about it when he landed in Lausanne in the spring of 1941 and that, like most young bourgeois of eighteen, he wondered why he was on earth—to do what? Nothing. (A discovery which loses none of its truth for having been conditioned by an individually desperate situation. The most fundamental truths are always discovered through individual situations. This does not mean that they are individual. Desperate situations furnish the means of discovering a fundamental absurdity of which they later appear as the contingent confirmation.)

This no longer means anything. I could continue through the years to this minute, but I feel it no longer has any meaning. I am no longer learning anything. It's becoming a routine. Tonight, coming down the Rue Saint-Sulpice (the street of failures; the first time I saw it, that's how it looked to me—overelaborate, angular, full of antique shops and dark apartments where I imagine those adolescents of the Latin Quarter have ended up, in overstuffed rooms where they outlive the hope of their revolt, becoming bourgeois, pious, and routine-worn), I told myself, "It no longer means anything, I can go on like this indefinitely, but I'm not learning any more. I have learned nothing, I haven't advanced a step except in theory and in knowledge. But theory remains inoperative. I don't know what to do with my life." Then (as in the spring of 1941, fifteen years earlier) he comes down the dusty street that smells of failure and wonders, "What can I do with my life?" and immediately this feeling is reflected in thought, in consciousness of the vanity of the thought of its vanity, then as if he were pulling out a plug at the bottom of this stagnant consciousness, everything flows out, assumes a direction. The consciousness of vanity is polarized by the project of writing about the consciousness of vanity, it is no longer merely the vain and suffering consciousness, it is here in order to bear witness to itself in the form of writing. (As in 1941, during the blackout in the Place Chauderon, looking at the sky, he suddenly realized the immensity of the universe and realized that the Place Chauderon, with its lampposts, its post office, its Vaudois and its blackout turning in the sidereal universe, had no importance whatever, neither it, nor he, nor the war across the border, nor men in general, nor thought—that it had no importance whatever and that it would take a detestable dose of stupidity, pretentiousness, solemnity, yes, abject solemnity, to attribute any importance to what was happening between the Place Chauderon and Warsaw, in some point of the sidereal universe. It was on this thought that he fed himself during the following months, supported by Valéry and Jean Rostand discoursing on frail-humanity-protoplasm's-pathetic-adventure; on this thought, and on its contradiction: that if nothing has any importance, then the consciousness that nothing has any importance has no importance. Yet it had an enormous importance, and he rushed to write this discovery, to write that it had no importance, to write that it had no importance to write it, to write that writing it had no importance to write it had no importance, and, caught in his own maze, to write about the contradiction of writing that writing has no importance.)

Thus, fundamentally I have not changed. Now as then, there is this sense of absurdity and this way of taking it as a literary theme, of making it his object aesthetically by living it in order to write it, and thereby to invent an aesthetic justification for it. I have explained this elsewhere; a consciousness driven to realize its own nothingness, to the vanity of being thus realized by its own nothingness, a consciousness incapable by its situation of living anything but the evidence of its own vanity and impotence, confronted with the fullness and unconcern of being, a consciousness which, immured in the universe, is nothing but a cry no one hears—such a consciousness cannot invent any other meaning for itself than itself, cannot find any other purpose than to be the cry it is not. I mean that such a consciousness, its cry unheard, knowing the vanity of its cry and yet unable to choke it back, having to express its existence as a cry and producing nothing but this deafening silence, such a consciousness finds no other means of manifesting its freedom save to will its cry as it already is; it wills itself to be as it exists (this is all it can be—itself), it doubles its cry, recovers it as the free product of its activity by re-creating it in the form of an object: it begins writing. And what I have written, day after day, was indeed cries, variations on the same theme, ceaselessly begun again, variations trying to shape this silent clamor in language, as if, by creating it in the form of an independent object, I could stop producing it in my own breath and, delivered, could then enjoy its contemplation; everything would be said.

And now the words rustle past, he listens to himself talking. And having talked a good deal (having accomplished his daily task, fixed for seven years now at two pages covered with a tiny handwriting), he can go to bed (or out for a walk), his conscience clear. Suddenly relaxed, he can enjoy everything: breathing the air, looking at people in the street, seeing the city with a painter's eye, as a vari-colored décor. He allows himself an "earned" respite; he is at ease with himself. After all, I'm not so bad after all, he tells himself. And if he runs into someone he knows, he begins talking almost lovingly. At least that's how it was for several years. Days that were sometimes terrible, during which he struggled to disentangle confused intentions ("If I can't clear this up, it's because I don't know what I mean"), punctuated by moments of euphoria. Why this euphoria? he wondered, still not forgiving himself for it, reproaching himself for it as a disturbing symptom; did it not bear witness that he was writing less to say something (to do something) than to "deserve" a moment's respite, as he had performed his "spiritual exercises" at twelve, that writing was a way to get rid of himself, and not an attempt to find himself?

Of course this was true for a long time. And as far as writing is concerned, I could readily busy myself with the same demonstration of a dialectical progression which succeeded so well in the case of prayer and which risks becoming a universal recipe, showing (1) that he began to write to appropriate French thought and to teach himself how to think—this was the period of his stylistic exercises; (2) that in 1941, thanks to the *Pensées d'un Biologiste* (of Jean Rostand) and to the "Petite Lettre sur les Mythes," the "Variation sur une Pensée de Pascal" and the "Soirée avec Mallarmé" (of Valéry, in *Variété II*), followed by *Nausea* (bought by chance—he had just found *The Imagination* in a secondhand bookshop; not once looking at it, he had bought it and a month later, in a Genevese bookshop, he had found both *Nausea* and *The Wall*. "Well," he had thought, "a philosopher who writes fiction. That must be funny." And he bought them), he discovered cosmic (or ontological) despair. First by thought; it furnished him the intellectual means of realizing that he himself was living this despair conceived in other people's words as if it were an exterior truth. Or perhaps by trying to reproduce in himself the despair he found in others, he succeeded so well that he came to the inspired realization that it was indeed his own. Tremendous satisfaction: a true experience at last; by imitating others, he encountered himself. So he too was capable of truth, or rather truth, a certain truth, was immediately accessible to him! He began writing sub-Valéry and sub-*Nausea*. This was a religious discipline—to provoke their experiences in himself, to pour his own experience into the mold of truth (that is, into theirs) and by doing so to accede to that humanity he recognized in them and felt himself lacking altogether. He wrote so that by resembling them he could become a Man: that is, could escape his individual nullity by transcending it toward the universal by means of language. (3) That having started out to become Other (or to interiorize Otherness) and encountering himself in others, his literary exercise now becomes ambiguous; he no longer knows what belongs to others and what comes from himself. He begins speaking of himself in their manner. He speaks subject to confirmation; the orientation of his thought, if not its concrete content (however little) is furnished him by them, confirmed by them. He writes under their scrutiny like a dutiful student; he lives beneath their scrutiny, since his own experience interests him only to the degree that it accords with theirs. Thus his literary activity is alienated and falsified from the start, as though deflected from its potential authentic signification by the fundamental religious intention which inspires it. I mean that he writes in order to dismantle (like a bomb) his own intolerable experience by transforming it into a pretext for literature and assigning himself the distant goal (aimed at in doubt and often in despair) of being a Man like Valéry or Morel. (He calls him Morel because They have corrupted the name J.-P. S. for him, because gossip and public stupidity have seized upon the name of this Man, whom he jealously adored, as an army takes possession of the body of a woman who, though a whore for them, is your beloved and whom you decide to call Kay or L [more pseudonyms], to keep her reality for you separate from her reality for them.)

Here at last is the beginning of a truth. He wrote, he says, in order to shape his cry in language. Yes, doubtless; but this is an a posteriori interpretation based on the objective signification of the act of writing. Yet this signification, true in the last analysis, was not dominant at the start. At the point I have reached (supposition 3), I was writing to become the man par excellence whom the French author was for me; that is, I was deflecting my lived experience from its original signification in order to transform it into a literary experience. He was deflecting his experiences from their primary meaning, beginning to live them with a view to a second meaning, as "experiences-for-writing," and the meaning of the acitvity of writing was to transform his experience on paper into the experience of one of these celebrated others whom French authors were for him. He did not write to be an author, but to recover his existence transmuted into literary material, invested with the prestige of literature; he wrote to get rid of his existence, to live its crying absurdity in vain no longer, to produce it as if it flowed from his project of writing.

Therefore, at this stage, he was still writing the way you pray. Literature, for him, was other people's business, and by writing he was trying not to become one of these others (that would have seemed a laughable presumption to him) but to palm off his existence on them surreptitiously, to have it taken over by literature as an emanation of that literature-of-others. And is he doing anything different today? Is he quite sure he is not still writing to transform his existence into a literary work which, joining other people's in the Pantheon of literature, would save him from the contingency of existing like Antoine Roquentin, dreaming of transforming his existence into something like his favorite song?

I know; the Pantheon is dead for me, and I no longer believe in its divinities; literature has lost its prestige. And yet, what am I doing now? If the evocation of this past disturbs him, if he feels he is no longer advancing, is still chewing the same cud as fifteen years before, is falling back into the same rut, it is because he recognizes himself in this period. Why is he writing? He started out proudly and enthusiastically, believing that with this autobiography he would forge a new instrument, a new means of apprehending the world. Now he doesn't know any more. Only this: If he continues on this road, he will achieve nothing more than a new attempt at literary lifesaving, or, what comes down to the same thing, of philosophical lifesaving: a claim to set an example, to derive from his own case the illustration of a universal Method; of finding himself included not in the Pantheon of literature but in that of general theories. He must find something else.

More precisely, he must find something to say. His initial enthusiasm derived from this: he thought he had something to say, had something he *could* say; he could address himself to dozens of young men he had run across who, without being half-castes, lived the contradictions that his own mixed background had led him to realize (he thinks) and, by speaking of himself, could help them to understand how man was defeated. But now he doesn't know any longer. If he had the impression of a good start, it was because he felt he was speaking to someone. Since then, by speaking, he came back to the feeling of speaking in the void. Retiring into a new, imperfect shell; conscious suddenly that he was existing like these young men yawning on the Boulevard Saint-Germain who, like him, cover sheets of paper every night, who write against the world, against their brothers, who grow furious when someone says what they are thinking because what is important for them is to say it first—they write to distinguish themselves, to be the person who manages to get printed by beating out his friends. Well, he has nothing to say to such men; they are the fascists of literature. There remain the others, the ones who are more interested in the world than in me. It is the world (and someone like me-in-the-world) that I must tell them about. Yet, at the point I have reached (1941), there was virtually no world. What I was saying I was saying for nothing, to destroy the thing said, to produce the sidereal silence by my self-annihilating words. To reconstitute this experience is to re-create that great silence over the Place Chauderon, far from Voronezh, Kharkov, Smolensk, Bengazi, far from the five thousand mud farmers who starve to death in China every year; comprehensible only to Philippe Henriot, to M. Peyer who considered that the Army, the defeat and the Marshal "formed" youth— "And you have no lessons to teach us; in your place, my boy, I'd be only too happy they let me stay in Switzerland, and I'd keep my mouth shut"; comprehensible to Federal Councilor Pilet-Golaz, who carried on a crusade against the Reds in the name of Helvetian culture while the cinemas showed UFA, Swiss (Hurrah for General Guisan and our brave farmer-soldiers!) and Vichy newsreels. To reconstitute this period is to write the solitude, the stupidity, the daily lying, is to speak in order to say nothing (which is one definition of poetry as good as another); it is to do what I was doing then: to write the way you pray, because you're speaking to no one.

There are two ways of writing, as Morel says: for men and for God. Well, when you cannot write for men because you have nothing to tell them, you necessarily write for God. You "inscribe in language a great silent cry"; you create pure literature, beautiful and useless as the pyramids, denying men and their world in favor of their Nothingness. This no longer attracts me. It remains to say how it did attract me for seven years. And it remains to be seen afterward if there is anything else for me to say and do. For, thinking over what I have written, it seems to me that, as usual, the key signification of the project to write was (or is) the one I have not mentioned. Namely, that writing for God, as Morel says, is a claim to establish, as a literary work promised to the Pantheon of bookstores, truth in itself. It is to claim to establish a true relation alone with the absolute. Like the believer praying, it is a claim to recover alone his true reality; it affirms that the latter is on my paper, that I am what I write, that this writing, materialized without the assistance of others, must also be accepted religiously by them as a sacred and incontestable text, since it was produced without their help. And the signification of my writings (imposed, forced year after year on the rare visitors; as soon as they began talking about something, he cut short the discussion and, rummaging in his files, read them a sacred text, reread it instead of explaining it, referring his visitor to the writing as to a definitive source) has for a long time been this: to establish my being-in-itself-and-for-itself on paper and thereby, deriving it only from myself, to deny all true reality to my being-for-others. Or is it the other way around—since my reality-for-others has no truth for me, to recover on paper my true reality, incommunicable in life for lack of interlocutions? Yes, it's probably the latter proposition that was true at first. But the result was the same. (Or is it the point of departure rather than the result?) For me, other people did not count; they were puppets, shadows encountered every day whom I never bothered to understand. We were not living in the same world, their truth was without effect on mine (and conversely). Yes, probably a point of departure; here is where I started. But a result too; I have so well developed this condition of an exile in a world (Switzerland) without truth—and of an exile from the real world, the beyond-the-Swiss-borders—that nothing I thought brought the Swiss closer to me; I thought against them, and our separation, a point of departure, also became the accepted result of my attitude.

He stops, he admires this regression which has twice brought him to see a point of departure in what he first took for the effect of his choice. For despite all his resolutions, he has a tendency to forget that choice, like scientific discovery, invents only what already exists. I mean that he develops only this or that objective possibility the world offers him in order to feed it on his freedom. Thus with the choice to write—it was produced by a religious attitude toward French literature (a new form of an old religiosity) and also by an intolerable solitude. Objectively null, being nothing but a consciousness of his nothingness confronting a totally alien world, he was immediately offered two possibilities: to annihilate himself, nothing as he was, in a world perfectly unconcerned with him, and this he tried; but since it was impossible without killing himself (and he thought of this constantly), he had to find, once he decided to stay alive, a meaning for his life. It could have only one (this is the second possibility): that of not having any. When you cannot keep from crying out though you know you will not be heard, you may as well decide that this cry which has no meaning has a meaning insofar as it has none—that it is in itself its own absurd meaning. This is where poetry starts. Philosophy too; and, once started, developing a style from the situation itself, it manages to attribute value to this style and to perpetuate this situation.

But what if the situation changes? This is what must be considered. I no longer know what meaning it has to write. I write to find a meaning. But perhaps this meaning, once the situation and I change, is lost. Perhaps having used up this gadget, I have "cured" myself of the project to write. "Cured" by writing—by writing the cure of a man who is writing his discontent with what he writes. And who therefore would write the renunciation of his project to write. And who, writing about it, would discover that he has transformed his renunciation of literature into literature. But this is a superficial paradox. He clings to his paper for fear of losing his desire to write, and so that he will have that at least. For fear of leading a commonplace life, of dissolving into anonymity and diversion, of getting to like life's pleasure, of enjoying the life of all these bourgeois whose condition he is beginning to share, of becoming one of them. And—a correlative temptation to which he must not yield—for fear of overvaluing as a heroic achievement his life during the forties.

Mollusks floating in an aquarium: the loquacious and Jesuitical Peyer, who effaced himself before Philippe Henriot when he came into the dining room first; the sugary Violette, turning forty, who discovered the value of her virginity by not having managed to get rid of it; the boorish technician from Aarau who cut up his meat and potatoes as if he were wielding an ax, loaded his fork like a shovel and thrust food into his mouth as if he were feeding a furnace; the two pimply adolescents who dared not lift their pale eyes from their plates; Helena, with her slit of a mouth, her Bourbon nose, her legs like columns, though not without her charm, dreaming of her German aviator, silent, desperately Nazi though she didn't avoid him for that (a little tenderness, even from a half-caste, might have saved her? She ended up in an S.S. harem, "proud," she wrote, "to be chosen to perpetuate the German race. I shall give the Führer an elite citizen")—he stared at them as at mollusks in an aquarium. Stuff yourselves, he thought. He dreamed of walking into this dining room with a revolver and without a word calmly shooting them down one by one, to punish them for stuffing themselves here instead of being in Smolensk, in Tobruk, in London, in Brazzaville, to punish them for the earnestness which permitted no doubt that they must perpetuate their life by eating, to punish them for the presumption that made them think they had the sacred right to live. Men were objects in the sidereal universe, worth no more than the cast-iron lampposts which, in the prescribed blackout, no longer lit up the Place Chauderon. He loathed these useless objects for the assurance which kept them from suffering from their absurdity.

So there was something wrong in his relations with other men (something broken which has not mended, for he startles them with the same look today—the idlers on the terraces of the Champs-Elysées, the hothouse plants in Saint-Germain-des-Près, the bonebreakers stuffing themselves with meat, the crimson faces on the Métro stinking of red wine, he hates the flabby efflorescence of human flesh, human meat, the digestive placidity, the burps and sighs); it is as if these relations, based on the affective links with a few who were close to him, with a place which might be called "mine" (geographical as much as social and historical), could extend to the rest of humanity starting from these links, and, once these were broken, had collapsed, deprived of their primordial instrument.

This explanation is valid not only for him. To sympathize with men, to regard them as more than a kind of gratuitous institution, you must doubtless be linked in friendship or love to some among them, you must live in complicity with the surrounding society—a complicity which keeps you from constantly questioning the habits, styles, "values" of others, a complicity based on the existence of a common experience of humanity, a common surface of contact with the world. A complicity (which is not necessarily complacency) on whose basis alone can an authentic solidarity be constructed.

But nothing linked him to the Vaudois of 1941. (Does anything more link him to the Parisians of 1956? That remains to be seen.) They looked prosperous, with firm flesh, singsong accents, big behinds sticking out under their jackets that seemed to squeeze them under the arms; they dawdled along in their well-scrubbed lives in the blue trolley buses, walked over the Grand Pont from the Place Saint-François (guarded at each corner by a temple of finance) to the Place Bel-Air in the shadow of its commercial skyscraper. Among their banks, their well-stocked stores, in their thick woolens and their cleanliness, they seemed to be living outside time, with comfortable salaries, a guaranteed future. "Think Swiss. . . . The Swiss housewife cooks by electricity. . . . Vaudois liberalism. . . ." Federal Councilor Wetter plows his field behind a team of three horses; Dr. Ruppaner leaves for the eastern front to tend the heroes of the Wehrmacht; Federal Councilor Pilet-Golaz sells Oerlikon guns to the Reich; General Guisan spends a half hour on horseback every morning. "Switzerland, faithful to its ideal of neutrality . . . unshakably loyal to the values of the Christian West . . . haven of peace and charity in this world at war . . . ," Switzerland produces clock movements, butter and potatoes,

Switzerland lets the German munitions trains through the Gothard tunnel, fires its D.C.A. shells beside the R.A.F. bombardiers and interns French Army deserters in work camps where they contribute to the landowners' prosperity.

Switzerland does not exist. He took a long time to find this out. Switzerland was watches, gold-stuffed bank vaults, precision machinery, postcard landscapes; it mobilized its shabby myths, its reform theologians, its brawny peasants to convince itself of its existence, but it did not succeed. Like Austria before 1938, it admired itself in its postcards, its pompous speeches, dug up its dead and chewed over its history, but its attempt at self-hypnotism bogged down in the placidity of a people sitting on six years of food and fuel stocks, a people who had nothing to defend but their comforts, who know that "neutrality" toward the Reich and the Allies was a joke, that official Helvetia would always and inevitably find itself the accomplice of the stronger. I did not understand that this "common experience of humanity," this "common surface of contact with the world" which I lacked was also lacking in the Swiss of my generation; this country was a no man's land abandoned by the hopes and fears of the rest of the world; its historical reality was its historical nullity, it exiled its inhabitants from history and immured them in comfort and security as in a prison. The situation of Swiss youth, as desperate as my own (though on another level), offered no toe hold in history, their Swiss-being was the reality of their non-being and their national reality the reality of their historical exclusion. They could share only this exclusion and this despair, deride the verbiage of the official ideology to commune in contempt and resentment of their nation, and seek beyond its borders, with a determination and a seriousness I have never encountered elsewhere to the same degree, truths which remained fatally abstract and alien, for which they conceived nostalgic infatuations, which they cut into slivers in the course of interminable and sterile discussions.

For Swiss youth too, there was nothing to do. They could not have genius, they knew that. They were set apart, they watched history pass by as he used to watch the trains pull out. They were carried in tow by the exterior world, which did not penetrate here save in muffled echoes, they envied other nations their sufferings and their problems, real sufferings, and they could only trail after the thoughts, the decisions which these foreign problems provoked. They studiously read their Laforgue, discovered surrealism and Gide twenty years late; they spent, like Pierre, twenty laborious years bringing out a study of Dostoevski. Today there are perhaps five hundred of them who read *L'Observateur* the way other men read the Bible, who have violent arguments about Yankee colonialism in Latin America, about African nationalism, about the Chinese revolution, about New Orleans jazz. They feel that their thoughts have no weight, that they are doomed to be spectators or imitators, to have only an opinion about everything, and that this opinion matters so little; the opinion of the stupidest Frenchman, Russian or American matters more. They too read, think, argue the way you pray: in the presence of the absolute, to summon up the absolute which for them is a historical reality that always belongs to other people, to have something to do, to do nothing. And yet, if they wanted to, they could turn the self-disgust in which they commune to action. What an exercise it would be to write a Marxist study of Swiss reality! International capitalism as a whole would be reflected in it, the world-wide influence of big concerns like Mestle, Ciba, Brown Boveri, Oerlikon. "Swiss liberalism" would come down from its ideological pedestal and reveal its export industries swollen with foreign capital planted in the four corners of the world. Paternalism, the inertia of bureaucratized syndicalism, the sclerosis of socialist thought, the impotence of Communism and the absence of any revolutionary outlook would be illuminated by the high professional qualification of a manpower working essentially for export, it too alienated in the laws of foreign markets and international finance—a manpower for which it simply has no meaning to claim the ownership of the means of production, since these means of production do not serve to satisfy indigenous needs, since they constitute wealth only when minted by export-import and public-relations specialists, since Swiss prosperity rests on investment and loans abroad of capital which has also come from abroad seeking sanctuary in the vaults of Swiss banks. Nationalize all this? First you would have to nationalize Wall Street and the City, start the revolution in France and Italy, constitute the Soviet States of Europe, to which the Swiss would allot four administrative cantons (and not a Federated Republic, for with its value as a refuge it would lose its national reality). A fascinating undertaking, stamped with the same sterility as this tedious country, since it ends up with the demonstration that there is really nothing to do and that, when you are Swiss, you must wait until the world has changed to change something at home; you must wait for salvation from without, impotent, reduced to stirring up thoughts which are only thoughts.

They felt this curse of being Swiss. They had at their disposal the most highly perfected instruments in the world—libraries, famous universities, modern hospitals, engineers, doctors, research facilities and equipment envied by the rest of the world; their borders were open to the intellectual production of every country. And all this abundance shriveled between their fingers, useless, good for nothing but making money, custard pies, comfort for four million lives for whom life had no meaning. Condemned to see humanity from outside, they could encounter it only by invoking an abstract humanitarianism, rejecting the historical density of human reality in the name of a bleating idealism: the Red Cross, Children's Aid, Mother's Day. From the reality of struggle they derived only the ideas it had provoked in others, and their philosophers (staring at the ceiling of the amphitheater, their voices toneless, bodies scraggly) analyzed these ideas which had become general and abstract, confronting them, rejecting them one by one in the name of the timeless truths of Plato or Descartes.

The best rebelled, but their rebellion was hopeless. They knew it; either it stopped short or it poured out as literature, and it was with literature that they ended up when they had not drowned their despair in the sour white wine that ruined their livers, or in the routines of their professions. A secret literature, rarely published. A's hermetic poems—A was a navvy's son, sent to the university on a scholarship, who began annihilating the universe with Mallarmé before corroding it with Prévert, then setting it on fire with the Workers' Party, ending up as a professor. B's secret poetry—B was a derided bastard who began with a Vaudois version of Nazism, before turning to Ponge, to Stalin, then to Sartre, ending up as an official writing in a flamboyant style once a month for a bulletin read by some hundreds of solitary amateurs. Poetry of solitude, of impossible love, of despair, of the starry sky for Jean-Marie and for dozens of others who sang their nullity or gravely, in tiny sects, debated utopian socialism and French policy in North Africa. Some went to Germany because they saw in Nazism a great, purifying wind of barbarism which would wrench them from stagnation and permit them to encounter history; and some left at night to join the maquis in Savoy and were ashamed to admit when they came back that they had found nothing or that they had been laughed home; and some smuggled gold for love of danger; there were painters who on rarely sold canvases tried to open windows on the universe or more simply to break the glass of the one that was imprisoning them; and finally there were those who remained in the Workers' Party from resentment of this stifling system whose dream of human brotherhood remained without any effect on their condition.

They were all exiles, abstract and arrogant because their situation offered them no means of communication with either the world outside or the core of the Swiss collectivity that was swathed in lifeless traditions, casting each man back into his solitude within a supercilious conformism.

If he had thought of this then, he might have liked these men, who were somewhat in the same boat as himself. But they were not thinking of this either; the situation they opposed so noisily remained the matter of their consciousness and was not grasped in any clear formulation. He did not know he might have transcended his own misery by sympathizing with that of others and by explaining the latter's causes to them. He was too full of his own woes, chewing them over and over, making everyone he met responsible for them.

"Date of entry into Switzerland? Proof of resources? Validity of passport? Military status? Purpose of visit?" He stared timidly at the bald, gray-eyed immigration official who repeated the same questions every three months, then disappeared with his dossier into the chief's office. Verdict? You will be given a visa. Three months more. Three months' reprieve. Behind the chief's padded door was a god who would apply his rubber stamp—"Granted" or "Refused." And above the cantonal chief of police came the Federal Chief of Police, and above him, at the top, the Chief of the Federal Department of Justice and Police. Justice and Police—you had to be Swiss to think up an association like that. He watched the official's gray eyes, and he felt guilty. The eyes were indecipherable, perhaps a trifle ironic, and he thought he could read in them what Peyer had told him over and over: "Play it soft, my boy. You're being tolerated here. As long as your German passport is renewed you'll be kept on; you're under the Reich's protection. But we know how far we can depend on the Reich's protection in your case. You're half Jewish, aren't you? You can't study in Germany. So you came to hide here. Nice that Switzerland exists. But you don't like us. Well, we don't like you either. There are millions of guys like you. They say they'd like to come here for three months, but all they can think of is how to stay. And you think we can keep them all? You think we'll keep you when the Reich tells you to go

back? And they *will* call you back—you too. For the moment
you're in the Ersatz Reserve Three n.z.v. N.z.v.—that means polit-
ically suspect. So you won't want to go back when they call you.
I can see it all—one of these days you'll ask for right of asylum.
Only that won't work, for you. You're not a Jew, are you? Your
parents are still in Germany, aren't they? You've been granted a
passport? Then you're not a refugee. They're keeping an eye on
you. I suppose you'll hide and then come and find us after the passport expires—a *fait accompli*. But we weren't born yesterday. You
won't get away with it. We'll come and get you some night, two
cops and a cattle truck, and bang, the frontier. Alien passbook.
Temporary visit." He looked into the gray eyes, the gray eyes
looked at him. Behind the padded door, the chief sent out signals.
Green light. Red light. White light. Go sit down, sir, you'll be
called. Silence. The usher's shoes creak. Identity card? Your appointment notice? Without an appointment notice, I can't do a
thing for you, sir. The gray old man glances around him; no one
comes to his support. Every man for himself here. Under the usher's
impassive eyes, they shrink down in their seats. Guilty. A perfumed lady comes in with a dog, whispers in the usher's ear. White
light. Green light. Please come with me, madame. The shoes creak,
the padded door opens on pale-blue smoke. The chief receives the
lady and the dog. Impassive stare of the usher wandering slowly up
and down the row of aliens. "Try and make a fuss," the eyes seem
to say. "No. You're afraid to. Good." Then down to his register
again. There is a law for each of you; you will be judged according
to your file. You will not know what's in the file. Nor the law. You
will testify all the same.

"Origin?"

He testifies, "Austria."

"You mean Germany."

Badly testified. The gray eyes examine him. "Austria has no
juridical existence. Do you intend to return to Germany?"

He squirms. If only he knew what was in the dossier. He tries to reason it out quickly. If I say no, I admit I want to stay; they'll deport me. If I say yes, I'm declaring myself a Nazi. They'll suspect me, but will they deport me?

"Yes," he says.

"When?"

"After the autumn exams. In October."

Something is written on the form. What? "Three months extension." The form is hidden beneath the ringed hand. You will be judged according to the file. First the chief; then the Department of Justice and Police. Testify. There is a law for each of you. For perfumed women with dogs, and for the others. The law is without appeal. Yes, there is an appeal in the marble bank: ten brown thousand-franc notes. Leave ten brown thousand-franc notes and the Helvetian Confederation will take you under its protection. Justice and Police. Rich communes and poor communes. The Swiss law says the poor are to be maintained by their commune. An indigent alien must not fall to the maintenance of his commune. The indigent remains an alien. Ten thousand-franc notes will soften the communes' hearts. The rich alien will be a peaceful citizen. Look for a poor commune; five thousand francs are enough to soften its heart. Then you have a ten-years visa. If you're not deported the day before the tenth year is up.

Two days a week a policeman follows him. It is forbidden to travel without authorization. The German consul looks at him banteringly and salutes, his hand raised. "*Heil* Hitler! Three months' reprieve. We don't know if we can renew your passport after that. Why don't you go back to Germany? Studies? Study, my boy. We understand each other."

The Germans have their police and their friendly informers too. "The enemy is listening," the signs said. That was it. The enemy was everywhere, he was surrounded by enemies, he was being watched, he was under suspicion, he turned around in the street to see if he was being followed. Do those eyes belong to the policeman who will put handcuffs on him and take him to the border? Undesirable. Under suspicion, undesirable, supernumerary, useless mouth; pursued like an escaped criminal, guilty in the eyes of all the police of the world; starting when someone whispers behind him in class, feeling the back of his neck shrink, avoiding all contacts for more than a year, regarding with resentment, envy and abject self-pity the groups that formed at the university, the couples flirting during class, telling himself, "They have a right to. They're where they belong, safe, with a future. You're eating their bread, they don't want anything to do with you. Dirty foreigner, *boche, Jude,* why should they want you around?" And, repeating this, feeling his old and ignominious desire to cry rising in his throat, the desire of the boy beaten up by his schoolmate, the lost puppy, the child scolded by his mother. He knew he was exaggerating; no one here dreamed of persecuting him, these people paid no attention to the Nuremberg laws or whether he ate their bread; anyone else in his place (his mother, for instance) would have tried to "make connections," but as a matter of fact this situation fit him like a glove—only too happy to be able to tell himself he was persecuted, suspected by all these police, despised and rejected by the whole world, merely a hole in the hostile universe.

This lasted more than a year. Not a single person to talk to. Dreams of persecution; supposed executioners imagined everywhere; the desire to become the victim he imagined himself. The hunger he inflicted on himself to save 140 of the 340 francs a month sent from Vienna (for how much longer?). The sleep he refused in order to read Gide, Ruyer, Broglie, psychoanalysts, characterologists (to be done with the human, to put each man in a characterological and typological pigeonhole, to pin him down like a dead butterfly, since he could not knock him down, to rid himself of these persecuting stares by reducing them to biochemical reactions, to escape the human realm into the sidereal universe).

The disciplines of the engineers' school (chemistry division) where he was officially registered because it was the only diploma recognized abroad (neither letters nor medicine were accredited) but also because he could exploit this practical consideration to mortify himself—until he no longer knew if he had chosen chemistry because They refused him the right to do anything else, or to do the opposite of what he liked, or to feel guilty for hating studies for which first his parents and later a philanthropic couple sent him an allowance soon reduced to 200 francs a month (out of which he had to save sixty for tuition and laboratory fees). An objective situation immediately exploited to victimize himself, the constant thought of suicide, and several months' accumulation of chloroform stolen from the lab with which he sometimes anaesthetized himself in the evening, supposedly to fall asleep, actually hoping he might not wake up again, or that he might catch pneumonia or a cardiac syncope.

He had reached this point by '42 when, moving out of the family pension into a little room without meals, he turned rationing and poverty into another means of mortification, imposing a regime of Maggi cubes and oatmeal at noon (plus a carrot or a tomato), a pint of milk, 225 grams of black bread and forty grams of cheese at night, giving away his meat and fat coupons (or trading them for bread), and glorying in the fact that he could feed himself for less than sixty francs a month, that he weighed only 117 pounds, his face looking rather impressive, he thought, emaciated and somber. He meshed in so well with his objective situation that he no longer distinguished what corresponded to practical necessities in his behavior from what resulted from his taste for mortification; what he refused because of lack of money from what he refused "because you're no good and good things are not for you"; to what degree the world was the totality of what was refused him and to what degree it was the totality of what he refused himself, a knife he turned voluptuously in his own flesh, an objective exclusion he interiorized in order to exclude himself. There was a real objective malediction, but instead of developing it, interiorizing it, choosing himself as cursed and excluded by humanity, he could, like C (a Berlin half-caste whose mother was in America), have grown a little mustache, worn striped bow ties, assumed a knowing look and prepared himself for a career as an industrial chemist ("Think how valuable they'll be after the war!"), or, like D, an Italo-Turk, have dissolved the world into odors, thrusting his huge, voluptuous nose into the necks of bottles, deciding that Switzerland was a big stupid cow for him to milk, a matter of passing the time until, having sniffed and made love all he wanted, he could become a great perfume tycoon, sending great aphrodisiac gusts around the world and using his millions to ride in an Alfa-Romeo, to promote some explosive enterprise (dynamite for anarchists, subversive publications or Communist night school, he hadn't yet decided).

D, C—they intended, in their fashion, to appropriate the world, to be smarter than other people, to prove they couldn't be kept down; they regarded their exile as a joke, a temporary condition, they adapted themselves to a situation in which he regressed to his infantile masochism in order to conform to complacently magnified prohibitions. Of the same social origin, what was so different about them? This in particular: they were spoiled children, persuaded since infancy by the adoration their mothers showered upon them that they had rights (this was obvious from the way E, grasping his fork, speared his food with authority, broke the lumps of sugar for his coffee, and—away, useless object!—set noisily down his cup in his saucer when he was through), that the world was there for them to make use of, while he had been convinced by his mother that whatever anyone gave him was the result of an undeserved generosity (". . . all I've done for you, and that's the way you thank me") and that he had a debt to others which he could never repay, a guilt from which nothing could redeem him.

This, at least, is what those first years of solitude and mortifica-

tion were good for: to provide him occasions to push his complexes
to their limit, to descend as deep as he could into the consciousness
of his guilt and his nullity, permitting him to grasp not the origin
of his attitude in his complexes but, in the empirical situation of
which they have made him aware, certain fundamental aspects of
the human condition, such as:

—that each consciousness is alone in its own eyes;

—that *what is* is the site of an infinity of possible meanings, all
equally unjustifiable and gratuitous, and has no meaning in itself
save that of not having one;

—that this truth—that being has no meaning which is not gratuitous and that every vision of the world is both unjustifiable and true
—has no special privilege, since it, too, is one truth among others,
stamped with relativity and guilt.

From these primary truths, one can derive an infinite number of
consequences. The one he derived is significant of his basic attitude and of his situation at the time:

—Each consciousness is a nothing colliding with the plenitude
of being; logically, it should annihilate itself in its own nothingness
in order to permit being to be. Yet it cannot annihilate itself, for
even its efforts to be the nothing which it is perpetuate it as consciousness, oppose it to being with a dramatic intensity, widening
its separation from being. Consequence: Existence is contradiction,
and to become conscious of this contradiction in no way permits its
resolution, but reveals consciousness to itself as a "metaphysical
fault" in the plenitude of being.

Moral: One must crucify oneself upon this fault with no hope of
expiating it save by death.

—Each consciousness has its own truth, but insofar as its truth
is necessarily exclusive of all other truths—that is, individual and
finite—it is also a fault. Total consciousness would include all
truths and yield to none. Yet such consciousness, far from sur-
mounting the guilt of its finitude, would raise it to its zenith, for

each consciousness claims to raise its truth to the absolute, and total consciousness, relativizing all truths and preferring none, rejects them all. In so doing, it raises to the absolute its particular truth (namely, that no truth is preferable in itself to any other). The latter must therefore return to the circle, renounce itself in its turn as a truth like any other. It can do so only by canceling itself out. Yet in canceling itself out it would also cancel out its original affirmation as to the equal truth and error of all truths and would leave intact the infinite diversity of individual truths, each tending toward the absolute. This total consciousness which would identify itself with total indifference (or with its own annihilation), is therefore both necessary and impossible. Its necessity satisfies the philosophical requirement. Its impossibility condemns philosophy to failure.

Moral: The only valid philosophy is the one which demonstrates its own impossibility and abolishes itself in silence. It is to this demonstration, in the form of an essay or a novel, that he has harnessed himself since '42, dreaming of demolishing everything in order to demolish, finally, this demolition itself, so that once everything is said, nothing would really have been said at all.

There are two kinds of commentary to make on this procedure, the one affecting its motivations, the other its reality (which will occasion new motivations in its turn).

Motivations

It will be fiendishly difficult to find a thread running through the overlapping "subjective" and "objective" motivations. However, here is one immediate impression: This crucified nihilism which delights in following the circles of its own contradictions reveals a consciousness in the situation. In other words, this nihilism claims to be timeless truth, and that already means two things:

1. Its thought has an ontological quality. It is interested in what is fundamental and irreducible: in essence. There is a historical

reason for this. This man's reality had fallen to pieces, he was divided against himself because the world was divided, and he could make no camp's truth his own—neither Judaic nor Christian, neither German nor Allied (in whose eyes, as neither victim nor enemy, he quite simply did not exist) nor Swiss. Ignored by history, he felt he was the world's victim, and this historical exclusion reminded him of his prehistoric situation as a child persecuted and threatened with abandonment. This is why he does not refer his nullity, his guilt and his exclusion to transitory historical events, but experiences them as a permanent and fundamental condition. He does not dream of protesting against this condition nor of changing it. He interiorizes it. It furnishes the themes of his thought. But this thought has an immediate signification: to destroy the unacceptable truths which oppose each other by seeking in their historicity a fundamental truth. By adhering to this truth he can (a) decide against all those who decide against him—in fact, against everyone, (b) decide in favor of himself against everyone by converting his own error into the only truth, (c) join the rest of humanity by disengaging what, in man, is irreducible. As a matter of fact:

a. If you are wrong in the eyes of every constituted group, you are excluded by humanity, and to decide against humanity is no use at all. It is merely a stylistic exercise, your demonstration of the universal error will be listened to by no one, you will be speaking in the void. More precisely, your words, assured of being heard by no one, addressing no one, are a religious invocation, an invocation of a suprareal absolute in whose eyes my absolute error would become right, would assume a meaning. It is a way of praying because no one can willingly suffer and be wrong for nothing, because the purely absurd (his absurd existence within eight equare yards of walls, his feeling of being immured by a motionless eternity where nothing ever happens, where nothing can ever be changed, a prisoner of life, so that the most reasonable thing to do would be to lie down on the floor and wait for death) is intolerable, and because there must be someone to accept this suffering, to give it a meaning and make it of some use. It is this someone whom philosophical thought (with the same justification as prayer) refers to; it addresses itself to "God," it calls God "total consciousness." It is for this consciousness, in behalf of this consciousness, that philosophical thought speaks, and speaking (writing, the only way of giving the unheard word a trace of objectivity) is the very act of conjuring up this absolute to which one dedicates oneself. To conjure up this absent presence is a way of short-circuiting all humanity, of speaking over its head, in its absence, and of absenting oneself (abstracting oneself) from it in a language alienated from humanity by being violently ground up until it has clots of nonmeaning and silence within it—in short, by making language serve the annihilation of the very humanity which it manifests. Which is to say that such language is poetic. Claiming to communicate nothing save the impossibility of communication, knowing itself to be useless, it is (even if it takes the form of the digression and the antinovel—that is, an appearance of prose) a trap laid for the world; apparently reasonable, this speech begins by seizing human reality in its snares in order to talk about them, but its discourse ultimately collapses into silence, nothing has been said. Thus the world is reborn from the annihilation of thought as unthinkable and unusable. In one sense, everything has been destroyed, and in another sense nothing has happened except nothing. The thinker has produced the verbal monument of destruction; he has recreated his own drama on paper; all he can do now is begin again.

b. By raising his error to the rank of the only truth, he took his revenge on all (everyone, in fact) who doomed him to silence and nullity. But this truth is not practical, it is poetic. It declares that error is universal and that he himself, in proclaiming it, in no way escapes it. It manifests the error of all truth and the failure or vanity of every undertaking—the misery of consciousness. The historically miserable consciousness deepens its historical misery by perceiving in it the sign of consciousness' ontological misery. It glories in this misery, assumes consciousness of it as the sign of its greatest lucidity; takes credit for it and contemptuously goes out to do battle with the complacent fools who conceal the consciousness of their wretchedness. Thus, thanks to the discovery of the essential misery of consciousness, historical misery becomes, for the concretely miserable consciousness, the instrument and sign of its election; because it is the most miserable, it is the most conscious. Despairing of conquering its misery, it *chooses* it, attributes value to it. This is why it must fail and suffer even in its demonstration of universal misery and error; this demonstration must not succeed, otherwise consciousness would emerge from its misery and nullity by having accomplished at least that much which was "positive" to lodge in. It will therefore demolish this demonstration by showing its vanity, by accusing itself of pride, and by proclaiming that the truth it has just expressed is itself impure; that this self-accusation also participates in the pride it denounces; that philosophy, truth and authenticity are impossible and misery not to be escaped.

c. In so doing, the miserable consciousness has the satisfaction of affirming something which seems valid to it, which prevents anyone else from speaking, wrings cries of admiration from some, and permits him to incarnate consciousness, once admitted to the sanctuary of libraries, in its abstract universal essence, consciousness made book and man, soaring above individual concrete consciousness and proposing itself as an appeal to their essential vocation—that is, as value. But this is a task which is not at all easy. This excluded and ignored consciousness can encounter humanity—that is, a form of universality—only by continually reducing itself to a kind of "final simplicity," by raising itself above its contingency (above the form and the concrete causes of its misery), by eliminating what might be individual in its experience and its discourse in order to present itself as consciousness-in-general, impersonal and disincarnated. It will take advantage of its concrete nullity to make itself absolutely null, in order to be no one and nothing and, thanks to its extreme poverty, to gain extreme wealth; insofar as it is indeterminate, it will be both the negation and the abstract possibility of all determinations; insofar as it is no man in particular, it claims to contain the possibility of becoming all men and of subsuming, in the form of possibilities in suspension, all that is human.

Yet this attempt is doomed to failure: for it knows that the "last simplicity" cannot be "given" but must be constantly *performed,* without ever being achieved, by the refusal to be anything at all, by the indefinite contestation of all possible determinations, and that this refusal and this contestation are attitudes determined by contingent motivations—preferred attitudes which exclude all other possible attitudes and constitute the individuality of this consciousness. It must therefore interrogate and contest even its attitude of contestation and interrogation; in its project toward final nullity, this consciousness collides with its own existence as that which separates it from its universal essence. It can indicate universal essence only as the unrealizable value which shimmers on the horizon of its self-denunciations, which becomes the key to its failure and in the face of which attempt is failure. But it claims this failure as man's final truth and, in proclaiming it for itself, tries to drag all men down in its wreck.

2. The exile's isolation and nullity, reinforced by infantile masochism, the attitude of persecution he returns to on this occasion as to an old habit, pushing the experience of his condition to a metaphysical extreme—this radical despair, if you like, is the meaning his empirical condition assumes in the light of his original choice, and this despair, in a sense, is comfortable; the vanquished, the impotent victim are safe "at the bottom of the heap," nothing can happen to them, nothing more is asked of them, they have nothing to do. To love failure (and it is clear that he loved it) does not mean one does not suffer from it. And suffering talks drivel; it is the consciousness of nothingness (consciousness that what you

feel and want is an objective nothing colliding with the massiveness of being, rejected and rendered impossible by it, and with no reality logically) which spontaneously tends (lacking any object in which to love itself, to actualize itself, to realize itself) to produce itself as an object; it cries, dreams, and, by choice, writes; it creates literary objects in which it substitutes its own nothingness, raised to the status of being, for the reality which it destroys by this narcissistic promotion.

Yet, the activity of writing, initially a solution of despair, has its own unexpected weight (for after all it is an activity, and to re-create your own nothingness is, without your having desired it, to *create;* I'll come back to this shortly); and the systematization of the despair's counteruniverse of despair in literary digression is one way of engaging yourself in the world. This way will provoke new motivations; it discovers literature as a weapon and a power, the power to dismiss reality and to prefer oneself to it absolutely. It writes against the world in order to destroy it; it gives the means to hate the world and discovers its resentment against it at the same time that it makes it real.

You despise me? I cross you out with a stroke of my pen. Language is a weapon. Through it, I appropriate the body of all thought, and I hold you prisoner; if I manage to incarnate in it thoughts which owe you nothing and which stand of themselves, I have won. I escape your laws, I oppose my own to them, my own law which is their opposite and their refutation.

You hold me captive in your universe? I *assume* this captivity and fling it in your face; it suffices that I desire this exile you claim to impose upon me, that I enjoy the sufferings you inflict upon me. You claim to possess me by your contempt, but if I *want* you to despise me, I escape you; you do my will instead of imposing yours upon me. I transform my situation without changing anything in it, by deciding, after the fact, that it is the result of my will and glorying in it. I interiorize the law imposed upon me and, without producing anything save an inoperative will, a mere "movement of the soul," I set myself up as legislator of an already given order, which I permit to remain intact, whose canons I adopt. The power is yours provided the interior freedom is mine.

This attitude of arrogant and touchy defiance can be encountered historically among oppressed minority groups when, incapable of overcoming oppression and considering it as virtually immutable, they become aware of the fact that for and in relation to their oppressors, they are different: Negroes assuming their Negroness, Jews their Jewishness, children their infantilism, reinforce the difference imposed on them as an exclusion from the society of men and reverse it as a weapon against the latter. I am a Negro and it is by this Negroness that I escape you; you claim to dominate me by it; but now I invest myself with it, and this difference that you claim to impose upon me, from the moment that I assume it, you become impotent to destroy—it marks the limit of your power; you have excluded me, but if I *desire* this exclusion as the place to which I am entitled, I represent it to you as your impotence to integrate me. The Otherness you have conferred upon me I wrest from you; you claim I belong to you because of it? I teach you that because of it I no longer belong to you.

Thus the victim wrests the initiative of his exclusion from his oppressor and transfers it into the movement of his freedom, but of an "interior" freedom residing only in the consciousness of his nothingness, invulnerable because it is dependent on the order that rejects it and impotent against that order. Strange freedom, accomplice of what destroys it and at its peak in failure. In one sense, it is nothing; in another, it is a sovereign operation by which nothingness happens. For this slothful freedom, though it produces nothing, nevertheless functions, it is utterly occupied acting out—like a role whose rules it has invented—what it is forced to be. This imposed being which it receives from without and in which it cannot recognize itself as its product, which it cannot produce because it is already there as the negation of itself by another, it begins to produce as value, that is, as an obligation-to-be. Its functioning consists of wanting what is—that is, of putting the world in parentheses in order to pretend to re-create it, starting from nothing; it makes itself the nonsite of the world, the hole through which being trickles away, evaporates in appearance.

The bad faith of this attitude is patent. I loathe its touchy, vulnerable pride, the intense, aggressive expression of Jews or Negroes flaunting their Jewishness or Negroness as it has been defined by others; their stiff ostentation whose *voulue* arrogance reveals the inferiority they pretend not to suffer from. These men are failures; so they have been made, so they choose themselves, but because they cannot *live* their role, establish its value, settle into it comfortably, they force themselves to *act it out*. They create a defiant façade, concealing their need for humanity in order not to have to suffer from the impossibility of satisfying it.

And yet this attitude is something like the dawn of a morality. Because they do not have the material means to make themselves free, yet will not be enslaved to their objective image as fabricated by others, they claim the only material freedom left to them: to be what they are. They ostentatiously alienate themselves in their objectivity because that is the only way they can declare themselves to be subjects. But since they have not invented the norms to which they submit, since the objective image with which they invest themselves remains inevitably exterior to them and can be neither recognized nor experienced by them as their human reality, these men are ascetics. Intense, concentrated, self-centered, censoring their sensibility in order to admit only the man within it who conforms to the social canons, they undertake an exhausting reflexive labor to create for themselves what they cannot experience or even properly create (but only hesitantly provoke in other people's consciousness). This immense labor upon the self leads nowhere, produces no action by which one can establish oneself, and aims, ultimately, only at defeating the self. Yet in its very nonproductivity it produces something: itself. Not much; just this: a kind of detachment, an absence—that is, the consciousness of the self as a nonsite of being. Since I cannot be this role I am playing, I am nothing—save for this indefinite power of acting a part and assuming appearances.

When a man begins acting a part, even the part objectively assigned him by society, and this part, since it does not affect his original situation, remains invalid for him, furnishes in the most favorable eventualities only a discipline and in the least favorable only a mask beneath which his contradictions increase, then this man exposes himself to the discovery that his reality is not what he does and seems to be, but an activity aiming at making him seem something which he is not, at producing appearances. He exposes himself to the discovery that his authentic reality is his acting; and this discovery will all the more probably appear as the gap widens between the part he plays (whether he is required to play it by society or whether he assumes it *faute de mieux*) and the original situation he lives—all the more probably in that this part does not permit him to assume his effective relation with the world and its contradictions. Conversely, there are men who have no objective possibility of assuming their original relation to the world by coherent behavior: unfitted for everything, bastards, half-castes, men torn between the contradictory systems of behavior imposed upon them by a divided world, a divided family, an empirical reality having no common measure with their primordial engagement in the world. The latter will inevitably play a part. No socially consecrated behavior engages the totality of their being or transcends their contradictions, all behavior seems to lead nowhere; they constantly feel they are playing a part and that everyone else is acting —cheating.

For the Southern Negro or the Jew in a racist society, this discovery is not immediately accessible. The part he plays with dignity or pride is the only one he can play; the part his oppressors play is sedimented in formidably efficient order. These actors are kept from consciousness of the ludic character of their freedom by the rigor of the social decorum and by an existing order arranged to impose their role to the exclusion of all others. Their role, defined by social praxis, is as difficult to modify as the praxis itself, impossible to question without interrogating the entire social order. The impossibility of modifying my role, or of modifying it without losing my place or my human dignity at the heart of the social order, impedes the consciousness of its inauthenticity and its ludic character. This is why such consciousness is generally achieved by men who are incapable, because of their history and their individual contradictions, of "playing a part" and who therefore have nothing to lose by prosecuting an order which excludes them in any case.

But in whose name will they conduct this prosecution? If only they are Negroes, oppressed for racial stigmas, or Jews, persecuted by a society unable to realize its cohesion in other ways! Then their exclusion has a social and economic substratum, a historical dimension; their alienation is social and they can denounce this society in which they were born, this world which they produce as well as the citizens with rights, in the name of their own ideal right to recognition and social integration, in the name of their legitimate grievance against this society which refuses to be theirs. They would have a problem, this problem would be social, its particularity would connect with the universal, for their prosecution of this society would be conducted in the name of a society to be constructed whose agents they would already be—in the name of the possibility of this society's becoming really universal (that is, just) —and in whose preparation they would be united with all the other exploited men for whom man is still to be created. They would have, if you like, a "cause" and a hope. They could create an ideology for themselves; their struggle would determine man's value.

Lucky devils, he would have thought if he had thought at this period, to be a Negro in South Carolina, a Jew in Poland, a citizen of an occupied country, to be able to touch oppression with your hands and point to its mechanism and its causes, to know that they want your head and that by wanting your Jewish, Negro or Polish head they assume an absolute wrong whose punishment can be demanded of history. But he was neither Jew, Negro nor Pole, a member of no nation or class, oppressed by no particular society, excluded from no community in which he might have claimed membership. The roles were assigned, there was none for him. (Requests for employment sent to each of the Swiss chemical works were returned with "appreciation and regret." "Influence" was brought to bear on a manufacturer to accept him as an unpaid apprentice ["And don't forget to say thank you"] but the manufacturer retracted his offer after having said yes to the "influence." Lessons given at cut rates and clandestinely, articles written for half rates and unsigned.) The world created itself without him, he was excluded for no tangible reason, except that his mother had set him down in Switzerland in 1939 after the scuttling of Austria (where he could no longer even claim the integration anti-Semitism had refused him), that the Reich had expelled him from his nationality as insubordinate, that Switzerland had no reason to recognize him as her son—a kind of lost object, fallen from someone's pocket by accident, whom no one mistreated, whom no one wanted to take responsibility for because the owner was perhaps still in the vicinity and because no one could see what it would be good for anyway. Then whom could he revolt against (if not the Reich; but in the eyes of the Allies, he had no existence whatever, and they were so far away)? And with what cause? No individual or general wrong had been done him; on one side they had let him escape; on another he was tolerated; on the third, they were unaware of his existence. No role was assigned him, not even that of a pariah. And if, with Switzerland for horizon, he had gradually discovered a human order in which everyone acts, deceives and steals, in whose name would

he have conducted a prosecution of that order? It is scarcely correct
to say that he was excluded from it; he had no right to integration,
even ideally, having no affinity with this community and no part in
its construction. No one defrauded him of anything. He had no
historical or social grievance, no individual "cause" that might connect with the universal. His grievance could only be absolute, and
his problem, and the solution to his problem. Absolute—that is,
metaphysical. Because he had nothing to gain from any constituted
group, had been neither excluded nor defrauded by any of them,
could be integrated into no society, even the best in the world, had
a share in no historical struggle, there was nothing in whose name
he could question the order that surrounded him. He had nothing
to reproach it for, save its existence.

Yes, here is where the final explanation lies. Since the wrong
done by Switzerland's hypocritical social order (as by Germany and
France) was absolute, the criticism he could make of it was necessarily absolute, therefore destructive. No community could repair
this wrong by a contribution of justice; the failure of all communities was their very particularity and their historicity, whatever they
were; the fact that every existing society is not a willed creation of
the mind but the development and the transformation of a body of
experience made up of innumerable products of past undertakings
—a great flabby body which you can animate only by assuming a
body which you either have or haven't, flesh which you never tear
yourself out of if you came into the world inside it, and which
you never incarnate yourself in if you were born outside it. The
defect of all societies, as of any undertaking, is to be incarnated, to
have its own style, themes and instruments that cannot be deduced
by reason, and which therefore cannot be assumed by reason.
Everything is always done "like this," "like that," permeated by the
smell of wine, vodka or beer, by historical and literary reminis-
cences, platform ties, local mythologies. Every human action, if you
prefer—and for him this was its absolute defect, what separated

him from it absolutely—was contingent, could not refer to an idea or to a distinct will and promoted only particular, fragmentary truths caught in the lime of historical density and unjustifiable a priori. Every truth was permeated by errors, comedies, lies and chance, and unless you were its accomplice by birth you could not belong to it. Everything that was, for him, was Other, the substance of the world was Evil.

You understand his nihilism now? It was the image of his situation. For him concrete, historical reality was always the absolute obstacle separating him from the others. He could join no group in its always individual and concrete tasks, for he had inherited the patrimony of no group. His situation resembled no other. He was not even persecuted and excluded by all communities and undertakings, for no one had bothered to exclude him, he had not even been granted a traitor's reality. Ignored, merely a dark, dry body floating in a closed world, with neither past nor place nor future, he was, in his utter nakedness, an abstract individual—his particularity was to have none. His particularity was his absence of particularity, his not belonging to the world of other people. Neither Jew nor German, nor Austrian, nor Swiss, nor French, nor refugee, nor friend, nor enemy, nor exploiter, nor exploited, he was nothing of all he had to define himself by. And being nothing of all this, he had to contest all this, to contest the Jewishness which rejected him among Aryans, the Aryans who rejected him among the Jews, the Germans who had committed national suicide, the French who despised him for being German *("Autrichien—autre chien")*, decadent and under suspicion, the Swiss who regarded him as the potential germ-bearer of a distant epidemic, to contest himself, finally, insofar as by his incapacity to be anything at all he was the obstacle which separated him from others and, by his perpetual contestation of others' particularity, the very source of this distance between himself and them. Yes, he had to contest everything, including his own contestation—the particularities because they are, in their contingency, the source of separation and division; and the contestation of the particularities because, in a world where everyone has a particularity, not to have one (to lay claim to the abstract universal) is to particularize oneself too.

Then what was it he wanted? He was not sure himself. He contested every particularity, not in order to obtain reparation or assert his rights—that is, not in the name of a particular, positive and historical purpose—but in the name of an absolute of abstract pity. He condemned banal and inauthentic existence ("All these people living because they've been born, shaped like jelly in the mold of their environment"), its rancid loyalties, its pride, its complacent needs and customs, and, by showing its contingency and absurdity, assumed an absolute superiority of contempt over it. He condemned concrete man in the name of an unrealizable abstract, conscious moreover that he himself fell within the scope of his condemnation. Everything that was himself was hateful. Here he joined all those other solitary and uprooted intellectuals, poets, theoreticians of the apocalypse—Aron, Sperber, Caillois, Abelio, Éliade, Malraux, Monnerot—who, incapable of participating in the struggles of their time, alien to its hopes, exiled from its history, either because they are bourgeois or because they belong nowhere, consider it from a sidereal viewpoint as an object and, being unable to pursue any objective with mankind, claim to raise themselves above it by prophesying the apocalypse; they want to terrify. Thereby they take revenge on this crawling humanity with which they cannot live (neither with the bourgeois, too stupid, nor with the Marxists, who do not offer leading roles in a period of revolutionary stagnation) and to which, by reason of their particular situation, nothing affectively links them save their resentment. *Déclassé* exiles, they take their revenge by doing their best to frighten the bourgeois, to whom they arrogantly announce their deserved catastrophes, and the Marxists, to whom they promise the guillotine or Siberia, or else by annihilating humanity in the name of Carnot's principle, by some mythological analysis or apocalyptic exegesis. All conduct their prosecution in the name of transhistorical and transhuman absolute. Prophets or poets, their language describes the uselessness of the world. They are solitaries without hope.

For him, the transhuman absolute assumed the figure of "total consciousness" (something like Hegel's "immutable"), and it was in the name of this consciousness essence, relieved of the contingency of existing and of the "metaphysical fault" of finitude, that he contested every particularity. I have showed he was doomed to this contestation by his factual situation. But he was not compelled to accord it value. Now, like the Negro flaunting his Negroness, he paraded his exile, wanted it to be absolute, claimed to derive it only from himself; instead of enduring it, he developed it on his own account by an unconditioned choice. He wanted himself to be the refusal of all particularities. He arrogantly refused everything that, in any way, was refused him (friendship, nations, society, history, the lives he would never live, expensive food, even food within his means), and by this proud and inoperative refusal he expected everything to be restored to him as an unused possibility—or, rather, as an ideal right; by this refusal of every luxury, every possibility, he declared an ideal right to them which he would not have deigned to take advantage of. He who was nothing and could be nothing turned his nakedness into wealth, his nullity into omnitude, his universal inferiority into an absolutely superior being.

This was one of the meanings which his fated contestation offered him. He had slowly discovered and developed this objective signification. It had first been indicated to him by others, by the anxiety and fear his questioning and destructive mind provoked in them (not understanding, at first, that he might inspire respect, that he who felt inferior to everyone might be considered superior to everyone, he finally plucked up his courage and acted this unexpected and Mephistophelian role that had been foisted on him), but it had not been original. The first meaning of his contestation, which the anxious admiration of an unexpected public enriched with an unforeseen signification, was that of an *ascesis;* to create a means of access toward others and pierce the barriers by which other people's particularities isolated him, he had to appeal to what was universal and authentic in them. But what was it? The question was vital; he decided that life was not worth living, unless he could answer it. But at the same time the answer seemed one that no man could give, for the universal could only be the negation of the particular; yet man exists as an individual, the mere fact of existing is a fall from grace, a separation and a fault in the universal. In consequence, existence was a fall, and man, like Plotinus' hypostases, "fell" from the One, and all attempts to reverse the fall were doomed.

He might have said with Kierkegaard, had he known his work, that "before God we are always guilty." But he had a horror of all religious terminology, which he considered an instrument for producing guilt, a war machine of each separate moralism. His atheism was limited to declaring that God, the universal, the immutable, did not exist, and that consequently the effort to achieve them was sterile. There was a moral to be drawn from this declaration, that guilt is not, as the mystic believes, a fault against an (abstract and nonexistent) universal, but that *mysticism itself,* in its contempt for finitude, and therefore for concrete men, *is a fault against the others who are really existing.* The exclusive love of God (or of the abstract universal) is guilty par excellence, since it renders itself guilty toward everyone by its contempt for human reality.

He had drawn this conclusion, but only to live it in laceration and without being able to renounce an ascetic morality. For if he favored a positive morality that would regard the universal as so much wind, he was no more than an individual among individuals toward whom he was absolutely in the wrong since he did not resemble them and could not join them at any point; a bundle of flesh battered about in the universe, he might as well sit down here and let himself die. If, on the contrary, he favored an ascetic morality, he found himself in the same boat with the rest, he was, like them, a wretched consciousness fallen from the universal; but if he was then just as incapable of joining them, at least he gave himself the sterile satisfaction of knowing his misery, of declaring it and, in declaring it, of drawing others with him in a common and irremediable fall from grace.

I should like to be able to say that he experienced the agony of being torn between these two moralities. I should like to be sure he unceasingly burned both ends of this candle, hating men in their inauthenticity and unable to forgive himself for this hatred, immediately blaming himself for it, mortifying himself in order to punish himself for it. But I cannot say this. He had, I think, no such high intention, and if in fact he burned both ends of the candle, if he did not definitely favor an ascetic morality, and sainthood, if in fact he was willing to be torn by the antagonism between these two moralities, it was for contingent reasons—for instance, because he had not the strength to despise everyone, to claim the consciousness of his misery as the sign of his election, and to declare himself prophetically in the right against everyone else; because, by virtue of his early masochist background, he still needed to conform to some order, to be persecuted, victimized and guilty. I think that was what kept him from taking his *ascesis* seriously, made him realize that his pursuit of the universal was necessarily a procedure accomplished in a particular and contingent way, that his arrogant contempt for others was, in its earnestness, at least as hateful as they were to him. I must therefore turn to psychology, must recognize that it was for contingent reasons—by virtue of a contingent choice reaching back into the marshes of childhood—that he could not embark upon an arrogant and mystical quest for the universal but saw in the contestation which he conducted against others another role he could merely play, which, in its contingent reality, he would still have to contest, because he who claims to be right against all other men is in the wrong toward them insofar as he has contempt for them and wrong *with* them insofar as he remains, like them, a finite and contingent existence.

Arrogant insistence on exile, indefinite contestation of the truths which remained alien to him, pursuit of the immutable which would afford him an absolute viewpoint over those truths, guilt for not being able to join the others on their own concrete grounds— it was by virtue of such heterogeneous motivations and not of an originally philosophical intention that he discovered a contradiction which was finally fruitful. A contradiction which originally, perhaps, was merely the "psychological" conflict between the obligation to contest everything and the nostalgia for an order which he could obey and which would unite him to other men within the truth—but which, experienced and interminably pondered, made him aware of the philosophical problem of the universal and the particular, the general contradiction of consciousness on the one hand being given as a fact and on the other wanting to derive only from itself. The philosophical project did not break like a storm in the blue sky, but as an attempt to subsume an individual contradiction by a fundamental contradiction and to justify his division-within-himself as a universally relevant insight into the human condition.

That, for him, was what the activity of writing was (writing anything at all, provided that an abstract thought was born under his pen and that the lived experience daily incarnated itself in ordinary words)—to manifest the world, in its contingency, as that which is desperately in excess; to question the inauthenticity of those (that is, of everyone) who act out the comedy of hope and deceive themselves about themselves by believing in some immediate redemption; then, having contested everything, to contest himself. A process starting with the concrete, dissolving it into abstractions, then turning back on itself in order to deny itself in its turn. The universal toward which it tended was, in the image of the very mass of the universe that crushed it, undifferentiated nothingness—nothing at all, not even itself. A dream of making itself a bomb annihilating everything by its explosion, including itself. A universal power of negation incarnated insofar as it refuses all incarnation; in sophisms, poetic contradiction, little prose poems which capsize meaning into nonsense, a speech into silence. And there was this too: He, who could be nothing and whose objective reality was always the reality of his exclusion and his solitude (Jew? yes-no; Austrian? yes-no; chemist? yes-no; etc.), he assumed his nullity as a refuge. To be nothing, invisible and indefinable, offering no surface to attack, taking refuge in the pure interiority of the negative; nothing but the faculty of pronouncing "the nonsite of every site." An ironist, really. His written thought constantly tried to bite its own tail, to step back from itself or to produce by interior monologue (a technique carefully studied and always disappointing) the image of the absence of all thought, the rustle of words evoking silence. A concerted enterprise of annihilation, tinged with self-punishment. To write was for him what flagellation is for the mystic: a way of raising himself above his particular existence by incarnating it in language, a vehicle of the universal, and then, because a spoken existence remains no less an existence, destroying again what has just been said. An interminable labor whose purpose is nothing, the immediate product always disappointing, but which, despite his intention, has a positive reality: A man starting out to be nothing and to say nothing learns to say many things not altogether commonplace, discovers that he can make himself understood and that thought, even when it tries to be the negation of everything, is a means of access to the universal, is universal itself provided it is coherent. It was in 1945, freed from the tedious chemistry courses by obtaining his diploma, that he began writing a treatise, already begun several times, in which he would make a systematic interrogation of every human attitude—re-creating and dismantling them, revealing their bad faith, then throwing them aside.

Reality

The goal, inevitably, was unrealized, but by seeking it he discovered this astonishing thing: *I exist*. That is, he was more than whatever he did and could do, even more than his being-for-others, since he could indefinitely undo what he did, act what he was not, deceive as to what he was.

He thought he was wrecked, that nothing he could do would be of any consequence (not even suicide, since he would not be there to experience it), that he was condemned to endure until death the tedium of life-on-earth-for-nothing, and that the best he could do was to annihilate his absurdity day after day by decanting himself into literature. Yet insofar as a man works, even without hoping for results, he exposes himself to surprises. Even when he thinks he is doing nothing but the "nothingness he is," by the mere fact of making his nullity objective, of creating precisely what he is as an aesthetic work, he learns two things: (1) he apprehends himself in the eyes of others as a determinate power possessing a certain efficacy; (2) he apprehends himself in his own eyes as a free creative function, free even toward his work. He discovers himself as a "general negativity."

"Reduced to the supreme poverty of power without an object," as Valéry says, he feels capable of no matter what, he is the absolute void. Everything seems possible for him at the same time and for that reason indifferent; his possibilities are always "no matter which," with one double limitation: everything is possible for him except that one thing should be possible for him to the exclusion of all others; or (the second aspect) he insists on nothing save that indifference which refuses to insist on anything. Nothing, save the nothing which he is and which constantly tries to coincide with himself in rejecting all determination—leaving it to the others as a slough from which he has withdrawn himself.

In this indifference (his room reduced to its minimum volume by black hangings; minimum utensils—one spoon, one knife, one bowl, one chair, one table, one secondhand bed; minimum of food; minimum of gestures, actions, acquaintances) there is also the least repose. It is an *ascesis*—continuous activity. It is (or wants to be) constantly vanquished despite all "temptations"—continuous creation, enormous energy expending itself for nothing, in order to produce nothing. This is the opposite of ataraxia. This man doomed to inaction, for whom the world is an impregnable fortress and whose impotence reduces him to the pure insipidity of being there, invests his pride and his freedom in the creation of nonbeing. An object discarded by history, stamped with every prohibition except the prohibition to live, remaining, like a plant, at the spot where he has fallen, his situation and even his life can be only endured. But since man defines himself by what he does, he sees his vocation in the activity of undoing, of destroying this inert thing that he is. Vocation is perhaps too much to say; destruction, love of nothingness is the objective meaning proposed to him by the logic of his situation. He verifies this law of existence: If you deprive a man of any possibility of declaring his freedom by actions, his freedom—since you cannot prevent him from being free—will manifest itself negatively. For it is impossible for him not to be free, and yet impossible to be free effectively. A futile contestation of a situation with no way out, his freedom is reduced to being the sterile negation of a factitiousness that cannot be transcended in any direction (that I am here, that the world is precisely such as it is). And since this negation cannot be inscribed in the real, cannot impose its stamp upon it by transforming it and by realizing itself in its action, it transcends itself as pure loss—it passes into the realm of the imaginary. It produces itself as sterile opposition to being, unable to be a fruitful opposition. It characterizes existence as a

dichotomy in which being—the absolute obstacle (that is, Evil)—
is everything which keeps freedom from declaring itself and in
which freedom, pure nothingness of all being, is identified with love
of nonbeing, with the affirmation of that which is not.*

He might have adopted Mallarmé's remarks on "the dreadful
sensation of eternity," on the "vain forms of matter"; might have
declared like Mallarmé, "I am perfectly dead"; or again, "In my
eyes, the only occupation for a self-respecting man is to stare at
the blue sky (*l'azur*) while dying of hunger." Too bad he never
bothered to study Mallarmé; he would certainly have taken him
apart—and himself, by the same token. He would have grasped
concretely what he already knew in the abstract: The poet, a nihilist
in the full sense of the word, cheats contemptibly. He describes for
others the horror of the world, his own wretchedness and solitude.
But he *wants* the world to be corrupted by Evil, he likes to describe
the Evil that corrupts himself. He establishes himself in his defeat
and converts it into his glory. He proclaims that man is great only
by his failures. He wants to fail admirably. He wants people to say
of him, "He suffered martyrdom and died because he was too pure,
too intransigent for his time."

This sad cheat constantly crucifies himself for the public. He
wants to recoup his real, historical, relative suffering by raising it
to the absolute, for all to see, in poems which bear witness to the
Impossibility of Man. He speaks from beyond the grave—*d'outre-
tombe*. He wants to be the fixed stare, laden with silent reproach, of
all the martyrs who were defeated by history yet whose unrealized
ideals persist (when anyone remembers them) like the presence,
beyond being and yet petrified by it, of the eternal Subject Value.†

---

* This is Mallarmé's "admirable lie": "Therefore I can deny all that exists
in order to affirm what does not. Admirable lie . . . I would witness the
spectacle of matter, of its being and, nevertheless, desperately hurling itself
into that Dream which it *knows does not* exist, proclaiming before the Nothing which is Truth these *glorious lies*."

† See in this regard *Saint Genêt*, pp. 178–83.

But what I most reproach this traitor for is that even while loudly proclaiming absolute Evil, he claims to take advantage of Evil. The whole world is Evil for him, because he has nothing to do with it; he therefore decides that the world will be useful to him, precisely insofar as it is useless, an absolute obstacle. He behaves like the saint who blesses his executioners and thanks God for his tortures; he *wants* the world to be the instrument of his failure and his martyrdom. The meaning of the universe in his eyes is to crush him so that he can utter his admirable groans. The world of Evil becomes the means of "glorious defeats." Then everything will be saved; Evil will have served to bring the value of man to fruition as a stubborn nothingness in the midst of being; the universe will be saved in all its horror for having produced the poet. Established in the imagination, contemplating himself through the eyes of a posterity which will curse his epoch, he re-creates this inacceptable life as his absolute purpose, sets out to desire it with a literary intent.

A facile, slothful solution which leaves everything as it was but which can nevertheless lead to a real way out if the writer can surrender himself and his literary prestige, can conceive of himself as the creative consciousness which he is in fact becoming, can make use of the dialectical resources he creates during his methodical search for a path—not in complacent descriptions of his misery. Methodical search for a path—he was far from thinking of that when, one winter day, he began writing in a torn notebook the first pages of "The Essay," determined that this time he would put everything into it, that he wouldn't go back to that novel of his, "Dead Life" (a description of despair and the vanity of life which he wanted to make monumental), before having shown that it is impossible to assume one's condition without cheating and that this demonstration itself was a kind of cheating.

There was no question of the "methodical search for a path," yet he was convinced that none existed; "The Essay" was merely an attempt at coherent thought. Yet to think coherently, even and particularly if you want to dismantle and demolish the absurdity and the failure of everything, you must be interested in everything, even out of hatred for everything; you must first understand the world you want to assassinate—and it is this passionate interest, passionate loathing for everything, which the essay "The Essay" will have achieved for him. When a man macerates for years in his masturbatory and metaphysicoascetic juice, it hardly matters whether he is interested in the world for "good" or for "bad" reasons; to be interested in them at all, even interested in cursing them, is already a first thread linking him to reality, and this thread, if he doesn't let it go, if he doesn't give up his demolition work, will perhaps become the path he was not even looking for but on which he will find himself traveling. Until the day when, discovering himself on a path in the world (though this day may never come and there is no certainty he will discover himself on the path if it does), he will consent to revise the motivations that led him there despite himself, so that finally— "Imagine, a path that I can take"—he can advance along it intentionally. But to advance along it intentionally he must revoke the very choice which led him along it despite himself.

He was ready neither to discover himself on a path nor to revoke his choice of despair. There were eighteen months to come before the first dawn of discovery, eighteen months which seemed an eternity to him because nothing indicated that he would ever emerge from them. He seemed, in fact, to be interminably sinking. Despair, moments of the terrible beauty of despair—like that December evening after spending the whole afternoon splitting logical hairs, dealing with the "illusions of the will," when he reached a point of such complication in his exposition, and yet of such vivid intensity of proof, that the verbal wall he was erecting suddenly collapsed and he saw himself, as if pierced by a bolt of lightning, chained to that illusory labor of abstraction and self-refusal; then he stood up, convinced of his capital discovery and that he would never manage to express that discovery and, in silent, self-coinciding anguish as he stood in front of the window, staring at the prostitutes' dolls in the window opposite, he smoked a cigarette butt that scorched his lungs. Like that Christmas Eve, in the soup of gray snow, watching all these people who had somewhere to go and who had money, the city, the world, the future, the law on their side, suddenly inventing the desire to do something he would remember and going into a bookstore full of people, carefully choosing, among the rare books, the two thickest and rarest volumes, and—feeling himself weak with fear, merely a scandalous object seized by the collar and handed over to the police, yet, in perfect opposition to this object, entirely the absolute subject residing in the complete negation of what he seemed to be—calmly putting first one book under his arm, then the other, walking across the shop, passing the cashier's counter and then behind it, slipping the volumes in his briefcase, and then, his briefcase stuffed with loot worth three hundred francs, leaving the store to sell his plunder down the street at a third of its value a few moments later. Moments in which he believed he was living—as if gathered up into an engrossing drama which lasted the space of several seconds without anything happening—the essential drama of consciousness. Like that summer night in his attic room in the Old Town, when he had leaned out the window before going to bed, suddenly seeing the deserted town, a heap of stones abandoned by a defunct humanity, and, on the sidewalk twenty yards below, the tangible possibility of his death, the intoxication of this possibility, while he had held his life in suspense, hesitating whether he should hold on or let go of the window frame. A moment in which he dissolved himself into anguish, convinced that this alone was authenticity, this instantaneous flash when everything was in question including the question itself suspended on the brink of suicide, that the rest of the time we only act out the comedy and fall from grace.

He called this the "neutral ethic of total refusal" ("neutral" for

the impossibility of choosing anything effectively, and "total refusal" for the contestation of all choices, refused by virtue of their
equal contingency), and it was an ethic of being: nothing, yet nothing aware of itself as a proud failure indifferent to everything, glit-
tering like a black diamond—what consciousness would be if it
coincided with itself as pure unqualified self-consciousness, omit-
ting, rejecting all being in its inessentiality.

Reality: The reality of this attitude was its hatred of everything
that determines man, and the poetic love of everything which is
the negation of that determination; the hatred of daily existence,
individual and inauthentic, and the love of the secret misery by
which (in the nostalgia for impossible elsewheres, dissatisfaction,
suffering) every man contests his particularity and reveals himself,
within his positive and objective reality, as a core of nonbeing, a
pure, solitary and miserable subject, escaping all attempts at realization—as failure. He began to probe for this essential and concealed
misery in everyone he met as their share of authentic universality,
by which alone he could communicate with them, assuming in their
eyes the disturbing figure of the kind of man who, seeing through
you, knows more about you than you know yourself, who—doctor,
psychoanalyst or chiromancer—possesses your truth that shines in
his eyes, fascinating but unrealizable. He began to hunt for souls
in misery; he considered the whores who lived across the street,
and not knowing how to talk to them, applied himself instead
to acting as midwife to their misery. This was a role that suited
him perfectly. And when he discovered a soul in pain and conscious of that pain, he felt a warm delight; when he fell in love,
it was with misery, the longing for the impossible.

With the boys he knew, it was the same thing. He had no friends,
because he frightened people, but his passion for other people's
miseries, his passion to understand others in order to put his finger
on the chink in the armor from which the miserable consciousness
ran won him many confidences. Boys came to him as to a kind of

confessor when they had problems, and he listened to them, explained their source and origin. For instance, that they were necessarily obsessed with the impossible because they were Swiss, that they were doomed to revolt, to literature or philosophy, because of their inacceptable condition, but that their revolt fed on what they were vainly and quite safely revolting against; that their great romantic loves would not batter down the walls of exile, solitude and mediocrity their Swiss reality had raised, but would merely offer a poetic evasion (an escape outside this society, in a locked room where they annihilated the social and historical order by making love *against it* with the pastor's daughter); that virtually nothing but literature or philosophy could open a window on the universal, but that this window was imaginary because thought would not batter down walls but nourished itself instead on its collisions against obstacles. Only this remained, to make misery conscious of itself, to resist the temptations of mediocre facility, and, by this gratuitous resistance, which, for the moment, had apparently no other purpose than itself, to maintain within this worm-eaten order—subsisting only by inertia and having lost faith in its ideological justifications—an entirely subjective demand for change which, on condition that it came first, would not let the objective occasion be lost when it presented itself.

This was a great deal of lucidity for a very little hope, and as his Swiss acquaintances grew older and found work (teaching, law and medicine) they began to accuse him of demolishing everything and offering nothing in return.

"I can't offer what our situation does not offer," he answered.

And Franck: "You stink intelligence the way some people stink under their arms."

And L: "You've found yourself—you write. That means you don't have to live. For you, everything is a pretext for intellectual speculation. Deep down inside, you don't give a damn."

Deep down inside, he didn't give a damn. It was easy enough

for him to advise against complacency in the given state of affairs, for, even had he wanted to, he couldn't have been satisfied here, alien as he was to this Swiss reality. He enjoyed the role of alien witness—other people's bad conscience. But as other people changed and integrated themselves, growing older, they stopped being as receptive to his lucidity and refused to share in his exile. They attributed to his psychological circumstances the vision of the world they had once agreed was objectively founded, that is, true, and which they now decided should be regarded from the perspective of psychological relativism. And there was a deeper misunderstanding: For these young bourgeois in the process of integration, the universal was *given,* they bathed in it as in the objective spirit of their society, and in order to join it all they had to do was surrender themselves to the promptings of the environmental conformism; for them the universal threatened engulfment in anonymity, and what was *not* given, what they could or had to conquer, was their individuality. It was by individualizing themselves, by making themselves distinct, that they conceived their freedom. For him, on the contrary, it was his individuality that was given; he was imprisoned by it as if by a certain impossibility of joining the others, as if by the others' propensity to consider him as "a case"; the universal was refused him, and it was by conquering it against his isolation, by transcending his particular problems, that he affirmed himself freely as transcendent. For him it was a matter of personal salvation to demolish psychological relativism and to establish an absolute hierarchy of attitudes—to erect a complete system in whose various echelons all values found their place. He had to reinvent everything human to justify not his own particular preferences but his refusal of this rotten and alien world, and the side he would take—after finishing this inventory of all values and received ideas—with full knowledge of the case, by virtue of universally valid criteria.

Such at least was the signification his work began to assume for him as he advanced upon it, advanced backward, recognizing the empty and artificial quality of his theoretical demonstrations and classifications, recognizing the sterility of an attempt consisting of the unfirm denunciation of attitudes arbitrarily grouped and which refused to fit into the original frame. And the recognition of the theoretical inadequacy of his framework, and of the fact that writing might become a road leading to other men, was doubtless furthered by three events occurring in the course of twelve crucial months: his meeting Morel; his breakup with L and, less decisively, with other people he was beginning to annoy; and his discovery of reality through journalism.

You

This happened early in June 1946. Morel had come to Switzerland for a lecture tour; and while waiting for "existentialism's pope," Swiss reviewers published various bitter-sweet opinions on the hopelessness of atheist existentialism and the depraving influence of this man Morel, who wallowed in nothingness, in the mud and the immorality of an "unrestricted liberty." The Swiss had filled the great hall of the Capitol movie house to overflowing at five o'clock in the afternoon in order to examine him, they had applauded French thought and the still fresh memory of the resistance, and that evening they had invited him to the "Friends of Art" (or something of that sort). And they invited me there too, because they wanted to show Morel that there were men right here in Switzerland who had read everything he had written. I suppose I was, in fact, the only one who had read everything. By the end of 1943 Morel had dethroned all the preceding divinities (Gide, Ruyer, Dostoevski, Valéry), I had steeped myself in *Being and Nothingness*, at first without understanding much of it, fascinated by the novelty and the complexity of its thought, then, by dint of persevering in my reading of this great object, infecting myself with it, adopting its terminology, raising it to the dignity of an encyclopedia which, since it treated everything, must have an answer to everything, and at last living in a universe having *Being and Nothingness* for its frontiers. Any experienced or observed reality was at once referred to such and such a page, where it was dealt with; Morel assumed the proportions of a demiurge; I imagined he had an answer for everything, since he announced that he had further answers in store, and I resented his keeping to himself the remainder of his thought, perhaps out of malice, to keep me on tenterhooks, or merely because he didn't care one way or the other; for I had the impression that he had thought of everything long before beginning to write a line, since in the first piece he had ever published ("The Transcendence of the Ego," 1936) he had already suggested the subjects he was still reserving, in *Being and Nothingness,* for a forthcoming work—pure reflection, authenticity, the "morality of reconciliation and salvation." In short, Morel was not a man at all, but God. (It was lucky, I tell myself now, I hadn't come across Hegel first! The German would have satisfied my craving for systematization and, conscientious as I was, I would have found an answer for everything in Hegel, would have shut myself up for years on end in the raving universe of his *Logic* with little chance of ever getting out, since first of all it took me three years before I escaped from the universe of failure constructed with the materials of *Being and Nothingness,* and second, Hegel was not the kind of man to jeopardize his whole system by questioning it or even admitting doubts, and third, I should never have been able, encountering Hegel, to realize he was a man and not God Himself.) Yet Morel was a man. This was a confusing discovery. He had turned up at the "Friends of Art"—short, heavy-set, looking somewhat disgusted by all these pundits who surrounded him and asked him academic questions about Heidegger and about subjects

explained many times over in *Being and Nothingness;* he was the
only man in the room who didn't look like a mummy, he gestured
as if to get some air, to dispel the intellectual fumes that concealed
the floor at his feet, knocking cigarette ashes on the professor's vest
and spilling wine on the judge's sleeve. He had a robust and oddly
concrete look, this Morel, occupying all the space around him with
his voluminous gestures (when he took a draw on his cigarette, he
lifted his entire arm to the height of his shoulder, so that it was
dangerous to come near him if you didn't want to get an elbow in
your neck) and hemming in the world as if he were weaving it by
his tireless gesticulation. Then, when he was sitting down, I leaped
for the chair next to him and there, for two or three hours, I asked
him questions, monopolizing Morel, more moved by his quality of
happy vitality (the life which he communicated to everything he
said or touched and which assumed a kind of evidence and truth),
by the real cigarette and the real glass of wine in his hands, than
by the familiar subjects we discussed. The evidence of all this,
which only Morel's person could communicate, was that this man
"loved life"—that is, loved work, resistance overcome, things and
people—that he had a horror of abstract ideas, that for him philosophy had to correspond to a search, a personal need, in order to
contain an ounce of truth, and that it was this search by which a
man tries to create a path for himself that interests him, and not
the fact that a man wrote or thought skillfully.

He discovered in Morel, for the first time in his life, the value of
generosity (or rather, generosity as a value): a way of wanting
to make men and things exist ("the passion to understand men," as
he was to write later in *Saint Genêt*), to discover at the heart of a
man's attitude a certain freedom at work, and to bring that freedom
to birth (or to help it be born) by discovering it. "And now, tell
me something about yourself"—a typical phrase with which Morel
received him eight days later in a Geneva bistro, granting him half
an hour of his attention and leaving him, despite a mutual incom-

prehension, the memory of the only true dialogue of his life, because everything, had there been time for it, could have been said and because the interlocutor's passionately comprehensive interest conferred for the first time on his own philosophical problems, and therefore on his person as well, a complete reality.

"All the same," Morel had said (and this was the point where they had ceased to understand each other), "you take up a certain amount of room on the earth's surface. What happens here concerns you too, doesn't it? You may think as you do in Switzerland, but if you had been in France, certainly you would have had to take part, to make a choice?"

"Gladly," I had said. "Which doesn't keep any choice made from being unjustifiable, so there's always a possibility of wondering, Why me in particular, here in particular, this in particular? And when you really wonder about that, you can't go on."

"But you exist none the less, and you necessarily make a choice, even in refusing to make a choice—even by abstention."

"I know," I said, "but that's not an argument. Because abstention is unjustifiable doesn't justify its contrary."

"You don't mean, though, that there's 'nothing to do'?"

"No. But since any choice is unjustifiable, how can I make one, knowing that?"

Morel thought for a moment. "I think you rather despise the concrete."

"Yes, I do," I answered.

"All the same, you're still something of an essentialist," he added.

I said yes again. And we stopped there. A man with a big black dog came in and Morel wanted to leave five francs tip. They told him not to. I was something of an essentialist and I despised the concrete. I wrote Morel a long letter which I did not send but in which I explained for the first time this scorn of the concrete: I was a man from nowhere for whom here or anywhere, this thing or that, made no difference, all meant the same, because no place was a "here" but only a "there or anywhere," because no work was actually his own but some task or other to which nothing neces- sarily bound him. Of course, *if* I had been French, I would have made a choice. I would have been forced to. Only I was neither French nor anything else, and I was forced to do nothing. All the commitments others had to make within relativity I had to make by an unconditioned option, without any necessity capable of mask- ing their contingency for me. I was not situated in relation to other people's undertakings. In the name of what would I commit myself? That was it, that was my problem. It admitted of no solution. I was a man in suspension, or sitting on a turntable with a circle of rails radiating out around me, which for others led somewhere, but not for me, I had no seat on any train. And so forth.

After which he left for Brussels to look for a job as engineer in the Belgian Congo. This was an attempt to commit suicide, but it failed. They did not accept him at the Upper Katanga mines. At La Forminière they did. It was 103 degrees in the shade in Brus- sels, an attic room with a dormer window cost fifty francs, and down below, in the Place du Midi, there was a fair and a honeyed voice that sang *"Un oiseau chante dans mon coeur"* from morning to night. The day before being accepted at La Forminière he had bought *Being and Nothingness* for L, because she was now his only link with the world, and he had written in it: "For L, what will have been truest for me, whatever I may say about it later."

He imagined the Congo as a uranium bath; he wanted to go there because it was unhealthy, in order to cut his chances of longevity by half and, after five years, to have made enough money to write for ten. And after five years of the Congo, he told himself, perhaps people would have forgotten that Austria was beaten and guilty and perhaps the ushers of the French Consulate would no longer slam the door in his face. At the offices of La Forminière, there were photographs of the Congo; a flat-nosed child was lying in his mother's arms; she was staring at him with bestial tenderness; half the child's face was eaten away by a canker, and in the background a palm tree was writhing in the heat; beneath it was a group of people—frozen, eternal. He would everlastingly have to wait for M. Merquell, and when M. Merquell came he would have to give him a letter from M. Tostet. M. Merquell had opened the letter. His fat, beringed hand hid itself beneath a pile of papers. When it reappeared, M. Merquell launched into an embarrassed little speech. "You understand," he said, "your case is extremely complicated. In the Congo, we take almost nothing but Americans any more."

He made a telephone call. He had white hair, a red face, his nose had been broken and a bone removed from it. "Personally," M. Merquell said, "I hate the Germans, you know. A race of barbarians. They should all be killed. All except the children, at least not the ones who can't speak yet. Are you Jewish?"

"My father is."

"Then you're Jewish. There's no reason for you to conceal it. I'm pro-Semitic, myself."

M. Merquell was sorry not to be able to do anything more for me than write a letter of recommendation to M. Jentgen; and M. Jentgen was sorry not to do anything more than write a letter to M. Berlage. M. Berlage was inclined to be optimistic and wrote a letter to M. van der Straaten. M. van de Straaten was on an indefinite leave of absence. Which was where the Congo venture ended. I returned to Lausanne, determined to "despise the concrete" no longer and to stop being "something of an essentialist." Passing through Paris (twelve hours authorized stopover) I bought *The Phenomenology of Mind.*

The second semester of 1946 was the great period. De Beauvoir brought out *The Ethics of Ambiguity,* Sartre *What Is Literature?,* Merleau-Ponty *The Phenomenology of Perception* and *The Yogi and the Proletariat* (alias *Humanism and Terror*), Jeanson *Sartre's Thought and the Moral Problem,* and Domarchi a Marxist article on money (in the *Revue Internationale*). Everything seemed possible, and because we felt we were making a new start, after seven years during which the old forms had burst open and theoretical intellectual activity had lost all sense of an object, thinking assumed a terribly important status. One could begin again as if at the zero point in practical affairs, and therefore in theory too; one could believe that theory would impose its imprint on practice provided it took action at top speed, or that a theory of money or a demonstration of the superiority of socialism would affect the course of history. Therefore one thought with zest, joyfully began the examination and redefinition of the most standard notions and controversies (for example, liberalism versus control; what is democracy? what is socialism?), asked questions which, normally, congealed or deliquescent societies prudently left alone, since in any case they can reach no effective conclusions, the chips already being down (for instance, what is justice? law? morality? the meaning of life?). One could say everything, and there was everything to say, and there was a public for every question because the facts had not determined any of them. (Five years later there would be neither public nor questions.)

Therefore, provided he managed to say something, writing—a gratuitous exercise of crucifixion—could become an action, and theoretical intelligence an element of reality instead of its sterile negation. Historical conjuncture accorded intellectual speculation an objective meaning, after having denied it any consequence for six years; it suddenly had an important quality, whatever one might say, and the stupidest writers all at once felt themselves called upon to be intelligent, to have something to say.

Historical conjuncture investing his plan to write, no matter how poeticoreligious it still was, with an objective meaning, it was the possibility of this meaning (to clarify the notions everyone was juggling, to prepare certain norms and criteria that might facilitate the choice of young men like himself, assailed by a multitude of possibilities, and permit them to orient themselves among opposing moralities) that he progressively discovered, thanks to the five works mentioned, thanks particularly to *What Is Literature?* and to Merleau-Ponty, whose rather empirical descriptions overturned his well-ordered universe by introducing into it their contingent nuances.

He felt himself spurred on by all these intellectual heavyweights, fearful lest before long everything would be said by them that he would like to have said himself, waking up at eleven in the morning obsessed by the image of Morel, who began to haunt his dreams, thickset and volatile, drawing on his cigarette, lifting his elbow, his round handwriting by this hour having already covered a pile of graph paper (in *Being and Nothingness* there was a mention somewhere of the "fresh vivacity of morning work"; and he had stolen from the publisher for whom he translated third-rate American novels a sheet from the second draft of *The Victors*), whereas, he himself hesitated listlessly on the threshold of a day which he must spend alone between four walls, squeezing out his two daily pages of dubious value after three in the afternoon, convinced others would have long since settled all the questions he tackled.

He wanted to enter literature as if it were a convent, to become not the peer (he did not feel worthy) but the honorable second of the protagonists of French thought, which for him represented universality and was comparable to nothing else except the Church because it expressed for him the Truth of the Present, dominated the historical controversy in the course of sacred conclaves, and because, in a general way, the intellectuals of French-speaking Switzerland lived with their eyes fixed on Paris as the Catholics did on Rome. Consigned to the sterility of provincialism, these intellec-

tuals considered Paris the capital of the mind and followed its dis-
putes, even the most Byzantine, with the same respect as that with
which the French Communist officials, made sterile and provincial
by the force of events, followed the sinister Zhdanovist controversy.

He was living focused on Paris and felt diminished by not being
there, writing as if he were and despising everything that did not
originate there. But this was nothing new.

The new element appeared one day in November 1946. He discovered that you could not live as if you did not exist, being both
pure mind and a man at the same time. And that it was perhaps
worth more to be a man, but that this was the most difficult thing
in the world. It was especially difficult because a man can realize
his own humanity only if a woman realizes hers (a woman and the
rest of the human beings around him, but particularly a woman),
because it is only for her that he can be a man totally.

I suppose I should set forth here a theory of the couple and of
the alienation of the couple in capitalist society, but this is precisely
what, among other things, I was doing at the time, thereby becoming an extremely irritating kind of man, a moralizer. The couple
cannot be a complete success, I used to say to L, unless each member desires the other's freedom more than anything else, but each
member cannot desire it concretely unless, through this individual
freedom, he desires a universal freedom—that is, if this freedom
has, in its singularity, a universal content, if we can collaborate in
view of a goal toward which each person transcends his cherished
ego; our separate freedoms cannot be desired concretely, cannot
encounter each other and acknowledge themselves except outside,
in the life of the world, through an object that serves them as an
emblem. Now, what have we, what can we do in common?

"You've found something," L said. "You write. What could I do
to help you with that?"

They saw each other on weekends, from Saturday afternoon to

Sunday evening. She made an hour's train trip to be with him, which made a fair hole in their budget (thirteen francs fifty per weekend, out of a monthly salary of two hundred and fifty francs, then three hundred, and then three hundred and fifty) and on the Saturday afternoon, after having looked into each other's eyes for five minutes, quite happy, and after having said "You," then "Are you all right?", then "What's new?", they had nothing else to tell each other. Then he said that their freedom must have a content, and she "What a pain you are." He would have liked her to do some writing, because her letters were often peculiarly good; she had tried and decided it wouldn't work. For a while she had thought of becoming a dressmaker, because she had a feeling for materials, for shapes and colors, but he told her that these were "small matters," aesthetic questions unaffected by morality, that the dressmaker was the accomplice of the bourgeoisie and in league with this class, since to have taste you had to have cash, and that it was unworthy to sell one's taste to wealthy people just because they had none themselves and thought you could buy anything.

"So, what do you want me to do?" L asked.

He answered that women were alienated by men and by androcratic society, and that she must free herself. How? He didn't have the least idea. ("Do something . . .") And besides, each human being must find his own way, and if he found hers for her, then it wouldn't be hers any more, since she would be doing something in order to please him.

After an hour of this sort of discussion, he felt he was wasting his time, and L collapsed in a corner of the bed and no longer said anything, looking vague and wretched, staring at him as if he were a picture whose evanescent meaning she was trying to discover, tasting the horrible solitude into which he was rejecting her once again. And he, confronted with this distant, mournful accusing glance: "You don't look very happy."

Then she grew angry because with him you always had to look

happy or else not happy, and she was sick of hearing all the time about how she was looking.

That night they went to the movies, and on Sunday they played chess, and when they separated for the week they felt defeated and melancholy.

It was on such an evening, when they were killing time in a café, that she asked him if he would be annoyed with her if she went to bed with another man. It was merely an idea, an experiment—just to see—which wouldn't come to anything, but she wanted to ask him first, all the same.

He told her that of course she was free, that it was only normal to want to experiment, that he wouldn't be angry with her, that in order to fulfill her womanhood she would doubtless have to sleep with any number of men. And he would be interested in hearing her impressions. He felt quite remote and rather generous, like a big brother, he had been very bored that day, but at the moment he felt a great abstract affection for her. As if that had been something he could still give her.

This leads me to believe that he had a possessive generosity. He spoke continually of other people's freedom (and liked to be asked to give advice) but on condition that others received their freedom from him. He would have liked to make them into his creatures, to produce them free and so that they derived, in their freedom, only from him. What he wrote of the adventurer could be applied to him: that, being unable to find himself in any concrete undertaking, contesting each in behalf of its share of failure, but nevertheless desiring his own freedom, he tries to incarnate this abstract freedom transcendentally projected as a pure value and a subjective requirement, to define it with superb indifference to all its possible concrete countenances, as though these were the appearances which it assumes but which he refuses to take seriously. The truth of this playful declension (namely, that freedom remains transcendent to its appearances, as the capacity to accord them to itself), he can make real only in others' eyes, and that is why the adventurer ends up as a writer—in order to recover the irrecoverable, to realize what action leaves unrealized. He drifts.

"You're drifting," L said.

His private concern was existence and freedom. He wanted to show other people how existence and freedom developed in their contingent aspect, were merely the verification of his general theory. He kept himself above them like essence above existence, the law above jurisprudence, and the state above the citizen. And he classified them. "You're an aesthete," he said to L, and to Franck, "You're a rebel." And he would explain to them the rank they occupied in the absolute hierarchy of attitudes. His relation to them was that of God to his creatures: a unilateral relation, in which he did not engage himself (he believed), making himself the witness of this relation as if he were not involved, analyzing the dialogue as it was spoken and constructing its theory. He acknowledged in others just enough freedom to admit the well-foundedness of his opinions, but not enough to contest them, for if they argued against him they were putting themselves in the wrong and he promptly demonstrated to them their bad faith or their resentment. ("How can you love someone when you know he is of bad faith?" Franck had asked.) But he immediately forgave them their rebellion or, worse still, sincerely affirmed that he had nothing to forgive, first (and this he actually said), because he didn't judge, understanding them too well for that, and because their mistake was not intended for him in particular, but for themselves, whom they were trying to mislead, and second (and this he did not say), because he was incapable of being angry with anyone, was too steeped in his own guilt and too conscious of the gift others made him by listening to him, to draw attention to *their* guilt.

I say "worse still" because his negation of others' defections toward him conferred a great nobility upon him in their eyes; they saw a generous forgiveness where in reality there was only indifference (it was not with him that they were involved, but only his ideas, and he, entrenched behind a wall of ideas, made himself actually absent from the terrain as an individual), and they felt unworthy confronted with such greatness of spirit. (Kay, reacting to the inhuman indifference of this negation of her own error, cried, "You can't just say it's nothing and act as if nothing had happened. Reproach me, blame me, get mad, at least show that it touches you." He drove her to despair by his way of reducing their personal conflicts to an aspect of conflict—"We're not talking about ideas, we're talking about you and me!"—and of being all the more detached and calm as she became more emotional; or of withholding from Kay a forgiveness she explicitly asked him for.

"Tell me you forgive me."

"But there's nothing to forgive."

"Yes there is. I was unfair."

"Well, it's over."

"Say you forgive me."

"Who am I to forgive you?"

Out of reach. Taking refuge in the realm of ideas, where all things are only their transparent reflection for the theoretical intellect, contingent illustrations of a general idea. I know that this is the most widespread philosophical attitude ("Philosophers have done nothing but interpret the world . . ."), the last development of aestheticism. In fact, the aesthete claims to justify the real by acting as if it were there only in order to annihilate itself (be annihilated) in beauty (in order to give birth to a poem, to a picture, to contemplative pleasure). And when the aesthetic "finalization" of the given can no longer be lived, or when the given does not lend itself to a livable aesthetic finalization, adapting itself to its object (or enlarging itself in order to absorb new regions), the aesthete substitutes the finalizing thought for the feeling and claims to make the world into a garden planted for and by the mind. He gives himself the satisfaction of seeing in the real *donnée* of general ideas only the confirmation of the latter. He explains what is by virtue of ideal abstractions which, in fact, have for their condition the existence of what is. Thus the philosopher by interpretation, as the aesthete by art, justifies what is and shows himself fundamentally a quietist— that is, a conservative; by interpreting what is, he demonstrates its "necessity" and permits himself the illusion of re-creating the world out of his ideas, whereas in reality he is only producing ideas which leave the world intact. Like the aesthete, he is a deserter from the real, to which he prefers the imaginary essence. His demonstrations are in fact always a posteriori (he lives, like Hegel, facing the past, establishing history's balance sheet and advancing backward) and retrospective (or retroactive), the only prospective philosophy, Marxism, offering itself as a denunciation of the philosophical atti- tude (and calling for perhaps still another philosophical clarifica- tion of its basis). Philosophy remains today the substitute for ac- tion of impotent thinkers (that is, thinkers incapable of effective action) who try to construct the world by means of thought, lack- ing the power to do so by action. It remains an aesthetic and reli- gious project.*

---

* In one sense, it will always remain aesthetic: It is the moment of reflec- tion by which the man of praxis, the historical man, "re-enters himself" and tries to seize the significance of action. And this seizure is to all intents and purposes always idealistic; it presents the subject as the unconditioned creator of significations and as the subject of history, whereas in fact he is always the object of history as well, inserted within it as an objective development whose meaning transcends his original intentions and whose significations, before having been created by him, were proposed to him by facts. Never- theless, what chance is there of humanizing the world and of inflecting its meaning, as far as possible, toward the "emancipation" of man, unless we attach history by thought as if it were our conscious work and unless we unreservedly ascribe it to freedom, in order to measure thereby the dis- crepancy which subsists between the real and the ideal—the degree of alienation? Marx himself did not fear this ascription, it was in fact the very basis of his critique: The world and the activity which produce it are and must be ascribable to man, and wherever this ascription does not correspond to a deliberate project, wherever it is possible only as an affirmation of right over fact, it brings to light (1) the alienation of freedom from its product; (2) an intention of alienation which exists as such in fact only by deceiving

Last development of aestheticism, the attitude of pure contemplation and disincarnated criticism drifting over his own relation with L. Above the battle, out of harm's way, until the day when L came in one November Saturday and, looking disturbed and overly playful, said, "That's it."

---

itself as to its own nature, and which its exposure contests and criticizes, for an intention that cannot be desired *as it is in reality* exposes itself in becoming conscious, and that is precisely why it is important to make it conscious, to present it to itself as subject, to call upon it to answer for its reality.

Philosophical reflection will therefore maintain all its rights in a Marxist society. But it will be only a moment of action in that society, integrated into action as a function of its constant criticism and readjustment. In capitalist society philosophical reflection cannot assume this function. If it criticizes the class of oppression, it is on condition that it cut itself off from or break with that class, for, unlike the revolutionary class, the class of oppression is not consciously engaged in the enterprise of building a human world. The criticism of this class will therefore be entirely negative, a summons to resign, since this class does not bear within itself the desire for its own emancipation but has produced this desire objectively only as its exterior negation, in the proletariat. Ineffectual, the criticism of a class which cannot be led by that criticism to renounce its own existence as a class is therefore perpetually tempted to take itself, in its ineffectuality, for its own goal, and to enjoy this state of affairs which it denounces; in fact, the latter offers to criticism the artistic possibility of laying claim to clairvoyance and the spirit of justice, of incarnating alone the humanist values in their ideal purity, and of harvesting from the very society it denounces the professorial functions and honors suitable to a distinguished mind. As for criticizing the action of the revolutionary class, in the hope of inflecting it in the "right direction," I hold that the philosopher would be unfitted to do so in a capitalist society and in a period of "class struggle," because (1) the revolutionary class is not yet sovereign, its action is still dominated by objective necessity much more than by a project of premeditated construction, and it is senseless to criticize an action dictated by objective conditions which cannot be ascribed to it but to the opposing class; (2) as long as the criticism comes from outside—that is, from the philosopher (who is bourgeois in any case and whose public is necessarily and particularly bourgeois)—it necessarily assumes the aspect of a class criticism weakening the cohesion, the discipline, the policy of the revolutionary party and will consequently be denounced by it; (3) since it is made from outside, this criticism is here again ineffectual, purely negative, and tempted to enjoy the superb solitude of the "spirit of justice," for it can in no way hope to influence the revolutionary party insofar as it remains outside it and thereby possesses neither its audience nor its confidence. If, on the other hand, the philosopher joins the Communist Party, he will realize at once both the political inopportunity of his criticism and its neces-

"What's it?"

"You know—I've slept with him."

There had been something else in his detachment and his possessive, abstract generosity. His attitude of pure contemplation was only an ethical exchange; he had a horror of asking anything for

---

sity but will not necessarily be better situated to render it effective, for (1) as a member of the party he will be committed to its discipline, and (2) as a bourgeois philosopher he will be the object of an understandable suspicion, which he will be able to dissipate only by giving pledges of discipline greater than other members', greater than will appear desirable to him for the efficacy of his constructive criticism.

His situation, whether outside or within the party, therefore remains unfortunate and manifests the objective fact that there is no place, in a class society, for a philosophy that is both good and effective. If he is unwilling to renounce either consciousness or efficacy, the philosopher can transcend the contradictions of his situation only by addressing himself to that thin fringe of the bourgeoisie which is more or less Marxist (but how many are there in France, where Hegel has only begun to be studied in the last fifteen years and where ignorance of Hegel makes most minds refractory to Marxism— also unknown in its philosophical basis, for Marx's most important texts, which are, I believe, also the most important texts of contemporary philosophy, have a current circulation of about four thousand), whose active sympathy is objectively necessary to the progress of the Communist Party. Therefore, to affect the party by means of the bourgeois Marxist fringe and on the other hand to deepen within the latter the influence of Marxism and of pro-Communist sympathy seems to me for the moment a possible procedure for the philosopher. But the effectiveness of this double and simultaneous contestation supposes a condition that is also double: (1) that there is an opportunity, even a remote one, for revolution—that is, that the revolutionary forces are objectively expanding—since this condition is necessary in order that (2) the Communist Party judges it important to preserve or to increase the progressivist fringe of the bourgeoisie, instead of turning in on itself and developing an ideological sclerosis, as it inevitably does in a period of stagnation or retreat of the revolutionary forces. Now, the first of these conditions has hitherto not appeared to be fulfilled (even if the objective presuppositions happen to be brought together, in fact) if the second condition is not also fulfilled at the right moment. There will not be an open, vital Communist Party without revolutionary opportunities, but the revolutionary opportunities will not become actual rather than potential if there is not a vital and open Communist Party.

That this procedure of a double and simultaneous contestation, whose concern for efficacity, moreover, contests the philosophic concern and vice versa, is not easy (not easy to know if and when and to what degree one does not attach enough or attaches too much importance to efficacity or to himself and he arranged matters so that he would never have to ask for anything. Originally this behavior was doubtless founded on his guilt complex. In his relations with others, he made himself into a self-effacing cipher (foreseeing the supposed requirements), for who was he to ask anyone else for something? Neither protected by

---

moral norms; if one puts too much confidence in the objective likelihood of a correction of errors and if one is therefore wrong to denounce the latter insufficiently, or if the contrary applies) the events of June 1956 make quite clear. The negative and complacent criticisms of both the party and the bourgeoisie, the "just" and the "leftist intellectuals," made a great show of triumphantly reproaching the other progressive intellectuals for not denouncing the Stalinist errors sooner and sufficiently; these "just" men believed that the Khrushchev report justified their having remained intransigent judges and entitled them now to be the only ones who had a right to speak, because they were the only ones who had always "seen what was going on" and unflaggingly criticized. Only, if this anti-Communist left had indeed criticized throughout, it was without any concern for effectiveness, but merely in order to feel justified and to be in the right against history. So if history (the autocriticism of the Communist Party) today confirms in part the criticism made by the intellectuals, it is in fact despite them and without their having any credit for it. For they are not interested in changing the course of history, but in incarnating against it certain eternal values. This is why, instead of rejoicing in the Communist Party's autocriticism and coming to its assistance, making themselves the mediators between the party and the revolutionary fringe of the bourgeoisie, they claim to see in the Communist autocriticism an additional reason for throwing discredit on the Communists "who were wrong all along" and to claim the monopoly of criticism. This is because in reality these distinguished minds feel their monopoly of "just" criticism threatened; if the Communist Party begins to denounce its own errors, what have they left to say? If their own previous criticisms are in part taken over by history, how can they still claim to uphold the cause of the true and the just *against* history? The only way for them to confirm the excellence of their pious intentions would be to help in their "historicization" now. But in order to do this they would have to give up wanting to be "just," and because they prefer the fine role of thinkers-above-the-battle to the efficacity of their thought and do not wish to give up this role, they apply themselves to demonstrating now (following *The Rebel*) that history is always bad and must always be opposed.

As for the progressive intellectuals who, out of their concern for efficacity, have hitherto toned down their criticisms, it is true that today they would have more influence over the fringe of the potential bourgeois sympathizers if they had criticized the party sooner and more openly. Yet had they done so, they would have been cut off from the party and their criticisms would have remained without effect. It is of no use having retrospectively been any order nor integrated, he was incapable of taking any of his desires seriously (of insisting on anything at all); confronted by someone else's desire, he yielded to it, it seemed natural to him to do so, since the other person believed in what he wanted—and also because to yield to someone else's taste was for him the only way of conforming (to an alien order). So by his attentive, self-effacing tolerance he appeared spineless and shifty, and indifferent too, since he never asked anyone for anything and let others be, pleasant enough when he was approached but never making the first step, never approaching anyone else. The objective consequence of this attitude was that he did not expose himself, always letting other people expose themselves more, in the solitude of demands without

---

right against history by oneself and too soon, for the important thing is not to be right in the absolute and before God, but to inflect history in the direction you want it to take. And in this regard, it can be more effective to say too little about it and to compromise oneself than to speak a great deal without result.

I shall have to return to this parenthesis later on, I believe. I interrupt it at the very point where interpretation should yield to the sketch of a plan of action, and that is why it still participates in the aestheticism mentioned above. It participates in it (1) by its interpretation of the intellectual's situation, by the justification it affords of his double contestation (which is perhaps not, after all, the best possible way out—that remains to be seen) and of the idealism and aestheticism of his position; (2) by the procedure of double contestation which I have just proposed and which, even if it be the best possible procedure objectively (and this too remains to be seen) tends to justify whatever taste and need I have for contestation. I am well aware that men capable of fulfilling the function which a given conjuncture proposes and requires (whether it be the case of a Quisling or that of a contester) are those who are subjectively prepared by a taste for this kind of function (by their "character," so to speak; Quisling surely dreamed of being Quisling long before history gave him an opportunity to do so, and that is why it was precisely he who discovered and seized this necessity—it corresponded to an a priori personal vocation in himself). But it is this a priori taste, too, which renders their affirmation of objective necessity suspect; they are too pleased that this necessity exists not to be under suspicion of having forced the interpretation of the facts and wantonly invented a necessity which was perhaps not so evident after all, and which they continue to proclaim when it has in fact disappeared. That is why the validity of the envisaged conduct remains to be seen.

reciprocity. He had received L, had let himself be attracted by her, without ever giving more than she asked, without the spontaneous impulse that might have made her feel he really wanted her. Did he want her? He didn't have the slightest idea, and that was his despair. She had exhausted herself for more than three months to obtain the slightest manifestation of reciprocity from him.

"Am I essential to you?" she had asked.

"Nothing is ever essential," he had said.

"Of course. But I think that for me . . . I think you're essential to me."

"You mean," he had philosophized, "you need to be essential to me."

"While you, obviously, are enough for yourself."

(And it had been the same thing afterwards with Kay. For weeks on end, after she had been turned out because of him and they had been living together in one room half filled by an enormous table, he came and went without saying a word, spending days over his papers and answering her in impatient monosyllables, while Kay, sick and knowing no one, not speaking a word of French, begged for a little of his time.

"You're enough for yourself," she said. "I'm no use to you at all. I make you waste your time."

He protested feebly. It was true that there was no room for anyone in particular in his life. No one in particular to whom he wanted to devote his life, because he did not count as an individual and therefore could not be concerned whether someone should grow attached to him as an individual. If he could hope to count, it was only by ideas that transcended his individuality; and if he could interest anyone, it was only so long as his ideas were at stake. To Kay, who would have let herself be cut into ribbons for him and who, one way or another [taking poison, marrying an old man, or becoming a nurse] would have destroyed herself if he had let her go, he had sent, in response to her questions, a dissertation on love and marriage: "You cannot give more than the other person is ready to receive. . . . You cannot commit yourself to someone for your whole life, unless by a purely formal and meaningless ceremony—because you cannot know in advance the circumstances which, in five, ten, or twenty years, will modify the meaning of your commitment and make it null and void. A commitment is valid only if you are free to confirm or revoke it. To negotiate for life is a formal and abstract gesture. That's what marriage is. Besides, could you swear that in twenty years you will still want to live with me?"

He must have grown remarkably thick-skinned to make use of such pretentious arguments at such a moment. She was trying to save their life together, he his philosophical point of honor. But she knew what she wanted, and he, although he accused her of living by false principles, knew only what he must want on principle. That is why, after long discussions, obliged to choose between Kay and principles, he discovered that the principles at stake were after all, from the moment that he was the only one to defend them, not so important, since they were now identified with his will as an individual quarreling with another will. He chose Kay over the principles, but ill-naturedly and without even realizing that she accepted for him—and without complaint—hunger and illness.)

He stared at L over a plate of saveloy vinaigrette, tried to "realize" she had been to bed with another man, and—as on every occasion when something happened to him which concerned him and which he could not keep himself from experiencing to the full, without the help of ideas and abstract principles, something that demanded of him some action or attitude that would affect the future—he escaped by means of aestheticism. He began to analyze what he was feeling or was going to feel ("You're going to behave like an ass and start suffering now"), what L must be feeling, and to compose a scene; to tell himself the present as if it had already occurred, to re-create it in his imagination, to recover himself as

its author (imaginary too, of course) in order to escape the intolerable intensity of actual experience. He was in fact living the scene,
the most perfect of all, in *Man's Fate,* where Kyo finds May again
after she has been to bed with a doctor from the hospital. ("He
wanted to so badly," she said.)

But he was not writing a novel now. Yet the temptation of making use of just this story in a novel, the complacency with which I
tell it, the attraction it holds for me do not derive only from the fact
that it is one of the few real incidents I have experienced, but
doubtless from the fact that I find gathered within it, as in an
archetypal situation, all the affective themes of my life. I am totally
concerned by it because totally challenged.

—Dismissed (but not right away); that is, excluded from the
community of men which was now confined to L. Yet he couldn't
complain of this exclusion. He had wanted it (abstractly, without
conviction) as he had always wanted, for years now, to rid himself
of everything that kept him in reality and forced him to exist instead
of merely thinking existence.

—Annulled, but by himself still more than by L. All that had
been necessary was that there should be something irreparable between them, that she should become for him, by that part of herself
which now had its truth in Someone Else, an independent freedom,
Someone Else herself, for him to feel dependent on her, wildly
dependent.

Of course, it was ordinary enough: You live for months or years
with a woman whom you take for granted more or less and who, by
virtue of a situation that seems quite settled, becomes a familiar and
rather tedious object. And the day this woman leaves you or "deceives" you, you discover you don't "know" her, or, rather, you
rediscover her autonomous existence, as during those first days together, and what is called her "mystery"—you realize that there is
a part of herself not adequate to her exterior as you know it, that her
look has a subjective underside, that for her the world and you your-

self exist with a taste and singular values you do not recognize.

But if he had merely rediscovered L's autonomy and subjectivity, it would perhaps have been excusable. Yet it was not. He knew that if she came back to him as before she would bore him as before, and that the value she now had for him derived from the fact that "before" had become the impossible. He loved the impossible for its own sake (as he had once loved A), he wanted to retain L's old reality for him because that reality, transcended and denied by her, was no longer anything but unreality, a being which she had been for him and which, objectively, was now nothing but nonbeing, the error which he insisted on maintaining against the evidence and for love of which he thrust himself deeper into nonbeing: a love of the impossible, a longing for nonbeing, perseverance in error, hours spent torturing himself by imagining her with someone else in order to realize (but this was impossible, and such impossibility comprised the irritating evanescence of suffering) the nonbeing of what she was for him and what he himself, as love of this nonbeing which he was henceforth alone to maintain in being, was—pure nothingness, existence of error.

To liquidate L would have been to liquidate his own aestheticism, his love of failure and suffering, his poetical attitude, his masochism, his choice of nullity, all suddenly reactivated, in which he fell back as into an old rut and in which nothing, this time, justified his falling back, for he himself had desired and provoked the occasion of his backsliding, persuaded that it would be quite easy for him to do without L, but when the opportunity presented itself he had not been able to resist the temptation, he had insisted on experiencing it as his failure and on thrusting himself voluptuously within it. Not right away, moreover. He had let the trap be set at some length, offering L his friendship (sincerely), accepting hers, constructing with her, starting from their enhanced independence, a more authentic dialogue.

Had they really set out to liquidate what was false between them and to build, starting from their unsettled love (and a love made impossible by their mutual defection—L's because she had adored him as a god, setting him too high to receive anything real from him and offering him no opportunity to give anything but the spectacle of his divinity; his own because he had not been able—even though he was bored up there—to get down from his pedestal and offer L an example of humanity instead of speeches), a relation of reciprocity? It was doubtful. If they had set out in this direction, they had in any case not succeeded in traveling far. He was dreaming of constructing a new love through friendship, and this time a true one—a utopia. To succeed he would have had to liquidate what was religious in L's love for him, and to manage that he would have had to be able to offer her more than anyone else on the human and physical level. Yet, despite several efforts to transform himself from a god and an idea into a real man, his metamorphosis had not taken place. It came too late. He was behaving like the discredited regime which, when the revolution is on the point of breaking out, suddenly offers all the reforms previously refused and, on the basis of these reforms, demands a reprieve—even more, demands to be considered as the incarnation of the revolutionary reforms conceived outside it. This regime that has not kept up with history will either be swept away or else, if granted a measure of confidence, will subsequently fall back into its former errors; what it has done under the pressure of events it will not be able to continue if the rebels lay down their arms.

Perhaps L felt this, but (just as the rebels cannot forget the former aspect of the *ancien régime* from one day to the next) she could not believe in the reality of such a change. For her he remained the remote divinity to whom sacrifices were offered on certain days, while more profane satisfactions were pursued elsewhere. She kept him like a precious relic in her jewel case.

"You, you're different," L said. "Even if I go to bed with other men, I consider you above all the rest."

He had considered this remark a terrible one. By it she, the only anchorage of his individual humanity, refused him the character of a man in order to maintain him in the capacity of a god or an idea at the very moment when he would have liked to descend among men—and the worst was that he had not stolen this exile among the divinities.

(It is only today that I understand what this sincere and "terrible" remark might imply of distress. Incapable of living only with an "unlivable" man [myself], whose tenderness was so furtive, who even in his way of making love seemed to ask forgiveness for his own existence; attracted on the other hand by a man difficult to reach [the other man], who in trying to dominate her revealed to her the "prey" aspect of her femininity and would have liked to despise her, she was unwilling to forgo either one. She had to hold on to the friendship and the esteem of the first in order not to feel herself fallen from grace; she needed the other's desire in order not to feel buried alive. In remorse and guilt she was living out the contradiction between her femininity and her humanity—between her social role of woman-as-prey and her unsatisfied need to accede to the universal as human transcendence. She did not see by what synthesis she could surmount this contradiction and tried to maintain both terms together by belonging sometimes to one, sometimes to the other. Her situation was typical of woman's condition in bourgeois society, which is, in immediate terms, hopeless. L had only the aesthetic satisfaction of playing her role as desirable object for the other man, of enjoying the new appearance she was assuming, or, rather, of enjoying her capacity to assume an appearance, and, in this *make-believe,* to catch him in the snare of his male pride, by agreeing to be the object he wanted her to be in order to slip between his fingers, since she was in fact only an object for him —an object simultaneously offered and not to be grasped, which transforms itself the moment you think you can possess it, ceaselessly offers you unexpected aspects, exasperates the male's desire for possession, satisfies it only in order to disappoint it at the last moment, thus sending the male back to his own subjectivity and seizing itself in his ferreting gaze as freedom object, that is as a traitorous object, a magic object, a disconcerting object. This is the game of seduction, and it is because woman finds, in the structure of her feminine alienation, no other immediate possibility of manifesting herself as freedom, and because the freedom object is perhaps the highest of the values offered by the situation, that her project of liberation, failing the actual transformation of the situation itself, rarely gets beyond that aestheticism which consists of play-acting beneath the master's eyes and of deceiving his desire for possession in complete security. A subordinate role, since it remains inessential; if the master is to be made to "fall" he must still desire to possess you; your freedom exists only as the object limit of his own, and since it is he who establishes your objectivity you depend on him. You deceive him, subjectively, but objectively he possesses you even in your deception. And then all he needs to do is turn his eyes away from you for your stratagem to dissolve into what it really is: false appearances which you assume, by the playful creation of which you escape him; but you do not escape him in your substance. You know the solitude of being for yourself the reverse or the denial of what you are for others, and of being for others a false being which denies yourself. And it is perhaps because your situation, in its contradictions and its solitude, resembles my own; because it consigns you to the contestation of the male universe at the same time as to that of your own particularity; because this ineffectual contestation is tempted to take itself for an objective goal [what can you do, how can you realize your subjective freedom in the given state of affairs?]; because your situation conditions you to a vocation as victim in revolt and as poet; because you rejoin the world of men only by making them forget who you are and who they think they are in relation to you, that I have sometimes thought I fraternally recognized myself in your misery and discovered only one way out of it: to write.)

Then he overpowered his bad faith and denounced the vanity of his aestheticism. He condemned her in order not to feel condemned himself. He said, "You don't mean anything to me any more." And she answered at first, "Flowers wither in stagnant water." She felt quite sad and empty. And later: "Go back to your books and your nothingness." She too needed him to be in the wrong. But neither she nor he was ever convinced that all the wrongs were only on the other side.

Out of all this there remained the conviction that a living man is worth more than a dead philosopher. And that it made little sense to torture another person for the love of an idea (and in particular an idea of love). That a life was not built out of fiats handed down a priori, and that in practice the intransigent fidelity to a priori thinking is the refusal of real existence. What use is it to have universal ideas in the abstract if these ideas prevent you from being a man, even if only in the eyes of a single person, and if in their name you refuse yourself to yourself and to another as well, refusing what it is that can make life livable? Is this an apology for compromise and resignation? I do not think so; and I think that we are all in this position. We glimpse a morality beyond the disintegration of our society, but because this disintegration has not yet reached its term this morality is not yet one we can practice. We know what the relations between a man and a woman (and other men) should be, but neither the man nor the woman of this relationship exists yet universally. In this a reason to offer a rejection to someone who comes to you, to send him away to die in solitude? (A question which I asked myself along with these others: Is the man who disapproves of the black market entitled to starve himself and his family? Is the man who denies the system of capitalist profit justified in letting himself die of cold and hunger in order not to compromise with the system by buying food from the shopkeeper around the corner? He will die; the shopkeeper remains. Refusal has a meaning only if it is collective, since its negation is then incarnated, assumes a positive aspect, becomes effective. As a solitary act, refusal is only an egotism, a way of preferring one's self in all its "purity" to the universe.)

"If we are together only for a moment," Kay said, "I prefer leaving now and taking with me the memory of our love intact."

He had equivocated for a long time. Then, that night, he had the revelation that if he let Kay go, if he had to remember all his life that she was dragging about somewhere between Rome and Bucharest, seeking refuge in her devotion to the sick or her duty toward a family, he could no longer look at himself in a mirror. If as a "philosopher" he refused to "compromise," as a man he would be a traitor and a coward. And then, if he was not certain he would be able to live with her, he was sure he did not want to lose her. He pressed Kay close to him and said with a sort of deliverance, "If you leave, I'll follow you. I couldn't bear to have let you go."

And after a moment he added, "Ever."

They knew it would not be easy. She because she would have to fight for her place against abstractions, be only a part of his life whereas for her he was her whole life. He because their life together virtually incarnated the contradiction between morality and life, between the philosopher and the man, the first not managing to raise the second to his own level, and the second failing to incarnate the first, each guilty in the other's eyes, tempted to sacrifice him or to sacrifice himself to him, to reproach him his existence as a defection (the man's defection against an ideal morality, the philosopher's against the reality of the man, of all other men). And as for the reproaches he could make to himself that he was neither sufficiently a man nor sufficiently a philosopher, but the living contradiction of the two, it had been fatal for Kay to make them to him ("I feel you could do without me so easily") and to herself ("Your life would be so much easier if it weren't for me"). And since they knew that this contradiction reflected the general contradiction of the world they lived in and would probably not be resolved in their lifetime (she believing she could never integrate herself in a socialist society, even if she theoretically approved of it; he that he must try to, if the occasion presented itself), a sort of division of labor was established between them: he represented for her her moral justification, she standing for the justification of his life as a man (wage earning submitted to, material pleasures accessible after three years of common wretchedness), his place and his mediator with the world that opened to her as if by magic. The episode with L had taught him this at least: that you do not transform men (or yourself) according to your a priori idea of their relationships, and that there is, between the evidence of what these relations should be and their effective possibility, the whole thickness of a world to be changed. That it is easy to gain acceptance intellectually for the value of ideal relations, but that intellectual acceptance is of no consequence when it does not find at hand the instruments of its accomplishment. That it was perhaps a praiseworthy enterprise to question oneself as to the ideal nature of human relations, but that it was neither up to me nor to anyone to reform humanity. That a priori moral requirements are only rootless notions which have opportunities to become effective only in the closed sector in which each person has a chance to act, but that as far as I was concerned this sector was neither the Negro problem in the United States nor the world revolution nor the emancipation of women nor universal peace; for no one, except the philosopher, proceeds from the universal to the particular; one must proceed concretely to attain the universal, from one's individual sector; otherwise one will have produced only an abstract idea incapable of taking any concrete form. It was during the first half of 1947 that I produced almost all the ideas subsequently developed (of which a good half remain to be developed). As for knowing what my sector is, this is not so simple to decide, and it is doubtless one of the objects of my present interrogation.

The spring day in 1948 when I said "Ever" to Kay, I did so in the conviction that she was my sector; not all of it, but at least the only tangible element of a sector all of whose other dimensions remained to be defined. For her, I was a man and I was responsible for my countenance as a man and for the course that her life would take; if I followed it I would perhaps succeed in the only concrete undertaking I could bring off: to make life livable for one person and, who knows, perhaps for myself too at the same time, even if, for that, I would have to take a job and for the most part lead an "ordinary" life.

Today I know that Kay was one of the moments of contradiction there are for a man who cannot accept the world as it is (either because the world is crushing him or because he remains a stranger to it), to accept it and even profit from it in details while refusing it as a whole. To accept it not in a spirit of compromise but "because there is nothing better to do," because the little that can be done is, in details, livable even when the entirety is not, and because the acceptance of detail permits some action in the direction of the transformation of the whole—but not enough, nevertheless, to be justified.

Yet I maintain that we must all live this contradiction, because we cannot (without staging an arrogant, ineffectual and complacent revolt) refuse altogether or transform at one stroke this world so inacceptable as a whole. There is no means of avoiding this contradiction, there are only opposing ways of facing it. The first, which is to content oneself with the little one, believes one can do while giving up doing everything—with the livable details of the corrupt whole, by concluding that things are not so bad after all; the second, more tempting, is to refuse the present, that is existence—and the temptation of finding it livable after all, because it is human—by taking refuge in the totalitarian ideological refusal of this world and its possibilities, by affirming against reality the purity of a future in which the contradiction will be resolved and by fanatically rejecting in the name of this future (albeit mythical and wasting away for lack of a relation with the present) all the world's "impure temptations." Implicit in our situation is the double temptation of the cowardly man who, because he would like to live well, would like to find things not so bad after all, and of the militant fanatic who, as long as the revolution has not been brought to pass, considers life itself a sin, a vice to which only the decadent bourgeoisie consents, and whose attitude leads him to imagine the condition of the most wretched as strictly unlivable, forgetting that their revolt has a meaning only because it implies the need for humanity which the fanatic censures in himself as a dangerous weakness. (And is it not evident in fact that I was speaking of Kay as if of a weakness and in an apologetic tone of excuse, as if one had to apologize for living?)

Hailed by the British Navy off the coast of Palestine, the *Exodus*, with a cargo of Jews rescued from concentration camps, was forced to turn back. It berthed in Port Bou in the spring of '47 and remained in quarantine there until ordered to return to Hamburg. The five hundred Jews on board declared a hunger strike.

A leftist weekly happened to ask him for an article about the incident; after which he began to write other such pieces. It was because the weekly wanted his articles, and because he had no other source of income, that he began to interest himself in current realities and discovered, at the same time, that he was qualified to speak of nothing to anyone, that he had no sector, no point of view that was really his. Unless it was the outlook of abstract reason, which consisted in demonstrating the absurdity of all politics (absurdity of the plans for the dismemberment of Germany, absurdity of the war in Indonesia and Indochina, absurdity of the belief in the continuing reality of the American monopoly of atomic power), and the viewpoint of the persecuted, the oppressed and the rebellious (Jews, Malagasy, Indochinese, American Negroes, Greek Communists, South African Negroes). This led to an abstract condemnation, in the name of high principles, of the established powers, to the demonstration that man is crushed by an inhuman history, that the world is bad and that the cause of its inhumanity could be summed up thus: The determining motives of human actions (capitalist profit with its struggle for markets and national prestige) cannot answer for and control their objective results; to obtain what they desire, men do what they do not desire.

But rather than set forth here certain thoughts on the capitalist regime, which I conceived (not having bothered to read Marx) from the contact with empirical reality, it would be better to try to understand these thoughts in the light of my relation to the apparent truth of this society: money.

For him, as far back as he can remember, money was something you received, stole or took but did not "earn," the fact of receiving it or taking it where it could be had being comparable to theft. Something that floats about in the human world like manna, is always appropriated by "those who have it" ("They have money," his mother used to say. "I don't have any more money. Can you give me some money?" "Where do you think I'm going to get it?" his father would say. "Oh," she said, "how I wish I had money the way they do!") and cannot be acquired except by taking it away from them. And to this end there are various ways (service, sale, borrowing, beggary) which all come down to inducing the possessor, by ruse or deception, to give you some of it, the sum he gives you having no immediately intelligible relation to what (if the situation arises) you offer him in exchange, but only to his own estimation of your needs, the need he has of you, the degree of sympathy he feels toward you.

(The newspaper paid him thirty to forty francs for an article three or four pages long and paid others up to sixty francs. "I can't pay that man less," the editor said. Another weekly paid twenty-five francs maximum.

Conversation with the editor of a Parisian daily:

"How much do you make?"

"About sixty francs."

"But that's pretty good!"

"It's not enough for the work I do."

"For a boy your age, after a year in the firm, I think that's doing very well!"

"You've just hired X, who doesn't do anything in particular, and you pay him eighty. And Y, who doesn't do half the work I do, makes seventy."

"I can't go into such considerations."

"But you can't keep me from making comparisons."

"Look here, Gorz, you know I'm very fond of you. But you're a boy without any particular needs. You don't have a car, you don't have mistresses, you don't have debts, you don't have a way of life to maintain. Now X needs a lot of money. . . .")

So a vast sector of society is organized in order to take money away from those who have it. (And since the latter get hold of it by depriving those who don't have any, they participate in a double exploitation—first they make people work to deprive them of a share of the market value of their product, then they make others work in order to be able to spend a part of the profit realized on the first. So it is the first group, farmers and laborers, who support at their own expense the workers of the luxury industries of which they are nevertheless not consumers.)

The only way to get hold of money—that is, to take it from those who had it—was therefore to satisfy a need the latter thought they had: to rent or sell oneself to them. And the only means of being freed from this prostitution was "to have money," by inheritance, by theft, or by lottery; then you could afford the luxury of doing as you chose. There were therefore those who "made every penny they had" by selling themselves, and those who paid for everything by buying themselves. And, between the two, the great floating mass of the middle classes who buy and sell themselves at either end, ignobly servile toward the possessors and ignobly scornful of the nonpossessors.

He, as it turned out, was one of those for whom everything was bought, except that he couldn't pay, a *petit bourgeois* without money. There could be no question of earning money; he had nothing to sell that anyone might have wanted to buy from him. Banished from the social machinery by being forbidden to work, he was well placed to observe this machinery in which each man is to the others what he is in relation to money, in which each man has money by having the money of other men. That was what a city was (insofar as a city is a market)—a human concentration which, by its extent and its density, appears to each man as a swarm of men objects. For each man, the city is the city of the others and he himself is the will to exempt himself from the common fate by profiting from the others without letting them profit from him. The city is born as the collective involuntary product of each man's individual will. Because the others pass through it or happen to be there, men have come there to profit from their presence, they have constructed houses and stores there, each man for himself, without a concerted plan, without perceiving that they were thus becoming for each of the others a part of those others and were producing despite them a collective work, not knowing it was collective, and a common fate which for each man, wishing only to profit from the others, consisted of exposing himself as one of the others to each individual's will to profit.

Urban society: a strange body whose reality is produced by each man's attempt to influence this reality and to exempt himself from its law. A human landscape which, by its density, overturns nature; where nature (the given uncreated) is for each man this quantitative humanity; where the exploitation of nature by man becomes the exploitation by man of the human collectivity considered as an external fact. Each man regards as natural laws the molecular laws of the urban collectivity, without realizing that he himself comprises a part of this collectivity, promotes its laws, and falls beneath their sway *by his very efforts to influence them;* the attempts to profit by the statistical laws (market, exchange) in reality establish these laws, verify them and perpetuate them without ever increasing the total number of opportunities. Man profits from men as if they were alien things (has nothing to ask of them or offer to them save money), without realizing that he thereby makes himself the promoter of a reifying order in which he himself figures only as an alien thing (demanding or dispensing money). It is because no one feels himself responsible for this alienating order that it continues to function—thanks to the myth, to which each man clings, that a man can succeed by himself in evading the logic of the system, that one can (and should) be the only man subject exploiting a collectivity of insects not deserving the name of men. The crematory ovens are within the logic of the system. And dictatorship too, of course, and this for two reasons:

First, because the truth of bourgeois society remains exterior to it as an involuntary consequence. When this consequence, by the activity of each individual, becomes detrimental to all, appeal is made to the providential savior who rescues each individual from the consequences of his own acts, but rescues him *from outside,* by external intervention, without asking individual sacrifice of him.

Second, because the public interest, in a bourgeois regime, is the interest of no one, is incarnated in no group whose activity would be consciously to the interest of all. There is not, concretely, a public interest common to both large and small real-estate owners, to consumers and dealers, to white-collar workers, farmers and factory laborers.

The abstract and formal public interest common to these antagonistic groups exists only to prevent each of the other groups from making its particular interest prevail—by assuring the state of an extremely relative independence as arbiter: by demanding its intervention against this or that particular interest which is too powerful—without each man's lessening his attempt, nevertheless, to make his own private interest prevail if he can.

The completely formal and negative public interest of each group therefore exists to prevent the victory of any concrete interest—but if it succeeds in this intention it must renounce in its turn any hope of victory.

This is why the private interests which confront one another at the heart of bourgeois society struggle against all the other private interests and *at the same time* against the state's power of arbitration, which each man tries to confiscate as the instrument of his private power.

Hence what is wrongly construed as the expression of the public interest (the power and the independence of the nation, the independence of the organs of administration and justice, of instruction and information, civil liberties, etc.) and as the "values" of this society is in reality only the consequence of antagonistic interests neutralizing each other and each one trying, out of fear of the others' triumph, to perpetuate the conditions of their antagonism. A result of an equilibrium of forces that is in essence precarious, the "values" and "liberties" of bourgeois society are also permanently threatened by each of the private interests in the struggle —for each of the latter is ready, as soon as it has the power to do so, to suppress the "regime of liberty" for the profit of its own domination.

The bourgeois liberties are in essence fragile, for they are not willed by any social group, except perhaps by a minority of professional liberals who have become the beneficiaries of a regime that has created them.

He began thinking about this apropos of the black market in France and of Gaullism in 1947. Particularly in regard to the invincible black market, by which each man thought he could exempt himself from the common fate (until the common fate no longer existed except as a fiction against which one took precautions), to the point where a people was composed in the majority of men who considered themselves specially privileged, and where exceptional privileges became in fact the rule: the struggle of each against all, hoarding, speculation, inflation, generalized selfishness and the masquerading of every need as a need for money. Money was the only universal value because universally desired, but an abstract universal, as if animated by a magical life, melting away between your fingers, which each man desired to own privately.

There would be material for a long dissertation in this contradic‹ tion of individually coveting what is a universal substance, since this contradiction, as it is activated in relation to money, sums up the fundamental contradiction of capitalist society (the individual considering freedom as his private affair and his universality as what he possesses by depriving others of it); * and perhaps I shall someday return to this dissertation begun during the winter of '47–'48 as if (while Kay wretchedly dragged herself about, eating nothing but oatmeal that they had persuaded Walter to pay for by taking him *en pension,* in return for a payment of one franc, around the huge, cluttered table on which they made a little room for three jelly glasses instead of plates) as if by this expedient he had finally found a means other than nihilism of pronouncing the annihilation of the world.

A dissertation, pugnacious little articles (and later venomous ones, each containing a discreet dose of poison, the materials of an indictment omitted so that the facts could speak for themselves): this was not an annihilation that he had in hand, nor a revolution, but a matter of getting paid by the bourgeoisie for assembling a

---

* See Marx, "The Jewish Question," *Philosophical Works,* vol. I, pp. 192–201, Costes edition.

dossier that would overwhelm it, to lodge himself in the capitalist world like a poisonous spider in the middle of its web, decoding the vibrations and rejoicing when things were going badly. To be the lucid witness and the judge of the world's absurdity. It was a taste for this attitude that found him, a year later, writing propaganda for the World Citizens, a movement he had at first rejected as a *petit bourgeois* manifestation, demanding the abstract union of equally abstract men of good will; presenting himself to strange audiences (Protestant youth movements, parish reunions, Quakers, etc.) as a decrier of Western politics; conducting the prosecution, before these naïve minds, implicit in bourgeois states; taking towards the world the viewpoint of a judge, the outlook of Sirius.

Nothing new, all in all, in this role that boiled down to saying "I am not one of you, I see you from a point where you cannot see me"; World Citizen—that is, a man from nowhere (and not from everywhere) contesting real particularities in the name of an abstract and unreal universality. A way of dissolving the concrete, while simulating an interest for it, in the abstract, and of denouncing it afterward in the name of his opposition to the latter. This said, it would be surprising if despite his dissertations on the fetishism of money, he had not been fascinated by its abstraction; money was the annihilation of the concrete in the abstract, the metamorphosis of real products into currency, of the thing into its imaginary possibility, the triumph of the imaginary (of the belief in the power of a piece of paper, founded on the belief of each man in the belief of all the rest) over the real, the denial of diversity, the suppression as well as the preservation (*Aufhebung*) of duration (duration of work preserved as savings after having been denied by its payment; duration of life and inactivity possessed by the assurance of having "something to live on" for a few weeks or years), the annihilation of concrete doing and being in a perfectly impersonal having that, since it is the only payment asked of you, permits you to pass unnoticed and silences all questions as to your passage. He who pays has no accounting to give, has no need to pay with his own person.

No need to look much further. I think that this time I have put my finger on the "original complex" to which all his attitudes toward other people refer (the silences, the horror of assuming any identity or role in the eyes of others—that is, the timidity—the avoidance of concrete relationships by theorizing about these relationships or by psychoanalyzing the interlocutor, the preference for relationships in which all that is asked of him is a theoretical intelligence, the refusal to pay with his own person in order to substitute ideas and to identify himself with them, the refusal to speak a common language and to say common things, the absence of spontaneity, the taste for self-annihilation) and from which other attitudes (masochism, effacement, what I have called "treason," opposition and contestation) flow as an empirical consequence. It will perhaps take quite some time to explain this, but I shall try, without falling into psychologism and still allowing historical dialectic its share.

I

THE TRAITOR

*What consciousness does in isolation is,
furthermore, without the slightest interest.*
—KARL MARX, "The German Ideology"

I must turn back to the place where I first touched on the original
complex which I should now like to clarify further for myself. I
have referred to the desired standard which regulates all our behavior and whose lack of realization causes the self-for-itself to feel
not so much guilty as in danger of loss, in danger of losing its
being, its value, its orientation, its place in the world. This is what
the psychoanalysts call the ego; this ego does not exist; it is an
ideal image of the self (an ideal "I"), thematized, often rational-
ized, drawn from a swarm of possibilities and temptations. It is the
image according to which the self-for-itself attempts to identify itself. To identify itself with what? With itself as Other. The ego is
Someone Else.

It is not an accident that I have spoken of myself throughout in
the third person. I had intended to give a theoretical justification
for this device at the end of my work, but what follows will probably dull my taste for such elaboration. This is because, aside from
all theoretical considerations, he has a horror of "I." More simply,

he has no ego—no character, no declared taste save that of effacing himself, none of that comfort of a man easy in his own skin, no spontaneity, no personality. For other people, he emerges from a mysterious silence only to manifest himself as a theoretical intelligence or, gaining confidence, to play with his instruments of communication: to play with language by puns, to play with his voice by making animal sounds—sheep, pig and duck—to play with his body by a grotesque gait or gesticulation. These games have an ironic quality: he destroys the very communication he sets up and negates the means of communication by the way he uses them. All in all, he emerges from silence only to create silence by self-destructive communication (or remains plunged in it by the impersonality of his theoretical discourse). It is not enough to speak of "a horror of the ego"; he has a *terror of identification:* a terror of being identified by other people with an ego that is Someone Else, a terror of saying more than he means or something different from what he means, consequently a terror of saying anything at all. Hence his voice is low, indistinct, monotonous, monosyllabic, and it easily goes unnoticed. And there has always been this terror, as far back as his conscious memory extends, back to the age when he was beginning to speak; it is the significance which communication with others by means of language immediately assumed for him; it has always paralyzed the act of speech. It is the most original and fundamental of his complexes.

I should have suspected this when I was describing his strabismus, his lisp and his childish stuttering. These are signs—signs (as is the child's anxiety to know if it is himself or only her son his mother loves) that the discovery of his existence for other people (that is, the discovery of his ego) has been a traumatism; that there has always been an intolerable disproportion between what he was for himself and his being-for-others; that his singularity, discovered simultaneously with speech (he asked, emerging from the darkness behind the heavy red velvet curtain, how it was that an eye could see and a head could think, dizzied at the age of four by the mystery of an external appearance—eye and head—doubled by the inner reality of sight and thought, the scandal of an inner reality having the object's appearance as its unrealizable contrary), consisted in never having adhered, like most other men, to his ego, his speech, his being-for-others as to the norm of an ideal and successful identity with himself.

They corrected his strabismus with glasses, his lisp with a metal loop, his stammer by mechanical exercises, and he spoke perfectly, but with a voice so low and so fast that his mother was forever complaining, "What are you saying? Talk louder! What are you mumbling about now?" and they nicknamed him Mumbler (*Nuschler*); even hearing the dreadful word kept him from wanting to speak. Then he learned to howl, to low, to whinny, bleat and growl, because these animal sounds, impossible to be mistaken, meant what they meant, their meaning was identified with the determined vocal possibilities of the animal—"natural" sounds without mystery, all intention inseparable from this simple-minded act of speech, since for the animal no other was possible.

With language the situation was entirely different; and language, for man, begins with the body. Previously immersed in his body as in the matter of his nonthematic experience, he discovered one day that this body which he identified with himself signified something for other people and that this signification escaped him. The experiential meaning of his behavior was stolen from him by a hedge of faces leaning over him which suddenly burst out laughing or delivered weighty commentaries (explosions of merriment which his first stammering provoked; childish witticisms repeated dozens of times by his delighted mother, who exhibited him to strangers as if he were a trained dog, making him repeat his pearls whose meaning escaped him), having received a mysterious message from his body. This body itself was stolen from him, it spoke to others in a language he did not know; he *was spoken* by his body. Unrealizable significations, intentions he was certain he did not have because he did not understand them, came to inhabit him from outside, establishing themselves within him like parasites that eat away the flesh or, worse still, the consciousness, without his being able to turn around and see them. He became for others an Odd Little Person of whom they spoke in his presence in the third person, a strange object (playing with the little wheels on the bars of the kind of cage they put him in at the age of two, he felt their eyes, their silence upon him; "I suppose he'll be an engineer," his mother said in her encouraging voice; for them, he beat on the wheels wildly; something was expected of him, what was an "engineer"?) before whom grown-up men got down on all fours and made faces and ladies went into high-pitched ecstasies. They saw something on him he was ignorant of, he "told" them something he did not know, they expected him to play a role. He did not understand them, he did not understand his role. They terrorized him. He hated them.

His entire childhood was spent under this tyranny of identification, for he was always required to identify himself with the role, with the ego his mother wanted him to play and necessarily imputed to him because that was how she wanted to see him. She saw him as she would have liked him to be, she showed him his imaginary ego as if in a mirror, and this ego was Someone Else, a lie, unless it was the other way around—unless it was *he* who was Someone Else, a lie. Yes, it probably *was* the other way around, his mother couldn't be wrong, she was sure to see him as he really was —so he was a lie, Someone Else, and guilty of not feeling the way she saw him. He was Someone Else, other than his ego, and being unable to identify himself with his ego condemned him to being rejected—as a lie, a ghost, a consciousness ashamed of disappointing and deceiving—into the outer darkness.

I suppose this is what is meant by "moral consciousness" (or the superego), this image of yourself which is always shown to you as what you are, and which, since in fact you are nothing else, you should be from now on, lest you lose yourself in the shadows of being nothing. You interiorize the requirement to identify yourself and, in order to conform to the ego presented to you, you apply yourself to producing it by "censoring" what contradicts it—that is, by thematizing only those elements in your intentions and behavior that confirm it—the rest, like the dark of the moon, remaining unknown (but not unconscious) for you.

There would doubtless be a difference depending on whether your ego is a real objectivation of yourself, originally corresponding to your real possibilities, or a false image presented to you by systematically misinterpreting your real possibilities, and which, not corresponding to them, can only be achieved by desire to deceive, to play a false role. In fact, your objectivation is never immediately true; you are presented (this is education) an unreal image of yourself in order that it will suggest possibilities of achieving it by your behavior. It remains to discover how you can adapt yourself and if, in the way you do so, the possibilities suggested (by interpreting you, decoding you, by *speaking* you, in the transitive sense of the verb "to speak") can be adopted and developed (because they already correspond to a rough draft of behavior) or if they remain alien either because you are simply being lied to about yourself or—it comes down to the same thing—because you are being tyrannized (by being made to feel that your ego does not belong to you but to others, and that in order to come into possession of it you must deserve it, pay for it with obedience as if it were something you had pawned, thereby contracting a debt which must be paid). It remains to be seen, in other words, whether the language which you are, in fact, for other people is revealed to you as your power over them or as their power over you, as your possibility of manifesting yourself in the intersubjective universe of speech, or as your fall into the *other people's* universe of discourse.

I know, it is never one *or* the other; but there is always one

aspect or the other which is dominant, and for him it was clearly
the second. Language (like the whole world, moreover) was the
exclusive property of his mother. She ruled over words in order to
rule over men by cascades of talk, holding her disconcerted interlocutors paralyzed, as if in a glue. Language was her kingdom, and
to speak was to enter this realm and immediately fall under her
jurisdiction. Speaking necessarily meant serving her in her own
language (since she confiscated it) and providing significations over
which she expected to rule incontestably. Speaking (and keeping
still) always meant saying what *she* meant, and the flood of words
that received his murmur (or his silence) made him say what *she*
thought or wanted to hear. He was a prisoner in the kingdom of
maternal discourse, fettered to the fabulations by which she identified him, and, unable to free himself from her verbal ascendancy,
could escape only by a stubborn silence. (An impression renewed
after eight years of wartime separation: Her welcoming words in
the station were like an attack, a spider web she was spinning
around him, binding his limbs, insistently reducing him to the appearance she wanted to find, assailing him with questions, exclama-
tions and commentaries to which there was no possible personal
response. "Let me look at you! My poor little boy! How thin you
are! Did you have a good trip? Could you sleep on the train? Was
it crowded? Oh, your hair! We will go to the barber tomorrow. You
can't go out with a thatch like that. People will turn around and
look at you in the street. Don't you go to the barber regularly? But
you must be dead tired! You certainly haven't grown any more
talkative in all these years! You look at me and tell yourself, 'She
doesn't even give me time to breathe!' Ah, these mothers! Come on,
we'll get a taxi. You can take a bath when you get home. You can
tell me everything then. But tell me . . ." Then he began staring
at her with incredulous amusement, trying to guess how long she
could go on talking by herself, and how many subjects she would
rush through once she got started. And then he had fallen into the

trap of her questions again; answering even one meant seeing that answer immediately crippled, maimed, swept into a verbal whirlpool from which emerged judgments, and a portrait of himself and further questions and demands that he deal with problems as she saw them. They began to quarrel, then he adopted the tactic of brief ironic replies, then stopped talking altogether because she was invincible, the verbal wall behind which she took refuge was not to be pierced, not even by someone whose voice was loud and whose breath long, because she wouldn't have the patience to listen to him. Then as for some twenty years he fell silent—the way his sister had fallen silent, emerging from her mutism only by defeatist sallies, verbal provocations uttered in a victim's accusing tone because she felt beaten in advance and sought nothing more than the proof of her defeat.)

To escape the kingdom of his mother's discourse, to elude her constraints, her eloquence, her judgments, her terrifying insistence on identification by protocol (to which the rediscovered photographs of his childhood bore witness: the year-old baby swathed in lace, wearing white gloves and a cap down to his ears; later in a beach robe by the Adriatic, or in pajamas, to prove that he had plenty of clothes; and then leaving this beach in midsummer, dressed in an overcoat and wearing gloves because that was how "one" traveled, wearing an overcoat whatever the temperature. An object of display, a symbol of respectability and wealth, clothes made the man, like the well-mannered formulas she taught him to recite)—that was probably why he had thrown himself early into the simultaneous refusal of language and clothes as if into a self-punishing *ascesis*. There was nothing else he could do. His mother expected a role of him which could only be played (she had spent her own life happily acting out such roles); but at the same time she discouraged his childish play-acting by demanding sincerity. He could not act the role of the well-brought-up, well-dressed, "cute" little boy to satisfy her ambition and at the same time feel

in accord both with his mother's requirements and with himself.
He was not in accord. Either he was acting and then he was lying,
or else he was not lying and then he was disappointing her. He was
disappointing her by what he really was, and realizing that he did
not come up to what was expected of him made him lose confidence
in his capacity as an actor. The expected role did not correspond to
his own possibilities, language was a dreadful trap, no ego was
presented to him that he could adopt and develop on his own. He
had to apply himself, force himself, make himself Someone Else in
order to prove at all equal to the part. He was living in the constant
terror of What have I said now? What have I done now?, transfixed at seeing his own spontaneous behavior petrified into criminal
acts supposedly premeditated, haphazard words construed as deliberate offenses or even as clever jokes; feeling himself exiled in the
other people's universe of discourse and incapable of finding a suitable expression, the consecrated formula which would satisfy their
expectation; incapable too of passing off as innocent (of being for-
given or even understood) the imbecile intentions which had made
him act and which, falling into the cunning universe of grownups,
assumed significations of an incalculable effect and Evil. So the
union between what he was for himself and what he was for others
was not accomplished; he had not achieved that outspokenness,
that ease, that amiable and talkative spontaneity of the "normal"
man—that is, of the spoken speaker who has managed to assert
himself as the subject of his speech or, rather, by alienating himself in it, by releasing himself confidently in his own commonplaces, feels himself able to act out the expected ego, feels in league
with those who expect this comedy of him, knows, in fact, nothing
but this comedy and desires nothing better than to be identified
with this ego They have chosen for him, thereby protecting it (and
protecting himself) against his solitude as a subject.

I know, of course, that the distrust of language, the constant fear
of being misunderstood, of being credited with intentions that were

not his but which others discovered in him as faults—I know that this complex lies deep within each of us, like the inevitable failure of communication, like our irremediable solitude. But I also know that we are not alone and that any authentic dialogue is based on the recognition of its own failure, on the recognition of the fact that we have never said everything and that everything still remains to be said. And authentic dialogue is impossible precisely when one of the two speakers refuses to recognize this failure and assumes something like an armor of impersonal language, an eloquence being spoken through him.

Yet his whole life was constructed on the belief that others were not in isolation, that they coincided with their impressive roles and were therefore not trying to understand him, but were expecting only a role determined in advance and which he could not fulfill. It is because he was convinced from the start of his essential incommensurability with other people's expectations, convinced of the immutability of the rift between himself and who he should have been that this rift was never closed. It was because of his guilt for not being Someone Else, like other people, that he had immediately accepted Jewishness as the confirmation of an exclusion he bore within himself. Who knows, perhaps he even provoked the stigmatization of his Jewishness by his timidity, his odd and deferential behavior, and perhaps his schoolmates would never have thrown it up to him had he not already designated himself as a victim. And because he was convinced he had betrayed the ego he should have been, he had done everything, objectively, to make this conviction a matter of fact. Lying in wait anxiously, timidly, for demands to identify himself, asking only to satisfy them and certain in advance that he would be unable to; accepting exclusion as normal, as almost foreseen; trying without conviction to play a role among the others and forever feeling alien to this role whose nature he left it up to others to define; then choosing this role, resigned in advance to its extraneousness and therefore contesting it even before having begun to act it; dreaming of a world where he would be judged only on the objective efficiency of his acts, where he could therefore acquit himself of his social role by the performance of a task exterior to his person, rigorously determined beforehand, in order to be his own master the rest of the time; attempting to acquit himself of this role with a payment of words and immediately pulling back into his shell; dreaming of a world without men, or of a conventional isolation, or of money, so that, once rid of his debt or far from any eyes, he would be happy being only what he would be for himself . . .

Many other mysteries were clarified in the light of this fundamental complex: his insistence, for instance, on changing languages (speaking a German dialect slang before converting to French) in order to get rid of his mother tongue, a term whose meaning now exploded with all its force; his predilection for foreign languages, which, in a foreign country, permitted him to offer other people words that clearly did not belong to him and were therefore nothing but a currency that did not engage his person; similarly his taste for abstraction, also a foreign language since: (1) it is not legal tender in normal interpersonal relations, and (2) when employed nevertheless, it excludes them. And his tendency toward opposition, also a refusal of ordinary speech, a negative attitude in which the subject, rejecting all identification as false, claims to derive only from himself; a tendency toward "irony" and "treason" in which the subject, confounding all attempts at identification, refers the interlocutor to the silence flickering behind the mask, presented as such, of his speech.

A horror of the serious and the conventional in every form, a repulsion for all the disguises (including dances, uniforms and feminine preparations) assumed ready-made, and particularly for the woman alienated from the prestige of her femininity and for the man who has surrendered the distinctions of his masculine responsibility, for both of them expect of the masculine interlocutor that he identify himself with a certain image of virility which was precisely the one his mother expected of him (the chivalric, strong protector, energetic, self-confident and imbued with the sense of justice and honor). A sympathy, on the other hand (almost a sense of brotherhood, in fact) for anyone in revolt against the requirements of identification—for Negroes, for colonized peoples, for women who, because they were unwilling to be a floral object, fragile, affectionate and desired, no longer expect anything from the "virile" male and are themselves no longer "someone" in the bourgeois society, which has not yet allowed them to constitute a new ego in place of the one they take exception to, the ego that is Other.

A taste for writing, last of all, for to write is to speak in the absence of others and to refuse them speech, it is to claim *Selbständigkeit* for my words, to forbid another person to tell me what he means (to "speak me"), constantly obliging him to ask *himself* if he understands the meaning of the text, the writer's intention removed from his grasp. To write, in sum, is to create a nocturnal reality hidden from other people's eyes, a reality they will never see, hearing only this language rising out of the darkness and falling silent when day breaks; the writer is an anonymous and invisible subject. This is probably why I hate talking about what I write and assume all kinds of pseudonyms, a way of declaring that the ego I must be is merely a disguise I disavow, and that I intend to recognize myself only in the nocturnal and nonidentifiable voice of my solitary speeches.

And here we come full circle. Because this reflection upon myself has been made in writing and intended its completion in the form of the text, it necessarily summed up and confirmed my fundamental choice to write because of my terror of identification. This text could therefore not hope to affect that choice; it participated in it.

The goal of this work must therefore be revised. Instead of writing to disidentify myself, to liquidate what I am (using the third person, addressing myself to no one, speaking in the void, creating for myself, under the eyes of an anonymous and silent public, an ego which, under analysis, I should have created for an analyst: the witness of "Myself as Someone Else" waiting for the intellectual detachment of my descriptions to be admired), I should write in order to define what I can be. But to do this, one must be two; to know what I can be I must know to whom I can speak, for whom I can be whoever it is that I can be.

This text has therefore not escaped what analysts call transference: it sums up perfectly the meaning and the nature of my relationship with others. It should now become an instrument for transforming this relationship. To begin with, it must from now on be written in the first person; and I have acquired at least the possibility of doing this, since at last the knowledge I have gained of myself meets my own experience.

This choice: Indeed it is a choice that is in question, since what was originally a terror of identification (an identification always made, treacherously, by other people, like a theft and a violation) was subsequently developed and thematized as a choice of non-identification, a choice to confess all alienations, even the objectivity of the act by which the silent subject, residing only in his private experience, falls into the world of objects and is there handed over to the exterior determinations applied to him by other people. And to motivate this choice, the infantile complex does not, obviously, suffice. It simply permits the explanation of certain terrors which survive in me, muted, like faint memories whose texture has been forgotten. It does not even permit me to explain *why* these terrors have survived until now. Fundamentally, it explains nothing (or everything, which comes down to the same thing); and so I return to what I was saying at the start: that this original complex has survived only because it has confirmed and

enriched itself during the course of my history with significations
that were not there at first; only because it has been instrumental
in disclosing a reality which urged it to develop itself, which confirmed it as a true grasp (that is, a grasp based on facts) of my real
situation, and not only of my personal situation—of the human
condition. This complex has not been a fit of insanity, nor the psychological residue of an infantile drama irrationally surviving the
circumstances that occasioned it. It has become the contingent establishment of a choice which has developed from this point as the
continual renewal of objective significations and dimensions in
events until it became a sufficiently coherent vision of the world
to be able, in certain respects, to furnish its own theoretical justification.

The dialectical process of the choice therefore seems to me as
follows: Originally there was a complex, an irrational attitude
assumed in childhood to avoid a situation the child had no means
of dealing with rationally. This original and dated complex could
in no case survive as such into adult life; if it survived as such in all
its childishness, it would be like the foreign body in a patient's
stomach, a meaningless accident to be dealt with by surgery. If the
original complex survives instead of falling into oblivion with the
rest of our childish attitudes, it can do so only to the degree that it
has become much more than the original complex it was at the
start. It is not the *attitude* of the child's original nonidentification
with his mother which is perpetuating itself, but a *project* of nonidentification which discovers in events forever new reasons for
development, forever new possibilities for refusing identification,
and forever new significations for this refusal. In other words, this
original attitude is invested, during the subject's history, with unforeseen and undesired objective significations which either confirm or deny it. To continue my recent image, the attitude "is
spoken" by the empirical event. The latter slips new words into the
vocabulary of its primitive "sentence," words which the subject has

never spoken, which are or are not susceptible of being integrated into his sentence, and which, when they are susceptible, *can* be integrated there or, in the opposite case, be discarded as "freak words," devoid of sense, which I am supposed to say but which I take exception to. The dialectical development of the complex into a choice is the activity of the subject assuming on his own account the words which events slip into his rudimentary sentence in order to enlarge the signification and the effect of this sentence. The latter can become still more complex and, at the same time, free, since the assumption of the "freak words" proposed by events is optional and since the place, the signification and the value I assign them in my sentence depends on me alone. The sentence which I happen to be saying at thirty is therefore quite a different thing from the childish stammer it started from. The latter is scattered through it like the words *"un coup de dés jamais n'abolira le hasard"* in Mallarmé's poem or like the fundamental theme in a fugal variation which can no more be reduced to its theme than it can be deduced from it. And just as the fugal variation, having reached a certain stage of its development, can properly transfigure its theme within certain limits and make one of its variations into the dominant theme, in the same way the choice that has been developed out of a complex can, within certain limits, return upon the latter and "transvalue" it. This at least in theory.

In practice, I still do not see where this discovery can lead or, rather, what I can make of it, for I see the indefensible contradictions of my choice, and I also see its productiveness. Finding it productive, I should like to follow it some of the way; observing the failures it is susceptible of, I should like to revise it somewhat. But how proceed at the heart of a personal choice in which everything necessarily relates to everything else? How renounce one's unproductive contradictions in order to preserve only the productive ones? How profit from a complex to the degree that it can serve as an image of the human condition, while at the same time liquidating it as a "complex"? How assert its consequences while at the same time liquidating its premises, resolutely perpetuating it in certain aspects and dissociating myself from it in others? No longer dependent on its affective establishment in prehistory, its status as a complex, would not my choice be deprived of its emotional scope (which inclines me—spontaneously, irrationally—to argument, reflection, the pursuit of contradictions) and become a fragile rationalism which perhaps could not withstand contrary inducements?

I know what the answer should be: You have just shown how much every man cherishes his complexes; you prefer to rely on the internal logic of a complex you yourself admit to be irrational and emotional in its scope, in order to persevere in an attitude which you consider productive, rather than rely on your freedom to persevere in the same attitude without the aid of a complex. Fundamentally you are afraid of your freedom, afraid of losing your complex because you might become "ordinary," like "everyone else," instead of preserving your precious and incommunicable singularity. You love yourself and you mistrust yourself. Your complex is a crutch without which you are afraid to walk, and yet are there not enough contradictions in your situation for you to go on thinking and arguing without needing a complex?

And the answer should also be: If the complex, to the degree that it is irrational, can protect me against contrary inducements, this is only because it is a structure of conduct heterogeneous to empirical reality, an element of the sentence that cannot enter into a relation with certain propositions of the mundane context. The complex is a permanent factor of disadaptation; it is here, precisely, that it is irrational. Yet if it forearms me against a complacent adaptation to the empirical state of things, the complex also forearms me against *any* adaptation, against *any* effective action. By maintaining a permanent discord between what I am and what is offered to me, the complex quite conceals the dimensions of the real and its opportunities, and it inclines me in certain respects to a sterilizing vision of the world. What I must now look for, then, is to what degree there are, in my empirical situation, real dimensions somehow passed over in silence by the interpretation which my original commitment imprints upon what will ultimately be my total discourse, to what degree these dimensions, insufficiently assumed or assumed by mistake, are perhaps those which would permit me to initiate the transfiguration of my choice, provided I center my sentence upon them.

What strikes me now is the time it took me to grasp my original project in its truly original sense. I have always had all the elements within my grasp. I have never strayed far from the point in my interpretations, and yet, while I was speaking of my "nullity complex," my "treason," my "masochism," I was not dealing with that "evidence" which the term "nonidentification" affords me. There is no doubt that I proceeded too quickly to interpretation by objective. I was incapable of deriving every possible advantage from it subjectively; for, as long as I had not clearly grasped my original project (or complex), it was impossible for me to decide what, in a dated attitude, was the objective signification of the situation in fact and what was, as a personal formulation of this situation, imputable only to me, subjectively.*

In attempting to grasp the signification of the nihilist *ascesis* upon whose contradictions I was crucifying myself I should doubtless have mentioned the Austro-German–Judaeo-Christian contradiction, as well as the nullity that exile imposes. But this contradiction had always existed, and the exile has lasted much longer than the nihilism. Complacency in the one as in the other, the preparation of speech that was no better than silence, could be understood

---

* Which confirms the fact that the subjective interpretation must come first. It is only if I single out my original choice that I can understand my history as a progress toward its meaning, as a signifying and gratuitous formulation of an empirical reality which extends, as I will know at that moment, far beyond what I have grasped of it.

only in the light of my nonidentification project, which found a marvelous opportunity for flowering in the empirical situation.

I knew this and even spoke of it, but without understanding it completely. Without understanding that I had created my total solitude because I had always dreamed of not existing for others. Without understanding that I was exaggerating my exclusion, my persecution, my danger, because I wanted to have an appearance which was totally exterior to me, imposed by violence, injustice and incomprehension; for only such an appearance could be totally impugned by me ("I am not the way they see me"); *for only so total an alienation could guarantee the integrity of an existence which wanted to be totally interior,* residing only in its consciousness of itself, deriving only from itself, never objectivizing itself. It was in order to reside entirely within myself, to offer no exterior hold upon myself, to remain nonobjectivizable and nonidentifiable, in order to be nothing ("null," as I was saying) that I adopted the contradictory and untenable position of the nihilist *ascesis* which resembles a form of sainthood. And so forth.

Mysticism, nihilism, the temptation of sainthood, treason, subjectivism, nonidentification, a tendency to martyrdom . . . This will to annihilate oneself was actually a formidable pride: wanting to be nothing that was determined, wanting to assume no ego in others' eyes in order to be everything in one's own—a solitary subjectivity; enormous and comfortable love of self: the consciousness which, in order to be immediately everything to the degree that it is a consciousness-for-itself, refuses to exist for others and to assume its finitude. This is the same kind of attitude we observe in Romain Rolland,* because he was an imperfect saint.† For whom was he writing? For posterity—that is, for God. What did he think of the Dreyfus Affair? That it was "a tide of madness" in which

---

* *Mémoires.*

† A good dissertation could be written on "Sainthood in Camus and Romain Rolland."

"the highest ideals" and "the lowest passions" were mingled. He felt that the massacre of the Armenians was much more important, much more interesting. He concerned himself with the massacre of the Armenians during the Dreyfus Affair because a Frenchman who in 1900 was interested in the massacre of the Armenians was a gentleman above the battle, above his fellow Frenchmen, playing the role of a generous and abstract humanist and refusing to define himself with regard to the problems of his time. He sacrificed *la patrie* to *la République,* but of course this republic was the republic of the future, which would include the whole world. Saint Romain was a citizen of the world for whom the Dreyfusards were only a "suspect mob" and their actions only "madness" and "frenzy." The truth is that Saint Romain put himself above the battle (or descended to take part in them only when his attitudes could have no effect) because he put himself above men (including the Armenians, for the latter were a convenient means of denying himself as a Frenchman involved in the Affair) and because the basis of his attitude was a contempt for men. "May God grant me battles, enemies, and jeering crowds . . ." Saint Theresa herself wanted to be "scorned, condemned, persecuted without reason," for "what does it matter, if in the eyes of the Lord we are exempt from the faults we are accused of?" Saint Romain wanted to be jeered by the crowds—first, because their hatred would indicate to him that he had nothing in common with his fellow men; second, because to be misunderstood and universally attacked while at the same time claiming to be right in the eyes of God is the ideal situation, in which you can refuse everything that you are with regard to others and can keep yourself entirely for yourself. "God alone" or "I alone"—the sense is the same when God is invoked against the "base passions" of the mob; you refuse to measure yourself by the common standard and deny your effective reality for others in the name of your superior and fictive reality for God; you refuse others any right to look at yourself, you put yourself in the position of a sacred subject, without a communicable reality. You are the One, the absolute and nonobjectivizable subjectivity; you do not act, you *are acted* by the human stupidity which brings it about that "a timid man with no taste for violence provokes animosity against himself . . ." This is Rolland, this is Benda, this is the leftist intellectual, this tortured and persecuted Saint-Juste who, when the colonized peoples rebel and assassinate the colonists, "finds himself forced to condemn . . . in the same breath both colonists and colonized people and for the same reasons." * Ultimately we come down to this: To be above everyone else, you must condemn everyone else.

Only it must be pointed out that to condemn only the colonists when you are a colonist yourself may also be a way of putting yourself above everyone else—to deny you have anything in common with your fellow men, to adopt before them, your only public and therefore the only public before whom you need disidentify yourself, the reasons of the other camp, to which everyone knows you do not belong. I am not saying it is wrong to condemn the colonists (I am convinced of the contrary), but I am saying that the attitude which consists of condemning only the colonists to whose faction you belong, no matter how legitimate and objectively well founded your condemnation, has also an objective signification of pride (to be right against everyone else, to renounce everyone else), so you may have adopted this objectively just attitude for indefensible subjective reasons. This is my case (what I was calling the taste for treason), and I am not alone.

Like many other men, like Ed, like you, probably, I am still tempted by what you might call religious Marxism. You know what I mean: an attitude that consists—by an extreme self-distrust, by a horror of your own masturbational subjectivity, by your

---

* Jean-Bloch Michel, "Present Situation of the Left," *Gazette Littéraire,* June 16–17, 1956. Cf. Camus: "When the oppressed man takes up arms in the name of justice, he takes a step into the kingdom of injustice."

experience of everything that is flabby, inconsistent and cozily solitary in yourself; by your need to have done once and for all with your own complexities in order to recover objectivity, the thread of the real and of history—in regarding men of flesh and blood as no more than so much putty and in explaining the misconceptions, stupidities and contemptible actions of Communist policy from the bird's-eye view of historical materialism; in considering the Communist parties as solid, totally objective entities to which you must unconditionally say yes or no, and say yes with the cowardly illusion of achieving historical objectivity, whereas in reality you achieve nothing at all. You remain outside, and it is only because you see it from outside—from the Sirius perspective of historical determinism—that you can consider Communism as an "objective process."

At least I am aware of this temptation, and I know that yielding to it leads nowhere. Not here and now. If, fifteen years ago, I had been living in Italy, there might have been some sense in joining the Communist Party there, as there would have been had I lived in Russia in 1900, or in any other country where revolutionary ferment confers effectiveness upon intellectual argument. At such a time, intellectual contestation would have launched me into action; I would have been obliged to adopt concrete positions, to abandon a destructive attitude of negativity for one of action. But at present the trap which the French Communist Party lays for me is that of a new abstraction, that which consists of justifying anything and everything by "the mechanisms of history," by the inhuman. If I joined the French Communist Party now (at my age and at this moment), it would certainly be for bad reasons: to "translude" (as Jeanson says) my contradictions and my obligation to live them for an illusory total objectivity; for the pleasure of being (as I was, long ago, on the side of the animals against men, on the side of the Reich's "cosmic forces" against the Jews and the rural Austrians), on the side of some supposedly implacable logic of the facts according to which what men want is only so much putty. (It is generally bastard children like myself who become both grand and petty inquisitors. From Malinovski, the insufficiently Russian Russified Pole who was the first informer from the Okhrana on the first Central Committee of the Communist Party, to Ordzhonikidze, to Dzerzhinski, to Zhezov, etc., not to mention less illustrious fanatics, fanatics are always intellectuals who are fed up with being themselves.)

Perhaps you will say that the fact of being unable to join the Communist Party except for bad reasons is a special situation, one limited to me (that there are many people who have excellent reasons to do so), and that in any case I encounter the same bad reasons in my decision *not* to join at present. You are surely right; only, the many people who have excellent reasons to join the French Communist Party are not the intellectuals; for a number of years now intellectuals have been quite superfluous there; their situation there is one of perfect nullity. And is that what I should choose? Let us be quite frank. For a man who at this moment is trying to transcend his nonidentification complex, this is not the way; the objective situation casts me back where I was at the very moment I feel subjectively prepared to emerge from it. But there is also the fact that ways are never *found;* ways are opened by advancing where there is no path. If the path had already been cleared, it would be too easy; one would merely follow it quite logically. The path's facility would become a snare, this ready-made role into which you lapse precisely because it is ready-made, reciting it like a prayer reeled off the tip of the tongue. And because you have followed it only by logic and not by starting from yourself as well, you remain fundamentally the same.

Now, although the situation seems paralyzed for the moment, although I do not see any objective possibility of proceeding otherwise, although the situation of the intellectual's nullity in France today refers me to my own individual nullity, I do not believe that all is lost. Rather, it is this objective nullity—which apparently confirms the subjective nullity but which derives a positive aspect from the fact that I am not alone in it, that there are thousands who experience it and vainly refuse it—which can become my link with the real, the instrument of its own transcendence.

I no longer believe, as at the outset of this work, that a man can change radically, can liquidate his original choice. But I am now convinced that by a careful analysis of his empirical situation, he can discover in his choice potential objective significations that permit him to reach positive conclusions. This is the whole question. You are never asked to change yourself altogether, but to learn to employ your resources, with full knowledge of the case, in view of a positive action (if you prefer, to learn to "dose" yourself with what you are in order to transcend yourself). This is the point I have reached. The "complex of nonidentification," since I have recognized it, has drained like an abscess. Instead of keeping the world at a distance like an enemy who must not be allowed to get a grip on me, I am learning to yield to it; to see it, to begin with, to taste its density, my presence within it, to listen to a man talking in the depths of his speech (instead of listening only to the surface of what he says). Not to feel quite so ill at ease in my own skin; to say what I think with the conviction that I am at least as sure of the rightness of my remarks as my interlocutor is of his; to be able to enjoy the passing moment, a light, an aroma, a look, a sound; to hold on to life, to want it to be full of all there is to be lived, including contradictions and risks that cannot be escaped—I am learning. I would not let anyone live it in my place. This is a task which belongs to me and in which only I can succeed. And if I do succeed, it is not I alone who will profit from it. Rather the inverse: to make a success of your life is to make a success of something that goes beyond it, that speaks and acts beyond it, externally, for all men. Which men? Not all. For I shall surely never be understood by those who say, "Listen, mister, you can talk about the Arabs all you want, but I *know* them!"; who say, "You don't know what you're talking about! I've *seen* Russians!"; who say, "When wages get back to normal we can breathe again!"; who say, "Sartre's ultra-Bolshevism"; who say, "You have a revolutionist fixation!"; who say, "The treason of the intellectuals, the Communist Party is in Moscow," "You always bite the hands that feed you." This much is certain: that I am on one side (the side of those who do not have enough and are not numerous enough to know they are a side), that I have no possibility of changing sides, that I will not change even if they try to buy me for the other side because it is "really" my own, and that the side I have chosen will always be the *other* side (that of men who suspect you, spy on you, watch for imperceptible impulses of subversion, pay some because of their position and others only for a job that can be demanded "because it's paid for"). I am on the side of those who have neither constituted Right nor Strength in their behalf, but only their own strength, which consists of ruse, bluff and the capacity to take advantage of its own weaknesses.

This is still not a profession of faith; these are merely facts. A fact that when a man is evicted, imprisoned for his opinions, censored, deported, boycotted, gagged, starved, it is I who am the target. A fact that the people who aim at me are the ones who surround me where I am and not the ones invoked by the exploiters of this part of the world as an alibi for their own violences. For me, for us, the violences of the socialist societies or of those societies attempting to become socialist in no way diminish the violence which surrounds us nor the necessity of opposing it. And if it is objected then that I could not express myself this way, could not denounce alienations in any other society than a capitalist one, I must reply:

1. It is precisely because the society is so constituted that I express myself this way.

2. The fact that I can denounce its alienations does not suppress them.

3. One does not denounce the alienations of a society undertaking to abolish all alienations in the same way as those of a society which is falling apart and which one is trying to change.

4. Criticism is not an end in itself, and the society which provokes and tolerates it has no reason to glorify itself thereby; it cannot take credit for the strikes or the political parties or the theoreticians trying to overturn it, for if it were not such as it is, there would have been no need for these strikes, these parties, and these theoreticians.

But is there really a need for them, a need for these theoretical and critical intellectuals, for these people who want to do only what they like, to say only what they think and feel, while the rest sell their souls and surrender to "objective necessities"? Is there really a need for these men who believe that "man is sick," that the world is sick, and who want the rest of its occupants to realize the totality of their unsatisfied needs, which are perhaps impossible to satisfy objectively? Is there a need for these troublemakers who try to be "the conscience of their times" and are therefore dangerous and useless to everyone, themselves included? Who offer what no one asks for in the hope that the offer will create the need? Who execute a commission no one has assigned them? Who are really the least important men in the world, and charlatans when they pretend to be anything else?

Is there any need for them? This is, in fact, the whole question, and it would take another essay to answer it. For on the whole, it goes without saying (but perhaps less than you think), there is a need for them, especially in a Marxist perspective. Because in Marxism there are two factors: a positive and practical plan of construction and a perpetual and methodical contestation of every alienation. It happens that these two moments have been separated by history; that Marxism's spirit of contestation has been atrophied

for many years, for to contest the alienations provoked by the
Soviet enterprise of disalienation was too dangerous a luxury; this
atrophy extended even to the Communist parties not in power (for
several reasons, of which one of the most important is that one cannot propagate in the French Communist Party the contestation of
French alienations and at the same time prevent the contestation
of Soviet alienations). Contestation has taken refuge in the
bourgeois camp, there remaining idealistic, negative, sterile and
aesthetic.

Yet this cannot continue much longer, if only for the reason that
although, according to good Marxist logic, material conditions permit the explanation of anything at all by way of alienation, they
do not permit the explanation (nor, a fortiori, the determination)
of a society where man, triumphing over his alienations, would be
his own product—that is, to be explained by himself alone, by his
purely human will. Therefore, either there is not yet, after twenty-
five years of transitional dictatorship, material basis for socialism
in Soviet Russia or else, what seems more likely to me, the contestation of the Soviet alienations will soon develop on this basis,
and the two moments of Marxism will again coincide. This will be
a tremendous "thaw," there will be work for everyone. In fact,
there is already such work if one believes in such a thaw, for it
must be prepared for. And to make it a success no ambiguity must
be permitted to surround the fact that it is in the spirit of Marxism
that the Communist realities are being contested, and not in the
spirit of bourgeois aestheticism. This is the most difficult point—
to be on the side of those one criticizes and to be separated from
them by the very hope one places in them; to contest their action
while at the same time recognizing that such action is not personally imputable to them, that the actors even in their errors and
in their inadequacies are also the product of a situation; to say they
are wrong without condemning them and without thereby claiming
the right for oneself, without expecting anyone's approval, espe-

cially that of the other camp. It is among contradictions like these
that one must remain in equilibrium.

Here I am, then, almost where I started. Is it not nullity that I
have just advocated? But perhaps, too, the intellectual today is
"nullity at work" (to paraphrase Jeanson)—that is, a nullity that
tries to make itself the instrument of its own transcendence; in
other words, the intellectual's last recourse, once he has recognized
himself as the least important man in the world, is to make a
weapon out of his disinterestedness. (His disinterestedness derives
from the fact that he asks nothing for himself and above all no
admiration for his "spiritual elevation." Here, I think, is the great
difference between men like Sartre and men like Camus. The first
speak with regard to a result, the second with regard to posthumous
glory in which is reflected, by anticipation, their arrogant judgment
of men.)

Here I am, then, almost where I started, but with at least this
certitude: The intellectual, if he cannot keep from being one, is
objectively on the side of the revolutionary forces, of historical
negativity,* and he must be on that side subjectively. This is the
intellectual's only chance of reality. In isolation he can do nothing
(nothing save amuse himself with the masks he is given and assist
those in revolt to spare themselves, thanks to literary negativity, a
certain amount of effort). If he ever acquires a certain power, it is
only the power to catalyze the diffuse will and the inchoate thought
which lie dormant in the facts and ask only to be expressed in
order to exist as such; the power to ask, since he is not physically
engaged in action, those questions which the actors undergo, to all
intents and purposes, without finding either the time or the perspective to ask them.

But to ask questions is not to resolve them; the man who knows
how to contest the reality of an action is also the man least capable

---

* By which I mean everything tending toward an appropriation of the
world by men and of the history which they produce in fact.

of influencing it in one direction or another. The answer to his questions, hypotheses and predictions will ultimately be made by others. The intellectual's literary negativity will never change the course of history, nor even acquire a shadow of reality if it is not included within the historical negativity of a class revolutionary by its condition.

This is why I say that if this class does not exist, or if we believe that it has lost its revolutionary vocation, then there is nothing left to do but to keep silent, for in this case the intellectual is finished altogether; what he says will be nothing more than the frivolous diversion of a society rotting where it stands whose members console themselves for their real impotence by their sovereign play of ideas. If speech retains a meaning (a meaning other than covering oneself with academic honors and feeding the amusement industry), it can do so only to the degree that intellectual negativity believes in historical negativity and attempts to coincide with it.

Only where else can I look for this historical negativity if not in the Communist Party, which (well or badly is another question) happens to incarnate it? I should tell you frankly that the junction point with the Communist Party remains for me, as for any intellectual not merely histrionic in his attitudes, the ultimate objective, and what prevents me from arriving at this point today is simultaneously (1) the material impossibility; (2) mistrust of the bad psychological reasons which such an adherence, in my present circumstances, would rest on; (3) disgust for certain procedures; (4) the conviction that this adherence would at present be as futile for the party as for myself; (5) the belief that a comprehensive contestation can soon become useful.

Useful, in fact, to the degree that it reinforces the historical negativity which the Communist Party happens to incarnate. This contestation will proceed in opposition to its objective if it weakens the revolutionary opportunities. It is not, either in itself or for me, an end in itself. In no case can it consist of criticizing the Communist Party in the name of timeless principles, pious hopes or its leaders' lack of intelligence. For the question which must be asked by anyone with even a shadow of Marxist training is not whether we know the personal qualities and defects of the leaders; it is whether we know the conditions of fact which have brought to and consolidated at the head of the party men having such qualities and such defects. Do we know whether these conditions persist or if their disappearance is already latent in the facts? Is the present leadership doing all that is objectively possible or, after permitting the movement to hibernate, is it uselessly perpetuating that hibernation and postponing an awakening by clinging to its own power? *

Yes, the intellectual's contestation has some use only if it corresponds to something besides his personal wishes, if it has opportunities to reinforce even indirectly the movement of historical

---

* Such is the question—and I call it "the question," for no one will ever possess enough of its elements to answer it with certitude. It is the role, the duty in fact, of the leaders to declare that material conditions in Soviet Russia and elsewhere still require discipline; that the construction of the material basis of socialism, for instance, is still incompatible with the open contestation of the alienations which this construction involves. But it is the role, the duty, in fact, of the intellectuals to contest the preceding affirmation, to make it apparent that the only way of knowing if the material conditions of bringing the transitional dictatorship to an end are at hand is to try to democratize that dictatorship. No one can say in advance who is right. No one can say outright whether the French Communist Party or the Soviet regime can be more democratic than they are. To know this one must contend, but in contending one must also know that one is taking risks. The stake of the struggle transcends the ideas in the name of which it is being waged. Therefore, if one is beaten one has no reason to complain. Personally, I am convinced that the intellectual—who has no material responsibility in the conduct of state and party business—tends to accord himself the *beau rôle* in contesting the leaders' action (as Trotsky and Bukharin, they who produced only ideas, had the splendid opportunity of scornfully criticizing a certain Stalin who, at the head of the administrative machine—and what a machine!—assumed all the dirty work). Could he do better in their place? We shall never know, for the men ready to assume material responsibilities in affairs of state will always, by historical selection and by definition, be anything but intellectuals. And the dirtiest trick that history can play on the latter is to bring them to power one day or another and to say, "*Hic Rhodus, hic salta!*"

negativity. But if this movement, in its only existing incarnation, is threatened, derailed or crushed, the intellectual is also threatened, derailed and crushed. If, at the decisive moments, he does not know how to fight beside the party and risk his life with it, he has abdicated and will not return to his privileged position. And if, the rest of the time, the party has no need of him, ignores him or jeers at him, he has only to wait. Perhaps the need will rise again. In this hope, and with the certitude that he cannot be right in isolation, he must avoid breaking off all relations with the party. This will perhaps allow him to contribute someday even more than is asked of him. For the rest, if he sees nothing more urgent to do, he may continue his work as an intellectual, but in the knowledge that his misery—the solitude and the unreality to which his requirement of total humanity is doomed—will come to an end only in a society where man, by producing the world, will produce himself as a total man; the knowledge that this production can be the act only of those for whom their humanity remains to be conquered; the knowledge that humanity has no debt to him, but that it is he who is the debtor, since, unlike those who labor for money or merely to survive, he can allow himself the luxury of having spiritual needs.

Once everything has been said, everything still remains to be said. My first text, in which I had wanted to say everything, fell from my hands like a bundle of dead leaves. I thought that this was the fault of its conception. But now the second is falling from my hands in the same way. Everything still remains to say; everything always remains to be said.

Hic Rhodus, hic salta. Yes, Rhodes is here. Among other things I have learned that I shall never be through beginning again, that my world is this white paper, my life the activity of covering it. I once thought life would become possible when I had said everything; and now I realize that life, for me, is to write; to start out each time trying to say everything and to begin again immediately afterward, because everything still remains to be said.

Yet I no longer believe that to write is the nearest approach to man's total realization. For some men in each society, it is merely the only realization possible. For some men who cannot ignore the fact that they bear within themselves a definitive flaw; something which has happened in their life makes it impossible for them to recognize themselves in the reality of the image which their acts create. Something has happened in their life, or it is their life itself, life in general—in which we are all incomplete individuals, incapable of accepting what we can be, ill adapted to our reality, devoured by needs which this civilization cannot satisfy. We are all potential traitors; each of us *petits bourgeois* betrays this society in his dreams, scorns his fellows, denies, in some nocturnal portion of himself, his daylight reality. What is offered to us? A laborious, narrowly specialized life at the heart of an enterprise which exceeds us and is even ignorant of itself; an ant life forever unable to recognize itself in the image of the world it contributes to produce. We are private men—deprived men, deprived of the human meaning of our specialized tasks, deprived of universality as real individuals working; cogs of an inhuman social machine which, as the mechanical resultant of our efforts, perverts our intentions and annihilates us at the very moment we produce it. Our need for humanity takes refuge in the private life, in nocturnal meetings and palavers, little orgies of vain dreams and discussions during which we destroy the society and the inacceptible reality it presses upon us. Which is why this society measures an individual's success by the number and the power of the means he acquires to hold the community at a distance, to escape the common fate, to isolate himself, to differentiate himself from all others, to build himself a shell against the world: a car, comfort, house, private property—all reducing his dependence on others and his contacts with them. This society considers as the crown of life the splendid isolation of the rich and refined property owner. But to those who would prefer not to possess, to isolate and to consume at the general expense, but to give, to communicate and to construct with and for all, this society has nothing to offer.

This society distinguishes itself by the profusion of instruments of destruction, evasion and disidentification which it puts at the disposal of its members. In the first category figures alcohol; in the second, the automobile (which, incarnating the negation of Here, makes Everywhere and Nowhere gleam across its hood and affords its owner the most illusory of freedoms, the apparent liberation from the constraints and requirements of life in common; * expending on automobiles a larger part of their revenue than any other nation, the French drive their cars *against society* in order to escape the common fate—their localization in a country whose future is shrinking—consuming in their carburetors their savings, the houses and factories they will not build, the nation's future, or what remains of it once the efforts invested in preserving the imperial past have been deducted); in the third category, eroticism, art and literature. All of us dream of being elsewhere and Other than we are. This too contributes to our reality. We are people who cannot endure the reality we represent "despite ourselves" except by contesting it or compensating for it by an enormous and often admirable

---

* Constraints and requirements which the drivers, racing by thousands on the road, rediscover and recreate there statistically as the resultant (desired by no one) of thousands of efforts to escape all laws, as a law which is therefore completely alien to them and which, caught in a jam advancing slower than a train or a subway, they have the illusion of being able to avoid thanks to their dexterity and to chance. The driver's freedom is that right Marx mentions: "to be able, in the framework of certain conditions, to take advantage of chance quite calmly." In the image of capitalist society, the drivers—each of whom hates all the rest and desires their disappearance, for they are pure obstacles for each individual driver—are in agreement only as to the necessity of perpetuating the conditions of chance by which each individual intends to profit for himself. But the possibilities of so profiting are mutually conditioned and limiting; the efforts to profit necessarily neutralize each other according to statistical laws.

production of the imaginary; we compensate by the profusion of our ideas for the profusion of facts which escape our grasp. We are terribly *intelligent*.

Whatever we say or do, we can never feel entirely real, there is a part of ourselves which remains unrealized, a part—of failure, of silence—which forbids us to content ourselves with whatever we live (do, say, are). An absolute distance divides us from our reality. The intellectual is the man who assumes this distance, who tries to recover the silence, the failure. The means of realization society offers men is not enough for him in this society, nor in any other; his sense of incompleteness exceeds his disagreement (or agreement) with the offered means of realization. He will never (I will never) be a great man of action; at best he will be an adventurer of action, impatient to get back to his desk to write what he has lived and thereby to recover the part of himself which action has left unrealized. I must invent the means of a complete realization which is impossible for me and whose means, for this reason, cannot be really existing means. I cannot claim that I will succeed in creating these means, nor that they will be worth more than those available to everyone else. I only know that like many others (and like every man, by right if not by fact) I must invent individual means to manifest man, and that the highest recompense I can hope for resides in this activity of creation.

It is this need for individual realization which the given means do not permit me to satisfy; it is this human need which an original contradiction in man exposes to the contradictions of his time and to its share of failure (experienced, though not thought, or assumed, by everyone); it is this need which motivates the work of art. It finds no satisfaction elsewhere. The work of art is the aesthetic manifestation of negativity, the contestation of the existing human reality. It acknowledges the fact that the constituted means of realization, whatever they are, which a society, whatever it is, puts at the disposal of its members are insufficient—by the mere fact that they are constituted—to manifest man totally. The work of art contests the constituted means insofar as by their objective solidity they apparently determine the man who in fact produces *them* and conceal from him the fact that it is he who produces these means, both man and nature alike. The work of art states that a production which is not conscious of producing and does not posit man as the origin and the end of its products has no value. It is freedom taking itself for an end to the degree that it cannot be satisfied with merely being given to itself at the level of the material means of its objective realization, but demands to be at the foundation of these means, to give them to itself. The work of art manifests the fact that man is always richer than what he is, richer in virtualities than what he can be, and that he must re-create himself, constantly reinvent himself, or else fall back into the automatism and the stereotypes of a dejected solemnity, being nothing but the "product of his product."

Art is disidentifying; it contests the identity which society conjures up in behalf of the consciousness-for-itself and which that consciousness assumes by the mere fact that it employs given means of realization; art is negativity and reflexive *ascesis,* because it puts freedom in essence (that is, on condition that it exist at all) at the source of human reality and thus restates the revolutionary requirement that man regain possession of himself (over and against his alienations) and continually re-create himself. But because it manifests only the (subjective) requirement of re-creation, because it indicates only the possibility of new means of realization but cannot by itself produce these means, which appear during praxis, art is ineffective, or, rather, becomes effective only when mediated by an action which it cannot provoke and which belongs on another level.

Then what good is rallying men to contestation if those who can

302 • • • THE TRAITOR

respond to this appeal (who possess the culture, the time and the money) cannot give freedom the means of making itself real, and if those who work, by the logic of their situation, at creating these means, those who *are* the revolutionary contestation in action, remain absorbed by more urgent tasks? Artistic creation remains both necessary and incapable, today, of believing in itself; cut off from the real revolutionary forces, its subjective demand for freedom has no other public than those for whom art is an alibi to avoid true freedom.

This is also a reason, I think, why I have not had the patience to create a work of art. I might have been able to ten years ago. Today I regard those who put beauty above all other considerations as being on the other side, on the side of those who believe in the right to possess, to enjoy, to eat, to command and to make their escape all by themselves. This book is in many respects the negation of art, a work of art which is trying to transcend itself at the very moment it comes into being, and which refuses to be an end in itself; that is why it is not a work of art.

I am not sure that I have kept all my promises. I now believe that subjective motivations are not so important. They no longer trouble me; they are fading. The man who succeeds, even for the "wrong reasons" (individual reasons), in committing himself to an action which transcends his contingent individuality, who regards the goal of this action as more real, more important than himself, who forgets his self-esteem and the ineffable singularity of his precious person to the point of no longer even feeling that he is making humanity a tremendous gift by declaring himself on its side —this man can say, "It matters little enough for what subjective reasons I have come to act this way, from the moment that I know that my objective reasons are real and defensible in the world's eyes; instead of worrying about my 'revolutionist fixation' or about the psychology of resentment in the proletarianized masses, why

don't you come to terms with the real state of things which psychoanalysis sometimes serves you as a pretext to ignore?"

It is only natural that the situation should give me back what I
have given to it, that I should find in everything I say or do at this
moment that shimmer of motivations, hardly defensible in themselves, of which I was speaking earlier. But, in fact, a situation,
provided one assumes it altogether, an action, provided one persists in it, always give back more than one puts into them and lead
by their objective logic beyond one's original intentions. Perhaps
the original choice of the bourgeois son was at the start, in its
subjective intention, a revolt, a treason, a disidentification. The
situation will have given him back all that. But more than that,
other people and history will have conferred on his egocentric
gesture an unlooked-for reality; the historical conjuncture in which
he functions will have conferred upon this gesture a signification
which overflows its first intention. Will he carry on this signification to the point of making it the dominant aspect of his project?
It is my behavior which will decide whether this gesture was merely
a juvenile crisis or the point of departure of a commitment resolved
not to let go of the thread, found by chance, of the real; to act it
instead of being acted by it. It is because the world always makes
us say more than we meant and continually puts us at a crossroads
of possible significations that we must, in truth, continually choose
ourselves.

But I cannot enact a commitment and invent a reality for myself
in isolation. I can only determine the direction and the side on
which I exist and, once this is done, launch in that direction an
action still necessarily without real weight, dependent on my fragile
and solitary will. After that, I must wait and hope that others will
return this action to me weighted with the reality they will have
conferred upon it. This is my present hope. I cannot go further by
myself. My reality is not within my power alone, it is also what you
will make of me. It will certainly exceed my intentions by a density

I cannot foresee (or by the nullity in which your indifference will maintain me) and will betray them in many respects; it will compel me to new intentions, new interrogations.

We have all begun by being "betrayed"; it is only very exceptionally that we have knowingly and deliberately engaged ourselves as we find ourselves to be. The reality of our "innocent" intentions has led us to be what we have not wanted to be. We have never done only what we wanted to do, but always what other people and history have decided we have done. Between the intellectual who, to escape this risk, isolates himself and wills his own inaction and those who with good intentions and pious hopes decline the reality which in fact they create, but of which they declare themselves prisoners, a way must be found.

We must want action to exceed its intention, for this is the price of its reality. We must want to be engaged by others more deeply than we thought or could be by ourselves. But to be capable of really wanting this (instead of producing merely an imaginary and vacant will, masking fatalism), we must still do so knowingly; we must know the total situation in which action, once performed, will take its effect, the side and the direction on which we want to be engaged. This is what I have tried to do. It is in the limits of this intention that I have agreed to be "betrayed" (that is, led further than I can go by myself); it is my reality in the eyes of those who are on the same side as I which is important to me. Not to bow humbly beneath their verdict, not to make myself their instrument, but to play according to the rules we have agreed on and in the determination of which a dialogue must be possible. While waiting for something better.

December 1955–September 1956